# THE
# GREENWOOD ANNUAL ABSTRACT
# OF
# LEGAL DISSERTATIONS
# AND THESES,
# 1985–1987

# THE GREENWOOD ANNUAL ABSTRACT OF LEGAL DISSERTATIONS AND THESES, 1985–1987

Compiled by Kenneth Brown

Greenwood Press
New York • Westport, Connecticut • London

The Greenwood Annual Abstract of
Legal Dissertations and Theses, 1985-1987
Kenneth Brown, compiler

ISSN 1040-3876



ISBN: 0-313-26486-4
ISSN: 1040-3876

First published in 1988

Greenwood Press, Inc.
88 Post Road West, Westport, Connecticut 06881

Printed in the United States of America

The paper used in this book complies with the Permanent Paper Standard issued by the National Information Standards Organization (Z39.48-1984).

10 9 8 7 6 5 4 3 2 1

# Contents

# Preface

The objective of the *Greenwood Annual Abstract of Legal Dissertations and Theses* is to provide convenient research access to all dissertations and theses accepted at United States law schools. As with most pioneering efforts, the objective has been attained only in part.

This first volume surveys the period 1985-1987 and provides information on 176 dissertations and theses. Although it is our belief that this represents much of the material accepted for the master of law and doctor of juridical science written requirements during the period, it is not a complete listing. In future volumes we will attempt to strengthen the coverage of the initial period while bringing the coverage forward. With the cooperation of American law schools, comprehensive coverage should be attainable.

*The Greenwood Annual Abstract of Legal Dissertations and Theses* is organized in three sections. The abstract section comprises the bulk of the volume and is organized alphabetically by author last name. Each entry consists of full author name; full title and, with few exceptions, full subtitle; name of the institution granting the degree; year the thesis or dissertation was submitted or copyrighted (these can be different from the year the degree was granted); the degree level (an "M" or "D" indicate master of law or doctor of juridical science materials respectively); inclusive pagination; whether the material has notes, appendixes, or bibliography; and a one-page or longer abstract.

The second component is a title index and the third is a subject index. The latter has been designed to be of use not only to law students and scholars but also to those in the social sciences.

We would like to acknowledge the cooperation of the law schools that have joined this program to date and those that made materials available for this first volume. In addition, James L. Hoover of Columbia and Willis Meredith of Harvard gave freely of their time and expertise. Finally, we owe a great debt to Ken Brown, whose untimely death robbed legal publishing of a remarkable supporter and this project of its first compiler.

# THE GREENWOOD ANNUAL ABSTRACT OF LEGAL DISSERTATIONS AND THESES, 1985–1987

# ABSTRACTS

Abbas, Akmal Kamel

ARBITRATION IN EGYPT: CRITIQUE UNDER CONTEMPORANEOUS VIEWS

Harvard Law School 1987 M

82 pages

Footnotes

The revision of articles 501-513 of the Code of Civil and Commercial Procedure of 1968 concerning private arbitration is and has been considered for the past ten years one of the most important issues raised by several Egyptian Jurists.

In view of the conclusion of a protocol between the Egyptian Government and the Asian-African Legal Consultative for the establishment of the Regional Center for International Commercial Arbitration in Cairo this revision is necessary if the Center is to function at all.

Ever since 1974 Egypt has pursued a policy of encouraging foreign investors to carry out new projects in all fields of the Egyptian economy. The policy often referred to as "El Infeltah" or the "Open Door Policy" is aimed directly at private capital and investments. As a result of this policy the volume of international trade between Egypt and the rest of the world has drastically expanded, after its limited growth in the sixties, when international trade was conducted by the Egyptian Government and its agencies in the form of bilateral treaties concluded with other states.

In fact, this policy and its effects, namely the increase of international trade between Egyptian public sector agencies as well as private individuals and corporations, has triggered the call of Egyptian Jurists for the revision of the Egyptian rules regulating private arbitration and in particular international arbitration.

The Egyptian economic policies of the sixties explain the lack of interest at that time of both jurists and courts in the New York Convention on Recognition and Enforcement of Foreign Arbitral Awards. This was so even though Egypt was one of the first countries to ratify the New York Convention.

In conclusion the author discusses international arbitration as it is viewed today. Certain aspects of domestic arbitration in both the French and the American legal systems are examined. An overview of certain aspects of the Egyptian system of arbitration is made in order to find out in what ways the Egyptian system differs from other national systems. The final part of the paper summarizes the most important considerations that should be borne in mind with respect to revision of the Egyptian legal system on arbitration.

Acevedo, Anibal

RECENT TRENDS IN CHOICE-OF-LAW AND THE PERSPECTIVE OF REFORMING THE CIVIL CODE OF PUERTO RICO

Harvard Law School 1987 M

94 pages

Footnotes

During the last twenty years the United States and Europe have experimented an incredible and interesting development in the field of choice-of-law. Although based on different experiences, needs and methodologies, it is possible to identify common trends on both sides of the Atlantic. Nevertheless, the possibilities of achieving a common language, methodology and understanding is far from reality. That does not mean that it should not become a common goal. The experience of some multilateral conventions that include within its members countries of both civil law and common law traditions show us that the endeavor is one with possibilities.

It is within this historical context that the enterprise of reforming the anachronic Puerto Rican Civil Code should take place. Puerto Rico is in an excellent position to get involved in a drafting of a new code in the area of conflict of law that could serve as a rapprochement between the European and American systems.

Puerto Rico is now engaged in a different endeavor; not in savings its Code but in adapting it to the present demands and needs of the modern Puerto Rican society. During this century, some minor and unsystematic amendments have been passed. As a consequence of the economic and social development of Puerto Rico, the Code in many areas has become outmoded. The realization of an integral reform is necessary and imminent. One purpose of this paper is to bring to the ongoing discussions in Puerto Rico a work which could be useful in redrafting the choice-of-law articles of the revised code. The reality and goals of modern Puerto Rico, with its political, social and economic interchange with the United States, its cultural and possible economic integration with the Caribbean and Latin

America, the importance of tourism in its future development, the presence in the island of many foreigners who live and work there but at the same time maintain relations with their respective homelands, the presence of many Puerto Rican in the United States, and Puerto Rico's location among the civil law countries and its willingness to remain within them, impose upon Puerto Rico the duty to develop a choice-of-law scheme that would take into account those realities and facilitate the achievement of their collective ends.

The fact that the Puerto Rican conflict of law is a hotchpotch of different theories and approaches complicates the reforming endeavor. On the other hand, that same factor has impeded the rooting of any specific theory. This opens the number of alternative for the drafters. They not only will have to re-write the Code, they will have to create a system from a bunch of contradictory baseless rules. Starting from scratch would give them the opportunity to create a Private International Law code that would positively contribute to the world developments on this field.

Aiura, Shinchi

REEVALUATING WALLS BETWEEN BANKS AND SECURITIES FIRMS

Harvard Law School 1987 M

62 pages

Footnotes

In this paper the author re-evaluates the Glass-Steagall Act of the United States and Section 65 of the Securities and Exchange Law of Japan.

The Banking Act of 1933, popularly known as the Glass-Steagall Act, mandated the separation of commercial banking and investment banking. The Act was one of a series of regulatory acts designed to insure proper supervision of certain bank practices. The Act has two main features: one is the establishment of the Federal Deposit Insurance corporation (FDIC) and the other is the segregation of investment banking from commercial banking.

Japan's Security and Exchange Law of 1948 was passed under the supervision of Occupation authorities stationed in Japan after the Second World War. The Law adopted almost all the security regulation statutes of the United States; the Securities Act of 1933 and the Securities Exchange Act of 1934. Article 65 of the Securities and Exchange Law was adopted from the Glass-Steagall Act at the last stage of the legislative process.

The Glass-Steagall Act is over fifty years old and the Securities and Exchange Law is nearly forty years old. Today, some parts of these statutes are said to be outdated and to require amendment. The issue of whether or not to repeal the statutes that prohibit commercial banks from entering into investment banking, in particular, has been most heatedly debated.

The "wall" between the investment and commercial banks has been actually lowered since these statutes were enacted in both countries. Even though the "wall" is getting lower, it is not a solution to the problem. It is believed that some legislative action must be taken to evaluate this problem.

In this paper the author focuses on the corporate securities business of commercial banks, putting an emphasis on underwriting activities. Security firms are permitted to deal in government and municipal bonds in both the United States and Japan. Discussed first is the statutory framework, and then examined is the legislative history rational for separating the two banking functions. Finally, explored is the alleged conflicts of interest and other concerns for concentration of resources. A possible answer is recommended for these alleged adverse effects, examining existing laws and/or future legislation.

Alexander, Daniel

ARTIFICIAL JUSTICE: RULE-MAKING, RULE BREAKING, CONSISTENCY AND CHANGE IN ENGLISH ADMINISTRATIVE LAW

Harvard Law School 1987 M

76 pages

Footnotes and appendices

Once in England there were two realms constantly at war fighting over the same territory and over the same people for the political heart of the country. Between them, invoked and alternately admired and despised by the leaders of each realm, policing their frequent skirmishes and battles, keeping score of the victories and defeats, and most important of all, declaring the lore, stood the judges.

The first realm was the domain of private rights and liberties, naturalized by their sourcelessness, echoing back to time immemorial through a noble tradition of common law adjudication, the judges forced to resolve disputes inside that domain as well as the disputes of war with the other. All productive economic mechanism, the imaginative lore told us, found their expression within that domain, which appeared as a hive of internal activity, but essentially sealed off from the public gaze. The lore conceived of procedural (due process) rights as operating to check arbitrary and misinformed territorial captures by the other realm, and act as a brake on artificial intrusion into and interference with this hallowed region of economic activity.

As far as constitutional doctrine went, the domain was protected by an unarmed guard - the presumption of statutory interpretation that unless there are clear words to the contrary a statute should not be held to take away private rights of property without compensation - a principle that, wherever possible, operated to make the overall boundary of this private domain subject to little change.

The second realm, the predictable lore said, was the domain of governmental action - a hive not of productive activity but of drones - elected representatives speaking through statutes, with what they ordered implemented elsewhere in the bureaucracy, generally by unelected officials. The second domain was rather different from the first in that it appeared to be a creation of the first but with a distinct and powerful identity of its own, generally content to leave alone the territory of one section of the first domain alone in exchange for greater fruits from another section. So far as there was a constitutional doctrine governing this domain it was that of parliamentary sovereignty - that those controlling that domain could, so long as they behaved in accordance with their own rules, do exactly as they pleased. This constitutional principle, far from providing the story with a neat symmetry upset the balance straight away. The dice seemed loaded in favor of the second domain in such a way that if it came to a serious battle it would inevitably win. The lore declarers slowly realized this but, for some years, fearing that to adjust the balance in any substantive way would incur the unrestrained wrath of the leaders of thee second domain during a period in which those leaders were trying hard to gain new ground - and fearing this more than the diffuse disaffection felt by those inhabitants of the first domain, they chose who to support - not only on substance but even on procedure.

Alexander, Vincent C.

THE FUTURE OF THE CORPORATE ATTORNEY-CLIENT PRIVILEGE

Columbia Law School 1985 M

258 pages

Footnotes and bibliography

Modern rules of adjudicative fact-finding have opened wide the door to the admission of probative and reliable evidence. One of these rules holds that the public has a right to every person's evidence. Similarly, modern rules of pretrial discovery allow a party to probe his adversary's claims and to prepare his own case by unearthing facts that might aid in resolving the controversy. In this regard, the Supreme Court wrote, "Mutual knowledge of all the relevant facts gathered by both parties is essential to proper litigation." On the other hand, the duty to give testimony and produce documents is sometimes excused because the evidence, though relevant, would reveal a privileged communication. The privilege for confidential communications between attorney and client is perhaps the most widely accepted privilege. A consensus is more difficult to discern, however, when the client whose communications are at issue is a corporation. Although few today would seriously contest the principle that a corporate client is entitled to the privilege, the scope of the privilege in the corporate context is a continuing source of controversy.

The principle tension caused by the availability of the privilege to corporations is its potential for the loss of a great deal more relevant information than is lost in the case of an individual. Since the privilege shields from disclosure only the words spoken to and by the lawyer, not the client's knowledge of the facts themselves, an individual opponent can be questioned about such facts with relative ease. A large corporation, on the other hand, often "speaks" to its counsel through many different agents, thus creating a potentially broad "zone of silence." In some cases, extracting the underlying facts from a host of individual employees may be not only burdensome but also impossible of achievement if the witnesses are unavailable or uncooperative.

The overall value of the attorney-client privilege is weaker in the case of a large corporation than it is when the client is an individual or a closely-held corporation because personal privacy interests are lacking. In addition, maximization of the potential benefits of the privilege by extending its coverage to all levels of the corporate hierarchy will inevitably create a blockage to truth in some cases. Furthermore, it is likely that the goals of the corporate attorney-client privilege can be adequately achieved in many circumstances without the necessity of taking the same monolithic approach that applies in the case of individuals. Thus, it will be argued that the traditional absolute nature of the corporate attorney-client privilege should be relaxed in favor of a qualified privilege that will provide flexibility without undermining the beneficial goals of confidentiality.

Almand, Lawson Robert

AN EXAMINATION OF THE REQUIREMENTS FOR DISSEMINATION OF HUMANITARIAN LAW TO THE ARMED FORCES CONTAINED IN THE GENEVA CONVENTIONS OF 1949 AND PROTOCOL I

George Washington Law School 1986 M

128 pages

Footnotes and appendices

This paper examines the sources of responsibility for dissemination of the humanitarian law of armed conflict contained in the Hague and Geneva Conventions and Protocol I Additional to the Geneva Convention of 1949, analyzes the international Red Cross standards for implementing the provisions and principles of those documents, and finally, examines and assesses the United States military's compliance with those requirements.

In examining the law relating to dissemination, there is merit in reviewing the origins and functions of the law of armed conflict in general. In order to demonstrate the law's relevance to members of the armed forces, there is a need to show why the rules are important and how they operate in conjunction with other military doctrines such as military necessity and economy of force. For this reason, the paper is divided into three parts and a conclusion.

The first part of the paper examines the source of humanitarian law and provides a broad base survey of the substance and reasoning underlying the law.

The second part deals with affirmative obligations to disseminate the law by providing an historic perspective and then analyzing current conventional obligations.

The author then examines the United States military's implementation of the law relating to dissemination. In addition to providing an overview of the U.S. scheme for compliance, two case studies of specific U.S. implementation are viewed. The first case study examines the results of a joint field exercise participated in by the U.S. in Korea in 1982 in which law of armed conflict problems were effectively presented. The second case study provides a view of the U.S. Marine Corps' law of war program through an assist from the Annual Marine Corps Law of War Course.

Amy, Lo Sau Han

CHINA'S SPECIAL ECONOMIC ZONES

Harvard Law School M

61 pages

Footnotes

Six years have passed since the PRC established its Special Economic Zones (SEZs) in 1980 to attract foreign capital and advanced technology to speed up the Four Modernizations. Four cities - Shenzhen, Zhuhai and Shantou in Guangdong Province and Xiamen in Fujian Province - were designated as the sites for the SEZs and were granted extensive powers to adopt special policies to promote foreign trade and investment.

Widespread attention was drawn to the creation of the SEZs as it is an important manifestation of China's Open Door Policy. More significantly, it represented an unprecedented attempt by a Communist regime to set up privileged enclaves within its boundaries to pursue policies which are essentially capitalistic in nature.

But far from being inhibited by ideological constraints, the SEZs have made rapid progress. Shenzhen, for instance, has been transformed from a negligible border town to a bustling city and industrial output has jumped appreciably. On a national level, the SEZs' experience in economic reforms have served to inspire and accelerate the whole process of China's Open Door Policy. This is amply reflected in the opening of the 14 coastal cities in 1984 and the 3 delta areas in 1985 to foreign investments. The SEZs' efforts in lawmaking have also set valuable precedents for the rest of the country. Indeed, within a few years, the SEZs have come to command a significance which is far out of proportion to their relatively tiny size and population.

However, the euphoria about the SEZs have subsided considerably in recent months as the PRC implemented a series of measures to stabilize its overheated economy and tighten its Open Door Policy. While the leadership was reiterated their support of the SEZs, changes would seem to be inevitable.

In light of these events, this paper examines the development of the SEZs thus far. Comparisons will be made on the investment incentives offered by the SEZs and those offered elsewhere in the country. Attempt was made to discuss the effects of other open cities on the SEZs and the implications of recent developments of their future prospects.

Aponte-Toro, Roberto P.

AN AFFAIR OF THE LAW, THE POWER AND THE HEART: THE CONFLICT IN THE ATLANTIC COAST OF NICARAGUA

Harvard Law School 1986 M

101 pages

Footnotes

This paper deals with Nicaragua, but it is not about "freedom fighters" and "devils". Different from the now common approach in most newspaper coverage as well as public relations rhetoric, this paper attempts to be a balanced juridical and political analysis of a human conflict taking place in an area bombarded with demagoguery, inflammatory characteristics, as well as real weapons.

The author looks at the conflict between the indigenous populations of the Atlantic Coast of Nicaragua and the Government of that country. This conflict is not immunized from the effects of the external variable which produces most of the rhetoric normally state in United States foreign policy. In this instance, however, it may be a grave mistake to transpose that variable as the only real cause of the problem. The conflict here is presented with more balance, and with less of a apocalyptic perspective. It represents an example of a human, legal, and political problem which has generated natural human reactions on both sides of the equation.

What the author attempts to do is to use the existing framework of International Law to present a juridical analysis which may provide a framework to accommodate both sides' interests in conflict; one that will perform precisely some of those functions that served as rationalization for the establishment of the United Nations Charter.

The process of building trust between the parties as to a limited right to self-determination and self-government, as well as keeping open the possibilities of increasing participation of the indigenous population in national politics so as to influence policies which may affect them, is a very delicate one, full of stumbling blocks. The issue of autonomy as managed in international law is basically a political construct. Traditionally, political forces within the boundaries of the state have imposed the answer to the question. Generally, it has resulted from a dynamic struggle between the forces of a dominant and a dependent party. The conflict has been considered an internal or domestic issue, as domestic as the conflict between a state and its citizens was before Human Rights legislation and jurisprudence came along. The issue is the limited right of an indigenous population to self-determination in areas which are most dear to them. Commentators and jurists have opened the doors to sustained military claims to secession. Not keeping a door open to non-military non-secessionist claims, may just be an invitation to further warfare and dismemberment of states.

In the environment of mistrust which prevails between Sandinistas and Miskitos, agreements, documents or papers do not mean much. The Miskitos do not trust any structure of government. Controversies then, should be solved under circumstances which provide the weaker party, the indigenous population or minority, with the opportunity to negotiate politically with the Central Government as if it were a domestic issue, each party having a free hand in their stands. But it should leave the door open to international intervention in cases of violations of Human Rights.

Arbess, Daniel J.

REYKJAVIK AND BEYOND: THE DEMOCRATS AND STRATEGIC POLICY

Harvard Law School 1987 M

74 pages

Footnotes

It will be a long time before all of the implications of last October's Reykjavik summit becomes clear. While the world may never be certain of precisely what President Reagan and General Secretary Gorbachev almost agreed to at Hofdi House, whatever it was transformed the scope of future U.S.-Soviet talks and altered the strategic debate in the West. Reykjavik represents a moment of truth from which there will be no turning back. For almost half a century, conventional wisdom has held that the deterrent power of the U.S. nuclear umbrella is the very foundation of the West's security, the factor responsible for preventing war between the superpowers. In a single stroke, the rhetorical flourish of Reyjavik seemed to throw that conventional wisdom into the wind. While the Reagan administration and most Democrats have tried to put the "visionary stuff," as Margaret Thatcher describes it, back into the bottle, Gorbachev's statements since Reyjavik seem to indicate that the Soviets intend to keep a world without nuclear weapons on the agenda well into the future.

Critics of Reykjavik have two choices: they can either defend the conventional wisdom with its strategic shortcomings and limited arms control possibilities; or they can advance another approach to arms control and deterrence based on a different set of assumptions. Defense intellectuals in the Democratic party have thus far adopted the first tack, criticizing President Reagan for making proposals inconsistent with U.S. defense strategy and security. This paper makes the case for the second choice by arguing that Gorbachev's proposal at Reykjavik and since provide the United States and its allies with an historic opportunity to address contradictions that have long plagued its strategy, and to harmonize U.S. strategic policy with emerging realities. The rhetorical commitment to a world without nuclear weapons has also fractured the traditional arms control community, leaving it unfocussed and inattentive to the larger issues. A part of the arms control community, represented by McGeorge Bundy, Morton Halperin, and Robert McNamara, and others, is promoting fundamental changes in Western strategy in the form renunciation of first use of nuclear weapons and removal of nuclear weapons from the normal military infrastructure. This group is vague about how, or whether, the requirements of extended deterrence are to be met in the absence of the threat of first use, and whether and under what conditions deterrence is necessary. Others remain committed to first use and strategic modernization as an integral component of extended deterrence. There is agreement on two agenda items - the importance of preserving the ABM Treaty, and the desirability of deep cuts, yet not total elimination of first strike ballistic missiles - but beyond that, little consensus on what are, and what are not, desirable and realistic arms control objectives, and how they fit with strategy.

Archambault, William Herbert

HOSPITAL CREDENTIALS ACTION AND DUE PROCESS: A FRAMEWORK FOR FAIRNESS

George Washington Law School 1986 M

43 pages

Footnotes

During the past two decades, economic and social pressures have produced significant changes in the delivery of health care in the United States. Hospitals, in particular, have experienced a dramatic evolution in their responsibilities. Court rulings in the 1960s, that hospital governing bodies have the duty to monitor health care and prevent harm to patients, have received broad judicial acceptance. Legislative, executive and professional recognition of this duty followed and is today evidenced by state licensure statutes, Medicare and Medicaid regulations and the standards of the Joint Commission on Accreditation of Hospitals. No longer seen as simply providing working space for physicians, hospitals are now expected to be active participants in the effort to provide only quality health care.

Hospitals cannot balance and fulfill their responsibilities to the public and their staff physicians without a well defined credentialing program. This process needs to include a system of selecting, monitoring and evaluating staff physicians. When it reveals a physician of questionable qualifications or one who exhibits suspect performance or behavior, the process must allow prompt, decisive and fair action. With an almost endless variety of possible circumstances, problems and personalities, a hospital must have a well conceived, objective fair hearing plan to meet this demand.

Whether or not a hospital agrees with the specifics of the guidelines presented in this paper, it is necessary to incorporate their underlying policies and legal principles into the fair hearing plan. The identity and role of the hearing officer, for example, can be prescribed in many legitimate and acceptable ways. But if the hospital, through the hearing officer, creates a hearing environment in which the provider is placed at a serious disadvantage (such as where the hearing officer is a legally trained advocate for the hospital) then the hospital may expect serious judicial challenge to adverse credentials decision.

In short, hospitals can no longer assume that their staffing decisions are "in house." While deference to professional judgment still exists, courts are becoming less reluctant to critically scrutinize the procedure and substance of peer review. There are many reasons, legal, economic and professional for implementing a fair hearing plan. If there are good reasons to ignore the increasing pressure for such a plan they are quickly disappearing under the layers of recent court decisions.

Ariens, Michael .

SUICIDAL RIGHTS

Harvard Law School 1987 M

83 pages

Footnotes

A paradox of American liberal thought may be best expressed by those not of it. The "debate" between Aquinas and Hume informs some of the terrain to be surveyed in appraising the ethical issues concerning a "right" to commit suicide. In a markedly legalistic society like the United States, it also is an aid in organizing the legal responses to acts of and attempts to commit suicide. Like most ethical issues presently confronting the people of the United States, there is an attempt to find a solution by resort to courts of law.

This legal debate requires a critical review of the relationship of the individual and the community in present American liberal thought. Modern American liberal thought postulates that the government or community must be neutral about what is good for both members of the community and the community itself. It also postulates that there exists a sphere of action which affects solely an individual. That is, there exists a boundary in which certain actions will only harm oneself rather than others. The neutrality postulate and the harm to self/harm to others dichotomy are best explicated by John Stuart Mill in his essay ON LIBERTY.

The structure of Mill's liberal paradigm in constitutional law is an attempt to alleviate the tension between claims of right by an individual and claims of community interest by the state. The author shows that this attempt cannot succeed in structuring a solution to a debate about a right to commit suicide, but can only result in exacerbating the tensions found in American liberalism.

The Mill paradigm is becoming the prism through which suicides will be viewed. The separation of the self from others is becoming complete. The vision of a community with substantive ideals and hopes is replaced with a collection of atomistic individuals who impose their goals, through law, upon the community. In this situation, an ideal of redemption or hope for and from the community can no longer exist.

Bane, Philip Howard

COMBINED WORLDWIDE REPORTING: LEGISLATIVE IMPASSE AS A RESULT OF THE CONTAINER DECISION

George Washington Law School 1986 M

66 pages

Footnotes and appendices

Attempting to read the future in a crystal ball made up of footnotes from a United States Supreme Court opinion and statements from politicians is certainly fraught with risk. Many legal scholars risked their reputations on an explanation of the Court's famous footnote number 37 in 'Commissioner v. Crane'. The legal community waited for thirty-six years before the Court explained what it had intended in that curious footnote. Predicting accurately the outcome of any legislative proposal is no more secure a proposition.

Notwithstanding the risk inherent in such a task, this paper attempts to deal with the issues expounded in the case of Container Corporation v. Franchise Tax Board, decided on June 27, 1983, and the recent legislative impasse at the Federal and State levels over resolving the application of the worldwide combined reporting method of unitary taxation to multijurisdictional corporations. These issues take on significance for the future because of the present significant political and economic repercussions resulting from the impasse over the issue of unitary taxation and its application to multijurisdictional corporations.

In Container the Court held that California's application of the unitary business principle to a domestic parent corporation and its foreign affiliates was proper. The Court went on to hold that California had no obligation under the Foreign Commerce Clause of the United States Constitution to use the "arms-length" accounting method as used by the Federal Government, which also happens to be the prevailing international standard in allocating income.

This paper introduces the subject by discussing the high degree of interest that this issue attracts.

Next, it discusses the mechanics of unitary taxation with a discussion of the issues Container did and did not resolve. The compromises reached during the worldwide Unitary Tax Working Group Sessions and Final Report is discussed. The Treasury Department's recently proposed legislation and spread sheet disclosure requirements is analyzed. As a result of recent legislative impasses at the Federal and State level, the paper concludes with a review of the possible courses of action left available.

Banks, David

HAWAII'S RESPONSE TO REGULATION D

Harvard Law School 1986 M

83 pages

Footnotes

From 1950 to 1970, the growth dynamics of the American economy lay in established institutions, but since 1970 these dynamics have moved to the entrepreneurial sector. Small and new businesses now provide the majority of jobs generated in the economy and contribute a significant portion to the business output and gross national product of the United States.

The scope of entrepreneurial activity, however, is proportionate to the availability of investment capital. For years small business interests have complained bitterly to their elected representatives about securities laws and their deadening effect on capital formation. Small businesses, in particular, have suffered from the disproportionate costs of registration at both the state and federal levels.

In the last ten years legislators and state administrators, in recognition of the importance of small business and in response to concerns about the cost and complexity of the federal/state securities regulatory pattern, have focused on rationalizing and coordinating the regulation of small offerings. In 1980 Congress enacted the Small Business Investment Incentive Act, which added section 19(c) to the Securities Act of 1933. This section authorizes the Securities and Exchange Commission (SEC) to cooperate with associations of state securities officials to achieve greater uniformity in federal securities matters, to substantially reduce costs and paper work, and to minimize interference with capital formation.

In response to the Congressional mandate, on March 3, 1982, the SEC adopted Regulation D, providing a coordinated system of exemptions under the federal securities laws for private placement and limited offerings. Throughout the development of the regulation, the SEC actively sought the cooperation of the National Association of Securities Act Administrators (NASAA) with a view to encouraging the development of a compatible and uniform federal-state exemption based on Regulation D.

The goal of uniformity envisioned in the promulgation of Regulation D has forced state regulators to rethink the conceptual premises of their exemptive schemes and to reconsider the competing needs of investor protection versus capital formation. This paper does not canvas the myriad of state responses to Regulation D. Instead it examines the limited offering exemptions under the Hawaii Securities Act and how they have been revised to facilitate federal-state coordination and the capital formation requirements of limited offerings under Regulation D.

The Hawaiian exemptions compatible with Regulation D are analyzed in detail. Special attention is given to the additional exemptive criteria applied to the federal regulation and the extent to which Hawaii has aligned its exemption requirements with those of Regulation D and the current ULOE.

Berry, Dean Clement

CORNELIUS v. NUTT AND THE CURRENT STATE OF ARBITRAL REMEDIAL AUTHORITY IN THE FEDERAL SECTOR

George Washington Law School 1986 M

79 pages

Footnotes

The subject of remedies is one of the most controversial and complex areas in the law of arbitration. Although there is no serious dispute over whether arbitrators can formulate and order remedies in cases where the facts indicate they are required, questions frequently arise over the source and scope of arbitral remedial power. Nowhere is this more true than in federal sector labor arbitration, particularly now that the Supreme Court has rendered its decision in Cornelius v. Nutt.

Despite the need for consistency between arbitral and Merit Systems Protection Board (MSPB) forums, the disparate formulation and application of remedies in like cases is unavoidable. The nature of the forums promotes some inconsistency and, in light of its implicit allowance of differing remedial powers, there is little reason to believe this is wholly at odds with congressional intent that otherwise emphasizes consistency. This is especially true where arbitrators have consciously sought to apply MSPB standards and procedures in arriving at an appropriate remedy.

Any difference in remedies actually devised would reflect the inescapable fact that reasonable people can differ as to precisely what needs to be done to make an injured employee whole. Moreover, given the largely symmetric power between forums with respect to the basic remedies (reinstatement, back pay, and attorney's fees), there is little reason to believe that grievants will base their forum choice on an expectation of quantum differences in remedial relief. Indeed, an employee with a meritorious claim will more likely choose a forum based on where she has the best chance of prevailing on the merits; remedies, though certainly of great importance, are of little use when one's entitlement to them cannot be established.

For these reasons, an arbitrator's general discretion to formulate remedies consistent with the applicable collective bargaining agreement and relevant statutes, rules, and regulations, should remain intact in spite of counter-arguments based on the Supreme Court's resolution of Cornelius v. Nutt.

Bessner, Ronda

THE CONSTITUTIONALITY OF THE GROUP LIBEL OFFENSES IN THE CANADIAN CRIMINAL CODE

Harvard Law School 1986 M

78 pages

Footnotes

In 1965 a parliamentary committee was established whose mandate was to study and report upon the problems associated with the dissemination of hate propaganda in Canada. The special Committee was instructed to prepare recommendations on the suppression and control of group libel in the event the Committee concluded that the situation was serious enough to warrant government action.

It is the author's view that a balancing of interests approach should be taken by the courts in determining the constitutionality of legislation which restricts an individual's right to free expression. The courts should carefully weigh the state's purpose in enacting the particular statute against the individual's right to speak freely on the subject of his choice. The courts ought to be vigilant in protecting the highly valued right of free speech and only uphold laws which are designed to protect important societal interests and which are narrowly drawn to serve these purposes. In addition, courts should give serious considerations to the adoption of the public forum theory. The courts ought to be more protective of speech that occurs in a park, on the street or in another traditional public forum than of expression which takes place on other public property.

The author also feels that the category approach to speech should not be adopted by the courts. There are degrees of offensiveness and harm which result from group libel, obscenity and the other categories of speech which have been designated by the American courts as unprotected by the Constitution. Only speech which causes substantial injury, tangible or intangible, to either the people to whom it is directed or to society at large should be prohibited.

The clear and present danger test is not a suitable standard for ascertaining the constitutionality of group libel laws and other statutes which place limitations on the right to free speech. Firstly, a speaker cannot be successfully prosecuted under this doctrine unless his audience responds in a violent manner. Secondly, the speaker's words may not produce the "imminent" violent reaction required by the clear and present test. Finally, the test appears to be designed to prevent incidents of public disorder from occurring and is little concerned with protecting the vilified groups from physical and psychological harm.

The courts of Canada are in the process of closely scrutinizing the various approaches taken by the American judiciary to the First Amendment. From the few decisions rendered since the inception of the entrenched Charter of Rights, it appears likely that the courts will employ a balancing standard in assessing the constitutional validity of such legislation as the group libel provisions of the Criminal Code.

Bolmin, Monique

THE ROLE OF THE INTERNATIONAL FINANCIAL INSTITUTIONS IN THE RESCHEDULING DEBT OF THE THIRD WORLD COUNTRIES: THE BAKER INITIATIVE

Harvard Law School 1987 M

60 pages

Footnotes

Since the beginning of the 1980's, the international debt crisis has become the nightmare of Third World countries. This situation, which reached a peak in August 1982, with the unilateral decision of the Mexican government to suspend the payment of its debt services, originated in a complex set of economics, social and political factors that have existed since the mid-1970's.

The amount of the external debt of developing countries has reached such an extent that it has not only impeded the development of less developed countries, but has also begun to seriously undermine the world economic systems.

The spectrum of the bankruptcy of U.S. banks after the Mexican collapse, the astronomical U.S. trade deficit, the social and political turmoil in some debtor countries are some of the main indirect consequences of the external debt problem.

Indeed, the Secretary of the U.S. Treasury, J. Baker, proposed the adoption of a new plan, which called for the application of a sustained growth policy by the major indebted countries, as the only solution to comply with the burden of their debt-service.

The Baker initiative includes the following three measures: implementation by debtor countries of a structural growth oriented policy, enhancement of the role of the multilateral development banks in the management of the debt, and new net lendings by commercial banks. This initiative, however, does not reveal any original proposals. In other words, these measures were already considered as necessary by a number of experts and advocated by many of the indebted countries.

The U.S. position vis-a-vis the external debt problem within the United Nations multilateral institutions since 1981, the beginning of the Reagan administration, has been characterized by the support of a tough policy, administered in a magisterially manner by the IMF. Furthermore, the U.S. government has always demonstrated its reluctance to encourage the action of the multilateral development bank in the management of the debt. In addition, these institutions were viewed by the U.S. administration and the U.S. Congress as some sort of "welfare agencies".

The purpose of this paper is to present the origins and the causes of the Baker initiative, and the consequences of its implementation. Analyzed is the role of the IMF and the World Bank in the debt management process. From this analysis, it is possible to identify the factors which led to the necessity for the adoption of a new strategy to administer the international debt crisis. Then considered is the consequences of the Baker plan on the policy of these two institutions, their respective role and the legal procedures used to enforce it. The impact of its implementation on the relationship between the industrialized countries and the less developed countries within the UN multilateral institutions is also included.

Finally a discussion is presented as to the extent that one country or a coalition can serve its own interests through the implementation of rules which take on the nature of an international rule, and which is supposed to be the result of an agreement between all the parties concerned.

Briones, Luis Fernandez

CURRENT TAXATION OF FOREIGN SUBSIDIARIES: A PROPOSAL FOR ANTI-AVOIDANCE LEGISLATION IN SPAIN

Harvard Law School 1986 M

105 pages

Footnotes

In recent years there has been a growing interest in preventing international tax avoidance and evasion. One of the avoidance scheme deserving detailed analysis is the use of foreign tax haven subsidiaries which accumulate income at low rates of tax, thereby deferring the higher rates of domestic tax. The importance of this problem is illustrated by the number of international congresses and organizations that have addressed it and by the increasing number of countries that have enacted provisions to prevent tax free accumulation of income by subsidiaries.

The International Bar Association surveyed the primary industrialized countries of the world and concluded that "with the exception of Spain" all the reports indicated that all other national revenue authorities are hostile to their own nationals using tax havens in order to avoid or minimize their domestic tax burdens.

As a consequence, Spanish taxpayers may easily divert their taxable income to tax haven corporations and defer, sometimes permanently, the Spanish income tax. For this reason, Spain must promptly develop coherent anti-avoidance legislation that will prevent wealthy taxpayers and large corporations from deferring or avoiding their tax liabilities through international devices.

One of the most difficult problems in establishing anti-avoidance measures is writing legitimate tax legislation. This paper addresses part of this problem by examining those circumstances that justify the current taxation in Spain of undistributed earnings of foreign affiliates, analyzing legislation of various countries on a comparative basis. The paper contains a broad overview of the problem of tax deferral on earnings from foreign investment made through foreign corporations. It also examines how various tax systems determine when deferral must be eliminated. The author then formulates criteria that would assist the Spanish Congress and Administration in developing anti-avoidance legislation.

The provisions discussed in this paper cannot be developed without attention to other aspects of anti-avoidance legislation. Such legislation must address a broad group of subjects in a unitary way. The specific provisions of CFC regulations will be affected by the approach chosen for dealing with other avoidance problems, such as transfer prices or the deductibility of payments to tax haven corporations.

Brown, Hank

IRA'S - A WAGE EARNERS PATH TO BECOMING A MILLIONAIRE

George Washington Law School 1986 M

78 pages

Footnotes

America has long cherished its image as a land of opportunity. Generations of working people have dreamed of becoming millionaires. Those dreams of wealth have been fired again by the potential accumulation of Individual Retirement Accounts (IRA).

A little over a decade old, the IRA is available to those who earn compensation. The program is an attempt to encourage savings for retirement by working people of moderate means.

The attraction of deducting contributions from taxable income and the prospect of tax-deferred earnings while funds are in an IRA have stimulated explosive growth.

The focus of this paper is to take an in-depth look at the Individual Retirement Account and explore its workings, potentials and shortcomings. While there is a wealth of information published on IRAs, much of it is out of date because of statutory changes and very little of it draws together the many sections of the Internal Revenue Code that impacts IRAs. This analysis adds to the current literature on this subject by; analyzing the advantages and disadvantages of an IRA, comparing the features of an IRA to other tax-deferred options, providing a comprehensive look at the various issues relating to an IRA, examining when one should borrow to fund an IRA, and quantifying the potential accumulation of assets by utilizing an IRA.

The current literature has made much of the point that IRAs are not for everyone. The author explored the disadvantages of an IRA, but the most significant include the 10% penalty for premature withdrawals, inability to borrow from or on the account, and the comparatively less favorable tax treatment upon withdrawal. While these disadvantages are important, they may be offset with advantages in other areas. The offset proposal for IRA contributions in the event you contribute to 401(k) and 403(b) plans is a significant deterrence to growth.

The individual retirement account has experienced spectacular growth and has the potential for more. While it can be extremely useful in saving and preparing for retirement, it is only one of many tools to achieve that end. It should never be considered an exclusive alternative, but a very valuable additional program whose potential usefulness will vary with your time in life, personal circumstances and financial resources.

Brown, Kyle Nelson

PARTIAL TERMINATIONS OF QUALIFIED PENSION, PROFIT SHARING, AND STOCK BONUS PLANS

George Washington Law School 1986 M

96 pages

Footnotes

The current economic climate in some industries is forcing more and more employers to close plants and divisions or initiate mass discharges or layoffs of employees which can have significant consequences for an employer's pension plan. A discharge of employees, with the resulting exclusion of the employees from the company's pension plan, can cause a partial termination of the plan, requiring the employer to fully vest all terminated employees in all accrued and funded benefits.

Section 411(d)(3) of the Internal Revenue Code (Code) of 1954 requires that upon a partial termination of a qualified plan, all benefits funded and accrued must be fully vested. However, Section 411(d)(3) gives no guidelines on what a partial termination is or how it is to be determined. The doctrine of partial termination has developed by case law, with significant assistance by Internal Revenue Service Revenue Rulings and other published positions.

A partial termination occurs in one of two basic ways: the exclusion of a segment or class of employees from the plan or the reduction of future vesting or benefit accruals for all classes of employees. These types of partial terminations have been referred to as horizontal and vertical terminations, respectively.

This paper examines several problems and interesting concepts within the doctrine of partial terminations. First, the history and evolution of the doctrine is covered. Next, how a partial termination is discovered is discussed, followed by the normal litigation procedure. The most controversial and uncertain area of the doctrine, how the existence of a partial termination is determined, is examined in great detail. Finally, the paper focuses on the taxability consequences of a partial termination. The currently 'hot' area of plan asset reversions to the employer upon termination is not discussed, except as to how the creation of such a potential reversion may cause a partial termination.

Bull, Stephen N.H.

LANGUAGE RIGHTS IN INTERNATIONAL AND DOMESTIC LAW

Harvard Law School 1986 M

95 pages

Footnotes

This paper addresses the issue of the legal rights available to individuals and people in relation to the use of language. The issues raised go not so much to the question of freedom of the content of expression, but rather to freedom of the manner of expression and specifically whether and to what extent legal authorities have the power to compel people to use or not to use any particular language. Conversely, the question is whether those being directed have any rights in relation to their choice of language, and if so what they are.

Analyzing the reasons that language is important to people should assist in understanding the nature of legal regulation of language. One fundamental reason is that language is an instrument or medium for attaining certain benefits. To acquire skills and knowledge clearly requires the use of speech to convey the ideas inherent in them. The denials of a language understood by the individual will result in the denial of education in the sense that education in a language which is understood less than perfectly will probably entail a less than perfect understanding of the topic. Therefore, education is a particular important benefit facilitated by language, since it is essential to the acquisition of many other benefits.

Secondly, a strong argument can be made that language is necessary to secure just legal remedies. There is a danger that a litigant who cannot adequately understand the conduct or implications of legal proceedings will not have his case properly decided. Thus, procedural due process involves the notion of parties being able to fairly present their case and understand and rebut the opposing case.

Thirdly, language ability is often a necessary prerequisite to access to power. For example, the right to vote may be denied on the basis of a literacy test which acts to exclude those entitled to vote, but who are not competent in the language of the text. Also, access to employment in the civil service of a country will often involve a test in the official language which may not be a language of all the country's citizens. Further, ability in a particular language may be a precondition to naturalization, to the issue of a passport, and even to rights of mobility within a country.

Finally, language forms part of the individual's psychological and social make-up. It identifies him as a member of groups, allows him to interact with other members, is a "significant base value for the performance of many different social roles."

Byrd, B. Sharon

WRONGDOING AND ATTRIBUTION: IMPLICATIONS BEYOND THE JUSTIFICATION - EXCUSE DISTINCTION

Columbia Law School M

105 pages

Footnotes

The justification - excuse distinction has experienced a revival in the theoretical literature of the past two decades. Although still highly debated and criticized, it can be formulated as distinguishing questions of wrongdoing from those of attribution. A justification concerns the wrongfulness of an actor's conduct. It presupposes the violation of a legal or moral norm but provides that this violation was the right thing to do under the circumstances involved. As such it addresses the nature of the conduct and can be compared with the norm expressed in the criminal law prohibition itself. Commonly recognized justifications include self-defense, lesser evils, consent, and law enforcement. An excuse, on the other hand concerns the blame we may fairly attribute to the actor. It not only presupposes the violation of a legal or moral norm but also the wrongful or unjustified nature of this violation. Accordingly, it does not address the correctness of the actor's conduct, but rather the culpability of the actor for participating in such conduct. It expresses understanding for the actor because of his diminished ability to conform to the legal or moral norms involved.

This diminished ability may be the result of personal incapacity or of the extreme nature of the situation in which he finds himself. Typical excuses are duress, necessity, involuntary intoxication, unavoidable mistake of law, and insanity. If this distinction is accepted it arguably has certain consequences with respect to the appropriateness of third party intervention and the right to exercise self-defense. Justified conduct, if seen as the right thing to do in the situation, may be assisted by third parties and may not be defended against. Excused conduct, if seen as the wrong, but understandable, thing to do in the situation may not be assisted by third parties and may be defended against.

The author argues that the content of justificatory defense can be determined or alternatively that if it cannot then neither can the content of prohibitory norms. Most importantly, it is shown, that the decisive characteristic distinguished justifications from excuses is the function rather than the content of these norms. Furthermore, it is illustrated that the issue of mistake relates to the actor's intent and thereby to a dimension of the wrongdoing - attribution distinction different from that of justification and excuse. Finally, the author shows that once the content of justifications is understood and the issue of mistake is properly ordered that the consequences of making a justificatory claim follow from the nature of that claim and, therefore, should have practical value and be reflected in the criminal law.

Caceres, Manuel M.

OIL AS AN ALTERNATIVE FOR PARAGUAY'S DEVELOPMENT

Harvard Law School 1987 M

47 pages

Footnotes

This paper analyzes the impact of oil production in Paraguay. Even though this is yet to happen, specialists are sure that Paraguay has oil reserves in the Chaco. This region, known as the 'Gran Chaco', is located in the central part of South American. The 'Gran Chaco' includes great territories located in Argentina, Bolivia and Paraguay. Oil production is already going on in Argentina and Bolivia, and Paraguay is expected to join these countries in the near future.

Paraguay has a lot to learn, and if its government is clever enough can make good use of other countries problems caused by the mismanagement of the oil revenues. This is why this paper mentions other countries' experience, such as Mexico, Nigeria, Venezuela and Cameroon.

It is especially interesting to know how the oil production will affect Paraguay's agriculture-based economy. What generally happens is that this big flow of revenues is spent domestically, bringing an appreciation of the rate exchange, leading a shift in the production from the tradeable sectors to the non-tradeable. Another consequences is that the traditional export sectors - in Paraguay's case agricultural products such as cotton and soybean - will suffer due to the decline of international competitiveness as a result of higher exchange rates. Moreover, while real wages increases throughout the economy, the gap between rural and urban wages widens. As a consequence of the latter, there is a huge rural migration to towns and cities. Paraguay can also learn from its own experience. Due to the construction of the Itaipu hydroelectrical project with Brazil on the Parana river - the largest dam in the world - Paraguay went through unprecedented economic growth in the 1970's. But this boom stopped in 1982 when the project ended. At this time the country entered a recession, from which it has not recovered completely. This could have been avoided if the government had controlled the effects of the foreign currency produced by the project.

What the country must keep in mind is that oil is a limited resource, thus it will end one day. So the country should not count on oil for all its development plans. The government, as well, should not rely on the oil revenues as a permanent source of its budget. This pattern is what happened in most of the oil producing developing countries.

Campanini, Cinzia M.

A MAN'S CASTLE: PARADIGMS IN FOURTH AMENDMENT REASONING

Columbia Law School 1986 M

96 pages

Footnotes

In this paper the author has attempted a miniature exercise in the jurist's self-consciousness. In reasoning about, and within, the law, one makes an endless resort to an often unarticulated tacit knowledge that conditions ones reaction to a problem, the Gestalt through which we share and formulate it, the mechanism for 'seeing' similarities to problem-examples on which we have been educated. This shared knowledge, expressed partly in unquestioned 'dogmas' and 'paradigms' provides the jurist with analogies as well as a set of privileged or admissible metaphors which determine what problems are perceived as 'legal', and how they should be disposed of.

It is believed that a first step to understand this fact about legal thinking is to inquire into that oft-used, but poorly understood, judicial tool which is commonly named 'analogy'. The author reconstructs a fragment of it, which has caught attention as a frequent topos in the law: that "the world changes," or that "the law is in flux," that "technological advance requires legal change." Clearly, the author is not denying here the fact of technological change, and the like.

What the author argues is that the law is able to cope with such changes only if the paradigms that permeate juristic thought are made to shift, providing a set of perspective-axes whereby we can see the new situation as a problem which deserves a legal solution. These paradigms allow the accommodation within old concepts and categories of such new problems: what is understood, for instance, as a 'contract,' a 'theft,' a 'search,' a 'seizure' varies with the paradigm, which embodies a different view of the world and of human relationships. A problem lies in their frequent co-existence or interference side-by-side. A paradigm is seldom totally abandoned, and analogy tends to perpetuate difficulties: for it permits new wine to be poured in old vessels, which may not be totally cleared of stubborn sediments.

Fourth amendment jurisprudence provides an invaluable lore for the elucidation of the fundamental concern of this paper. When the decision is made to bring certain discrete factual occurrences within the net of the law, the key role is played by paradigms that provide an interpretive framework for those facts.

Canales-Zambrano, Gregorio G.

ASPECTS OF MEXICAN INTERNATIONAL TRADE: THE GATT AND THE BILATERAL RELATIONSHIP WITH THE UNITED STATES

Harvard Law School 1986 M

97 pages

Footnotes

Since the late 1970's Mexico has become the third commercial partner to the United States after Canada and Japan. On the other hand, the United States is Mexico's main trading partner by far.

The purpose of this paper is to analyze from a legal point of view the bilateral trade relationship between Mexico and the U.S. as it is now, and how it would be affected in the assumption that Mexico joined the General Agreement on Trade and Tariffs (GATT). Also it deals with internal U.S. and Mexican trade laws, and commercial policies.

Trade between two countries is important for its economical, social and political implications. There is an assumed conclusion that a free trade, or at least in a more liberated trade, between a rich and developing country with a high per capita income and a poorer less developed country with a low per capita income, would make the rich country richer and the poor country poorer. Although in more general terms, traditionally trade between countries has been beneficial to both in many ways. It is clear that in one way or another that what happens in either Mexico or the United States affects the other country. In a sense the future of both countries is linked together.

On a fair bilateral trade both Mexico and the United States should benefit. One country has a competitive advantage in some areas like cheap labor, climate, natural resources, geographical location and population, while the other country has a competitive advantage on different fields such as high technology, huge capital resources, economies of scale, infra structure, a big and sophisticated market, among other. A fair trade between the two countries would lead them into an economic convergence rather than into an economic divergence. In a good negotiated outcome, the interest and concern of both would have to be taken into account.

From the Mexican point of view, it is not possible to analyze International Trade without taking into account the bilateral relationship with the United States, and the GATT at the same time. Both are essential to its International Trade, which is why the author deals with some aspects of both in this paper. Trade is only one aspect of the complex relationship between Mexico and the United States. Illegal immigrants, foreign policy, tourism, drugs, foreign investment, the enormous debt, are among the most controversial points that dominate the bilateral relationship.

Canseco, Alfredo Ferrero Diez

MODERN TENDENCIES OF TORT LAW AND THE CONCEPT OF INSURANCE IN THE PERUVIAN CIVIL LAW SYSTEM

Harvard Law School 1987 M

81 pages

Footnotes and bibliography

The subject of Liability and Tort Law has always been considered important. This importance will undoubtedly grow, in so far as mankind keeps its irrepressible and accelerated progress. New risks are born constantly, which society somehow will have to absorb, because it will be impossible for individuals to cover the economic losses derived from them, and the victim will not be repaid. The legal system through different mechanisms created by society and the State, an reflected in legislation, will be in charge of relieving the economic problem caused by those losses. It is important to remember that the liability problem is basically an economic problem. Mere coexistence causes an illimitable series of relations and links which puts everybody's right in constant contact and jeopardy. First and utmost priority must then be given to the compensation of the victim and the social diffusion of the economic burden of loss.

The theory of social distribution of risks and losses exposed here, has as one of its premises, that the majority of accidents are the result of risks created by everyday changing modern life. Society's liability is evident if we consider that it consciously accepts the benefits derived from those risks. According with the theory, the economic cost of loss (except for fraud and gross negligence) must be shared by the community in order to prevent the burden from falling upon anyone in particular.

According with the complex economic problematic in Peru, the premiums of the compulsory liability insurance cannot be too high so as to not be an incentive for the purchase of this insurance, and in this way be an incentive for the potential insurer to violate the compulsory regulations that request the purchase of the compulsory insurance. If the latter happens, the victims from the uninsured motorist will increase, so as to make the system ineffective. The premium of this compulsory insurance must not be so high so as to make better for the insured to bear the risk of having to suffer itself the consequences of the damage he caused, instead of being protected, previous payment of the premium, by an insurance company.

The conjunction of the Compulsory Liability Insurance and the Voluntary Insurance, working together toward the public interest of satisfaction of the victim, might well be a solution for the problematic of tort law in this regard. The first step now is to implant a Compulsory Insurance according to a social and economic reality.

Carlson, Louis Davidson

THE LAW OF ARMED CONFLICT IN INTERNAL CONFLICTS: THE AFGHANISTAN CONFLICT

George Washington Law School 1986 M

144 pages

Footnotes and appendices

The purpose of this paper is to explore the law of armed conflict applicable to internal conflicts, especially the application and effects of Article 3, common to the four Geneva Conventions of 1949, focusing primarily upon its application in reference to the Civilian Convention where it has primary application in fulfilling its humanitarian function. The continuing conflict in Afghanistan will be used as a point of reference, and as an example of specific problem areas in applying the humanitarian law of armed conflict relating to internal conflicts in general, and the common Article 3 in particular.

Subsequent developments in the law of armed conflict related to internal conflicts will also be discussed, to include the 1977 Protocols Additional to the Geneva Conventions of 1949, and their status and contribution to the humanitarian law applicable to internal armed conflicts.

In the modern world it is becoming increasingly difficult to identify any armed conflict as being "purely domestic," or even as being "not of an international character." It is noteworthy, however, that since World War II, what have been designated as "internal" conflicts have been the most prevalent form of armed conflict.

In the first two decades following World War II, more than fifty new nations came into existence. It has been stated that eighty percent of the victims of armed conflict since the war have been the result of civil wars, largely related to these developing countries.

Since the effective control of international violence and coercion and the maintenance of a world legal order is the most basic task of the international community of nations, the development and application of customary and treaty law pertaining to contemporary "non-international" armed conflicts is of utmost importance.

Cavanagh, Edward D.

DETREBLING ANTITRUST DAMAGES: AN IDEA WHOSE TIME HAS COME?

Columbia Law School 1986 M

118 pages

Footnotes

Since the passage of the Sherman Act in 1890, successful plaintiffs in private antitrust actions have been entitled to recover three times the actual damages awarded. Originally embodied in section 7 of the Sherman Act, the mandatory treble damages provision was later incorporated into section 4 of the Clayton Act and made applicable to all actions in which private plaintiffs sought recovery under the federal antitrust laws. In the intervening century since the Sherman Act became law, the antitrust debate has concentrated largely on issues of substantive liability.

While the desirability of the mandatory treble damages remedy has been challenged from time to time since 1890, scholars did not focus seriously on antitrust remedies until the 1970's. In the last decade, mandatory trebling has come under intense attack from economists and legal scholars. The debate has broadened, and the detrebling movement has gathered momentum. Most recently, the Reagan Administration unveiled a package of legislative proposals calling for sweeping changes in the antitrust laws, including detrebling of damages for most antitrust violations.

The fundamental question explored in this paper is whether mandatory treble damages remain a useful tool in enforcement of the antitrust laws. A number of factors underscore the need to re-examine mandatory trebling. The historical justification for mandatory trebling is unclear. Moreover, the antitrust laws are somewhat imprecise; the line between what is permitted and what is forbidden is not always clear. The treble damages remedy may pose a trap for the unwary individuals who think they are complying with the antitrust laws and may not only deter socially beneficial conduct but also encourage inefficiency by discouraging traders from "playing it too close to the line," thereby increasing costs and lowering output. Mandatory trebling thus raises serious questions of fairness and may lead to awards which far exceed the economic harm caused by the defendant's malfeasance.

Finally, trebling may encourage prosecution of baseless suits by parties seeking to use the antitrust laws as a whipsaw to effect a quick settlement. On the other hand, the wisdom of detrebling may be questioned especially at a time when government enforcement efforts are narrowly directed at a few readily identifiable types of misconduct and courts through doctrines such as standing and antitrust injury are making it more difficult for plaintiffs to recover. In addition, this paper will examine possible alternatives to mandatory treble damages and analyze whether any such alternatives provide a viable replacement for the present system.

While the data generated by this study furnished some useful insights, they are nonetheless limited and does not provide any definitive guidance on the question of whether the treble damages remedy should be retained. In particular, this study does not address the fundamental question of the fairness of multiple damages in antitrust matters.

Chadha, Amit Singh

A HISTORICAL, POLITICAL, ECONOMIC, SOCIAL, RELIGIOUS AND LEGAL ANALYSIS OF THE ORIGIN, CAUSE AND RISE OF TERRORISM IN THE NORTH INDIAN STATE OF PUNJAB...

Harvard Law School M

145 pages

Footnotes and bibliography

No event in Indian history since Independence has reverberated throughout the country as violently as the recent happenings in the Punjab during those days known as "Operation Bluestar." The killing of innocent people by suspected terrorists, the passing of draconian laws by the government, the assault of the army on the Golden Temple in Amritsar, the assassination of Prime Minister Indira Gandhi, by her two Sikh guards, and the ensuing violence against the Sikhs, and later an unprecedented electoral mandate to the ruling political party form the background of this discussion.

To understand the situation in all its dimensions, a brief historical sketch of the origin of the Sikhs, their psyche, philosophy, and ideology is presented.

A brief politico-historical account of the Akali movement in the 1920s outlines its post-Independence rise as a strong regional political party in the State of Punjab and its subsequent conflict with the national Congress party for control of the State of Punjab.

The paper discusses the consequences of the Parliament's enactment of acts like the Terrorist Affected Areas Act, the Disturbed Areas Act, the National Securities Act, and so forth, which are shown to violate the constitutional prohibitions.

Possible solutions under Municipal Law are examined as well as potential remedies under international law.

The Sikhs, it is suggested, must recognize that they must remove the terrorist, separatist, secessionist, and extremist labels which have been stamped on them. They must make themselves powerful economically, socially, and politically so that they develop power to influence public opinion by publicizing their just demands and the injustices they have suffered. Public opinion, a too available to every minority, can pressure sovereign governments in their domestic functions.

The Indian government, on the other hand, must stop it attempts to obscure or justify its past actions and must try to identify and understand the root cause and nature of the whole problem. The government must view the situation in a wider perspective and stay above the trivialities and political infighting for power. To satisfy the minorities, it must open itself to more public scrutiny. If legislative restrictions are enacted, the government must ensure that they are fairly applied and not grossly misused.

Chan, Jeanette K.

THE HONG KONG INTERNATIONAL ARBITRATION CENTER: AN ALTERNATIVE FOR THE PEOPLE'S REPUBLIC OF CHINA

Harvard Law School 1986 M

106 pages

Footnotes

Dispute resolution by way of arbitration has become a ubiquitous provision in business contracts relating to the People's Republic of China. Generally, the Chinese parties prefer to settle commercial disputes by friendly negotiations or consultations, and failing resolution by such means, the matter will be referred to conciliation by two third parties. Arbitration is a system of last resort for the settlement of disputes. Litigation is generally distrusted. Researchers have suggested several reasons for the Chinese preference for arbitration over litigation. Whatever the reason, the conclusion seems to be inescapable one. Failing consultation and conciliation, dispute resolution has to be by arbitration, regardless of the nature of the transaction, the amount of money involved, or the nature of the dispute, and indeed whether the dispute is a fit subject for arbitration.

The search for an appropriate arbitral forum then becomes an issue that continues to haunt China traders and their advisers. As this paper illustrates, the question is not an inconsequential one. Stripped of all the technicalities, it boils down to this: where and how should the arbitration proceed?

Many cities and organizations have been proposed as locations and places for providing an arbitral forum. None, so far, seem to have emerged as dominant choices that is satisfactory to both the foreign and Chinese parties. For years, the Chinese have preferred to arbitrate in Beijing, a choice which is almost inevitably rejected by the foreign party who is in search of a neutral third-party forum. Alternatively, the Chinese have pressed for arbitration in the country of the defendant in a dispute, but that is also unsatisfactory to the non-Chinese party due to the possibility of manipulation and uncertainty. Arbitration in a third country has now been acceptable to China. The Chinese choices of a third country is usually Stockholm, Sweden. Stockholm is indeed the unquestioned leader of arbitration in East-West trade. However, putting aside the issues of physical location, and cultural and language differences, it is doubtful whether the expertise Stockholm has acquired in trade primarily between the USSR and the West equips it to handle the kind of problem likely to be faced by parties involved in the present-day China trade. China is opening up to the West for industrialization and modernization. If anything, China is going West. The imposition of a model based on trade with the Soviet bloc is out of step with these recent developments.

Other possible choices to provide an arbitral forum have been adopted by a process of geographical elimination. An American party will end up in a forum somewhere in Europe. An English party will find itself somewhere in continental Europe. For continental Europeans, it could be anywhere except on their home turf. In addition, the Chinese have been adamantly resisting the International Chamber of Commerce arbitration in Paris.

Another city has emerged with a very ambitious plan. Hong Kong is bidding to become an international arbitration center, with special expertise in the area of China trade. The paper then compares the legislation applicable in Hong Kong and Sweden, and their respective arbitration institutions and arrives at the conclusion that Hong Kong offers more to both the Chinese and foreign parties in arbitration. Finally, it raises the potential difficulties and hurdles Hong Kong faces in establishing itself as the prime international arbitration center for China trade

Chen, Che-Hung

TAIWAN'S FOREIGN DIRECT INVESTMENT: CURRENT STATUS AND FUTURE POLICY

Harvard Law School 1986 M

55 pages

Footnotes and appendices

Foreign direct investment use to be the kind of economic activity undertaken by developed countries, such as the United States, Europe and Japan. It was in the early 1980's that people began to sense developing countries' participation in such international business.

The newcomers are different from their forerunners in many respects. To mention a few, they are generally smaller in size, less advanced in technology, and almost unknown. Their international managerial skills and ability to remote control are less developed. Although economic and business administration scholars have already proposed various theories to explain the developed countries' foreign direct investment, none of them can be properly applied to these newcomers. A popular view is that there must be some advantage for firms from developing countries to choose foreign direct investment rather than other forms of business. Such advantage is mainly that they export technology appropriate to the local environment, which is usually labor-intensive and located in other developing countries. These analyses undoubtedly help one to understand better why firms in developing countries decide to run their business overseas and how they exercise their business judgment.

However, the government of a developing country normally assumes much of the responsibility for economic growth. An economic activity like foreign direct investment, which influences the whole country so profoundly, is certainly the object of government control. To grasp a more complete picture of the foreign direct investment by developing countries, it would be useful to study its legal aspect in addition to its business aspect.

The purpose of this study was to use Taiwan as an example in examining what is the general attitude towards foreign direct investment, how the government controls it, what are the difficulties Taiwan faces, and what are the possible solutions. The author first described its development and then analyzed relevant laws and the underlying policies.

Chittur, Krishnan

PERIMETERS OF THE BUSINESS JUDGMENT RULE: A STUDY OF THE LIMITS OF DIRECTORIAL DISCRETION

Harvard Law School 1986 D

376 pages

Footnotes

Directorship as an institution has evolved rapidly in the past decade. This evolution is primarily due to increased public concern with intra-corporate accountability, and a growing clamor for social responsibility on the part of the corporations. While these have been recurrent themes in academic writings ever since the turn of the century, the functioning of large, publicly held corporations became a political issue only in the 1970s. The general distrust of authority imparted singular significance to the question of who controls whom in the corporate structure. The board's role and functioning, thus came in for critical analysis.

Although Congressional sentiment for over half a century has been that directors "should be held responsible to the unsuspecting public for their neglect", that seldom occurred in practice. Consequently, corporate management was essentially unconstrained, and converted the corporation into the "first successful institutional claimant of significant unregulated power since the nation-state established its title in the sixteenth and seventeenth centuries". In this Mecca of competitive business, the Chairman of the Securities Exchange Commission had occasion to complain that corporate management was "too often complacent, self-perpetuating, and unresponsible".

Change was inevitable, historically speaking. It was sparked by two phenomena in the late 60s and early 70s. First, in the investigative climate of Watergate, spirited pursuit of large-scale corporate malfeasance became the order of the day; reformists working with missionary zeal soon established beyond question that disreputable conduct was rampant in reputable places. Second, academicians of repute wrote extensively revealing the failure of the law to allocate the cost of corporate misbehavior properly.

The author discusses in detail the corporate structure, the role of the directors, and the Common Law Standard. Considerable analysis is included on hostile takeovers, the poison pill, and their impact on the stock holders. A section is devoted to special litigation committees in derivative suits. This covers existing curbs and judicial review of SLC reports. The paper concludes with a section on the "rule and close corporations". This includes the unique considerations, judicial intervention, and the error in approach.

Chowdhury, M. Sirajuddoulah

UNCITRAL, INTERNATIONAL COMMERCIAL ARBITRATION AND THE MODEL LAW

Harvard Law School 1986 M

77 pages

Footnotes and appendices

The ever increasing transnational transactions in the field of trade, commerce, and investment among different nations of the world of both market economies and planned economies are faced with more and more disputes arising out of their business dealings. Growing economic and commercial interdependence between countries with different economic and legal systems requires coordination of efforts to deal with issues such as the settlement of disputes between states and nationals of other states.

Because conventional litigation involves enormous time, costs, and jurisdictional complications, more attention is being focused on alternative methods of dispute resolution, especially in the fields of transnational commercial and investment disputes. Thus, to avoid the uncertainties and complications of foreign litigation, the alternative of international arbitration is gaining ground. The use of arbitration for the settlement of commercial disputes is used world-wide, in the market economies as well as the planned economies, to overcome the artificial barriers created by national frontiers, to develop a system of international justice, and to deal with issues which hitherto have been found to be intractable.

In 1966 the United Nations General Assembly established the United Nations Commission on International Trade Law (UNCITRAL). UNCITRAL has 35 members representing countries from all world regions.

The paper examines the attempt by UNCITRAL to develop a model law in international commercial arbitration with the aim of promoting more development in the field of world trade and business through the dispute settlement mechanism of the international arbitral procedure. The Model Law developed by UNCITRAL provided a comprehensive procedural framework for the arbitral resolution of the disputes arising from a broad range of international commercial transactions. It provided for party autonomy in fashioning the arbitration process, reflected the principles of fairness, and included basic provisions for the functioning of arbitration proceedings.

The timing of the project is propitious. There is a growing interest in international commercial arbitration on the part of potential litigants as well as arbitration institutions and practitioners. England and France, among other countries, are taking legislative or other steps to improve their arbitration climate for international business disputes. Canada and Hong Kong are taking appropriate measures for legislation of the UNCITRAL Model Law.

The creation of regional arbitration centers in Kualalampur and Cairo, possibly to be followed by a Lagos center, is evidence of the will of the Third World countries to offer viable alternatives to what they consider the unjustified monopoly of the traditional arbitration centers. Adoption by states of a modern Model Law on international commercial arbitration might well become a test of their acceptability as an arbitration form.

The salient features of the UNCITRAL Model Law are revealed as being especially geared to international commercial arbitration. The validity of the Model Law is shown to be particularly applicable in the present state of international arbitration.

Since the objective of the Model Law is to contain within it the whole of the arbitration law of the countries which adopt it as a model, any adaptation of its terms must also fulfill this objective. Its underlying concept should lead to a comprehensive, self-contained, and explicit restatement in one enactment of the whole of the law applicable to international commercial arbitrations in every country willing to adhere to the concept of the Model Law in principle.

The use of the UNCITRAL Model Law on international commercial arbitration for the settlement of commercial dispute would be applicable at worldwide level. The procedure would be used both in industrialized and developing countries, assuring a better justice in complex international business transactions and related dispute settlements.

Chua, Karin S.M.

CHOICE OF LAW RELATING TO NEGOTIABLE INSTRUMENTS: COMPARING THE AMERICAN AND AUSTRALIAN APPROACHES

Harvard Law School 1986 M

132 pages

Footnotes

In this paper a comparison is made of the Australian and American approaches to choice of law rules and methodology affecting negotiable instruments such as bills of exchange and promissory notes.

In these jurisdictions, the legislature has either restated or modified common-law rules. The relative merits and demerits of the Australian Bills of Exchange Act 1909 and the Uniform Commercial Code as it applies to negotiable instruments is assessed. As the Australian legislation is based on the U.K. Bills of Exchange Act 1882 and because of the unique relationship between the Australian and English legal systems, much of the discussion considers English decisions.

Negotiable instruments are unique because they combine both contractual and proprietorial characteristics and because of the fact that the assignment of a negotiable instrument constitutes a major exception to the general principle that as assignor cannot convey a better title than he already possesses.

Not all commentators agree, however, that the rigidity of legislation for choice of law is necessary helpful. It is argued that in the particular area of negotiable instruments the British and Australian legislation has been cast too rigidly and the American legislation, although aimed initially at flexibility and yet comprehensiveness, has unfortunately led some courts to encourage the application of the lex fori, and consequently, forum-shopping. It is argued that in this field the judge-made law in both jurisdictions was probably superior.

An outline of the Australian law is presented,

and this is contrasted with the American approach noting some of the differences that have been observed between American and Australian choice of law rules and methodology relating to commercial contracts generally. The flexibility of approach in both jurisdictions towards commercial contracts are contrasted with the rigidity of the Australian legislation concerning negotiable instruments.

Cooper, Graeme Stuart

REVIEWING THE BENEFIT THEORY OF TAXATION

Columbia Law School M

116 pages

Footnotes and bibliography

Taxation is often thought simply to be the way that governments finance their activities. This belief is accurate but incomplete: on the one hand, governments finance their activities by many means of which taxation is only one, and, on the other hand, they use taxes for purposes beyond the mere raising of revenue. In modern societies, taxes have become the means to many ends.

Taxes can assist a government in its attempt to regulate the functioning of the economy and are also able to be used by governments as instruments to achieve various desired social goals. Taxes are used, often as if blunt instruments, to achieve economic goals: stabilizing the economy in order to moderate the consequences of changes in a country's production, encouraging increased consumer spending, or stimulating reductions in unemployment and greater business investment. The burden of a tax, or the benefit of an exemption from a tax, will be an incentive, often a sufficient incentive, to encourage a citizen to undertake desired behavior or cease other behavior. Finally, governments will interfere with the economy and use taxes, particularly the income tax, to seek the deliberate redistribution of income and wealth.

The critical analysis of any tax is usually undertaken by reference to a number of recognized criteria which can here be reduced to three. The first is a criterion of fairness or equity. The concept underlying this criterion are twofold: first, that taxpayers who are in an identical position ought to be treated equally and, for those who are not identical, the tax burden should differ, a heavier burden falling on those who meet some second order criterion, such as being better able to bear it. Some attempts have been made to identify a temporal aspect of equitable tax treatment. Another, but less well recognized implication of this principle, is that all kinds of receipts which are essentially income ought to be taxed identically. The second is a criterion of simplicity. Again, two distinct ideas are involved. One is that the liability to submit to the tax burden and the amount on which the tax is to be assessed should not be difficult to determine. The other is that the administrative costs associated with raising each dollar of revenue should be as low as possible. This includes both the taxpayer's compliance costs of providing the information necessary for the assessment to be made as well as the bureaucracy's costs of making the assessment and collecting the revenue. The third criterion is economic efficiency. The base upon which the tax is levied should, unless otherwise intended, be economically neutral so that it does not distort the operation of markets in the private economy by influencing matters such as choices about goods and services to be produced, methods of trading and forms of investment.

Governments ask a great deal of tax systems. It is not a sufficient goal for a tax merely to collect the desired revenue. It must do at least that, but the means adopted by the government will then be expected to conform as much as possible to the constraining criteria described. In other words, the means must be circumscribed - not necessarily to ensure a more effective accomplishment of the ends, but to conform to other criteria, extraneous, in some respects, to the task of raising revenue.

de Castro, Marcus R.

THE REVISION OF FORMALISM IN CRITICAL LEGAL HISTORY

Harvard Law School 1986 M

79 pages

Footnotes

It is perhaps part of the lore of present legal thought that "the history of modern jurisprudence may be characterized as a continuing attempt to find an adequate alternative to formalism as a basis for legal justice." The critique of formalism can thus be seen as the predicament of the current jurisprudential debate.

This discussion concerning the critique of formalism develops two main theses. The first is that the critique of formalism is not complete without a critique of objectivism. Arguments are offered to explain why categories such as social vision or ideology cannot remain alien to legal analysis. The second thesis is that the articulation of the critique of objectivism with that of formalism leads to the redefinition of legal rule as constitutive discourse. The connection of legal doctrine with categories that account for social change yields a conception of legal reasoning that is more consistent with the idea of legal rule as an instance of constitutive discourse, rather than with the notion of legal norm as formal or ideal prescription.

To understand the articulation between the critique of formalism and that of objectivism in connection with the visionary and the revisionary perspectives of the critical argument is the first of the two general objectives pursued. The second objective is to examine the elements that account for the rationality of the revisionary argument. It is argued that the project of the transformative possibilities of law is only acceptable if the critique of formalism is combined with that of objectivism. It is further argued that the revisionary critique of formalism yields a standard of rationality that can be understood as a kind of discourse that embodies the formative elements of social institutions, which cannot be pressed into formal rules nor into the frozen ideal structures of visionary theories.

The account of the formalist attitude as presented in its classical version is descriptive, without articulating the problems that inhere in the formalist theory of law. The formalist conception of legal doctrine as a practice is exposed. That the visionary critique of formalism undermines the basic postulates of the formalist theory of law is demonstrated. The concept of legal analysis consistent with the visionary perspective of the critical argument is developed. The model of justice that emerges from a visionary critique of formalism is connected to one basic set of notions, which can be thought of as consistent with an enlarged concept of formalism. The notions that account for the enlarged concept of formalism are not relinquished in the process of the theoretical elaboration of the visionary theory.

With the implications of the visionary critique of formalism revealed in their problematic character, it is further argued that one can conceive of an alternative theory to the systems of thought elaborated by formalism and by the visionary perspective of the critical argument. The revisionary alternative to the theories that generate the formalist and the purposive or visionary models of justice could have the consequence of radically denying the possibility of the prevalence of an institutional practice that is similar to what is known today as legal doctrine. It would be a radically destructive approach. It is assumed that the elaboration of such a revisionary theory of law must be guided by the consideration of the fact that the best alternative to the formalist and visionary theories would be that of the transformative possibilities of law.

The revision of formalism is therefore indicated as one way to understand the relationship of the critical argument with the transformative project. The revision of formalism in this perspective corresponds to deep modifications of both the formalist and the visionary theories by way of concessions made with respect to the criteria of rationality of legal analysis. These modifications are shown to lead to a redefined practice of legal analysis. This redefined practice must be one in which the concept of legal reasoning must be modified so as to incorporate, through institutional shaping, the consideration of ideals that arise from the formative elements of social institutions.

de la Espriella, Adriana

DEROGABILITY OF JUDICIAL GUARANTEES DURING STATES OF EMERGENCY UNDER THE AMERICAN CONVENTION OF HUMAN RIGHTS

Harvard Law School 1987 M

45 pages

Footnotes

This paper responds to the question presented to the Inter-American Court of Human Rights by the government of Uruguay. These questions refer to the scope of Article 27 of the American Convention of Human Rights, which contains an enumeration of non derogable rights even in exceptional circumstances. Among the rights enumerated as non derogable, the mentioned article includes the judicial guarantees necessary to protect these rights. The Uruguayan government has asked the Court to establish what exactly are those judicial guarantees that cannot be suspended in times of emergency.

The Convention itself contains, in general, three types of judicial guarantees that all the signatory States must implement in order to ensure the protection of the rights recognized as fundamental by them. Those guarantees are the right to habeas corpus, the right to fair trial, and the right to judicial protection. The concrete question before the Inter-American Court is then, if the right to habeas corpus, the right to fair trial and the right to judicial protection can or cannot be derogated in emergency situations according to Article 27 of the Convention.

The problem has no easy solution. While it is precisely during emergencies that governments need to concentrate their powers and be subjected to more flexible controls than usual in order to overcome or prevent the crisis, it is also during emergencies that the citizens have more need to guard themselves against arbitrary decisions, abuses and violations of human rights.

The judicial guarantees that must be preserved during states of emergency relate directly to the controls and checks to the exercise of authority that can guarantee the proper use of the extended powers. Their importance cannot be sufficiently emphasized; they refer to the preservation of the rule of law and of human dignity at all times.

States of exception are by no means remote possibilities. On the contrary, they are more frequent than desirable, and specially in Latin America. In fact, "since 1950 every Latin American nation has utilized the state of siege as an emergency means to govern because of threats to internal security". Therefore, the question of the derogability of rights during emergencies must be present and serious concern for the guardians of the American Convention of Human Rights. Unfortunately, Latin America has also been a dramatic example of how emergency powers can be turned into institutionalized abuses and violations of the most fundamental rights of the human person. The safeguards and guarantees that must prevent those tragic experiences from occurring are precisely the question presented before the Court.

Dennis, Robert Davis

TRADE REORGANIZATION

George Washington Law School 1986 M

107 pages

Footnotes and appendices

The United States currently faces a severe deficit in its international trade account. Although political economists writing on the subject blame a plethora of problems on the trade deficit, most will agree that the deficit adds to inflation, buffets the value of the dollar, contributes to unemployment, promotes protectionist policies, and heightens world tensions. For example, today nearly five million Americans are currently involved in the manufacturing of goods for export.

The irony of the United States' trade debt, however, is that it reflects both the strengths and the weaknesses of the American economy. The fivefold rise in the deficit since 1982 demonstrates not only lost foreign markets but an expanding domestic economy that has also been the impetus for speeding the development of countries such as Brazil and Mexico.

The days when the United States saw itself as an economic island so independent that it could all but ignore the rest of the world are gone. Now for the first time in decades, many across the land openly wonder, "How can America compete?" To this important question there has been no shortage of analysis or proposed solutions.

Economists, for example, blame the rapid American recovery, which has attracted imports (combined with a spotty recovery abroad, which has dampened exports) on America's poor balance of trade. Bankers, on the other hand, cite the over-valuation of the dollar and interest rates, which also promote imports and retard exports. Lawyers complain that protectionist practices by a host of countries are sapping United States markets and at the same time refusing to yield their own to foreigners. Businessmen argue that the competitiveness of United States exports is a function of all three determinants; openness of market, price, and uniqueness of or demand for goods.

The purpose of this paper is to examine whether trade reorganization would help solve America's trade troubles and, if so, which of the proposals is the most promising in terms of its effectiveness and likelihood of passage. In order to analyze the proposed organizational legislation, it is first necessary to review the development of America's foreign trade policy framework.

Denzler, Beat

JURISDICTIONAL CONFLICTS IN FEDERAL SYSTEMS: A COMPARATIVE STUDY

Harvard Law School 1986 M

108 pages

Footnotes

This paper analyzes and compares federal law bearing upon adjudicatory jurisdiction in the legal systems of the United States and of Switzerland. Despite their different sizes the United States and Switzerland have similar constitutional frameworks. Both nations are federations characterized by the parallel existence of several rather independent state jurisdictions overlapped by a federal legal order, creating the typical federal environment in which various interstate conflicts can arise and multiply. Both countries face the problem of allocating jurisdiction to adjudicate among the states or cantons, and both have adopted a federal solution as to this issue. The solutions differ greatly, thus providing for an interesting basis for a comparative study about the question of how a federal system can approach interstate jurisdictional conflicts.

Interstate jurisdictional conflicts differ in many respects from multinational conflicts. The strong bonds among the states of the same nation and their citizens as well as other national policies are elements not given in an international context. The proper functioning of a federal system may require an adjustment of conflicting state interests. Unlike in the multinational context such an adjustment can be imposed even upon non-consenting states through federal law. The availability of such higher level legal order is a unique opportunity of a federal system, allowing the adoption of original and "creative" conflict resolutions, scarcely achievable in multinational cases, the jurisdictional systems of both the United States and of Switzerland being illustrative examples.

The paper focuses on the following set of questions:

What is the source of jurisdictional law?

Is there a federal approach to the issue of interstate jurisdictional conflicts, and if so what is the regulatory mechanism adopted?

Have the jurisdictional provisions the feature of an "individual" right or of a jurisdiction-allocating "federal" rule?

The paper covers in detail the features of federal rules that regulate adjudicatory jurisdiction. This is followed by coverage of the American solution through analysis in terms of federalism, and concludes with the Swiss solution which is also analyzed in terms of federalism and compared to the American solution.

Devieux, Ketty G.

FOOD AID POLICIES AND INTERNATIONAL LAW: THE UNITED STATES FOOD AID PROGRAM (PL 480) AS IMPLEMENTED IN HAITI

Harvard Law School 1986 M

93 pages

Footnotes and appendix

In the twentieth century, the United States (US) demonstrated an increased tendency to intervene in the affairs of the Caribbean nations, through both military and economic involvement. In addition to open or covert use of force, the US has also economic assistance as an instrument of its foreign policy.

The context of the Haiti/US relationship is discussed in terms of the United Nations International Law Principles of Non-Intervention and Cooperation among Nations. The paper focuses on the US Food Aid Program Public Law 480 under which food is provided to Haiti. It analyses the provisions and conditions stipulated in the agreement signed by both governments in the light of established norms of international law on the respect of sovereignty of nations and cooperation for development. The text of the agreement appears in the appendix.

It is true that no country has achieved development on the basis of foreign assistance. It is also true that food aid cannot be expected to create employment, produce valuable works, improve nutrition and at the same time be efficient and reach the poorest people. However, considering that the developing countries cannot do without aid, it is imperative to attenuate if not abolish the negative interdependence characterizing their relations with the industrialized countries. The realization of self-reliance also presumes a major shift in the developed countries' policy of dominance by which is maintained the structural dependence of the developing countries.

The paper proposes the channeling of the overproduction of the surplus countries to an international organization, such as the food and

Agriculture Organization or the World Food Program, for distribution. These organizations are in a better position to work efficiently as a result of their increased resources. The developing countries would secure a continued access to food without any condition of political nature. As the distribution would take into account the appropriateness of the food available to every country that qualifies for it, the adverse effects on self-reliance objectives would be minimized. Moreover, such a solution would help separate food aid from the donor's aid program. There is generally little doubt among development economists that aid in cash is preferable to aid in food, since even in famine situations the problem is often lack of money to buy food rather than lack of food to buy.

Dias, Ayesha K.

HOBSON'S CHOICE IN THE FALKLANDS: DECOLONIZATION OR SELF-DETERMINATION

Columbia Law School 1987 M

196 pages

Footnotes, appendices and bibliography

The Falkland Islands, situated in the South Atlantic, comprise two large islands (East and West Falkland) and some two hundred smaller islands comprising a total area of approximately twelve square kilometers. The estimated population of the Falkland Islands, at the end of 1984, was around nineteen hundred, excluding military personnel and contract workers. This population has been steadily declining but its composition remains virtually unchanged. With a few exceptions, all are of European descent and most are of British origin.

The Falklands have been (and continue to be) the subject of a long, emotional, and bitter dispute between Britain and Argentina, both of whom lay claim to sovereignty over the Islands. A great deal has been written about the legal bases upon which these claims are founded and history is interpreted (and at times manipulated) by both claimants to lend credibility to their claims.

British claim to sovereignty over the Falkland Islands are based on discovery, conquest, settlement/colonization, and acquisitive prescription. There are significant shortcomings under international law with each of these bases claimed. British discoveries at the end of the sixteenth century form the basis for their claims to the Falkland Islands.

The author briefly enumerates the historical claimed legal bases, and is convinced that they are virtually obsolete and irrelevant to the present day problems.

Included in the paper are discussions on the seventeen years of bilateral negotiations, the Falklands' War with emphasis on the challenge of international conflict, international diplomacy and mediation, and principles of international law. Also provided are some warnings and lessons that resulted from the Falklands' conflict, and how Argentina became a victim of the United Nations law and practice of self-determination.

The author then suggests alternative "modern" international law concepts which he feels have more to offer for the resolution of the complicated and vexing problems that the Falkland Islands continue to pose.

DiBattiste, Carol

FEDERAL RULE OF EVIDENCE 412 AND MILITARY RULE OF EVIDENCE 412: ARE THEY SERVING THEIR PURPOSE?

Columbia Law School 1986 M

68 pages

Footnotes and appendices

Over seven years ago, the Ninety-Fifth Congress of the United States enacted the Privacy Protection for Rape Victims Act of 1978, Federal Rule of Evidence 412, "to protect rape victims from the degrading and embarrassing disclosure of intimate details about their private lives" during the course of a rape trial. In doing so, they followed the lead of many jurisdictions which had already enacted rape shield laws. Not only did Congress seek to change the federal system's evidentiary rules, which permitted a wide ranging inquiry into the rape victim's sex life, but they also hoped to provide a model rule for jurisdictions without rape shield laws.

Military Rule of Evidence 412, modeled after the Federal Rule 412, was adopted for military practice in 1980. Its purpose is basically identical to that of its federal counterpart: "to shield victims of sexual assaults from the often embarrassing and degrading cross-examination and evidence presentations common to prosecutions of such offenses."

To effectuate their purposes, both Federal Rule 412 and Military Rule 412 have identical provisions which restrict the admissibility of evidence concerning the victim's sexual behavior. Whether the restrictive provisions of Federal Rule 412 and its military counterpart unduly infringe upon the accused's sixth amendment right to confrontation and compulsory process continues to generate much discussion and controversy among commentators.

How do the federal and military courts interpret the "constitutionally required" provision? What sexual history evidence is being admitted and why? Ultimately, is the purpose of the rules being eroded? This paper evaluates the present effectiveness of Federal Rule 412 and Military Rule 412 in light of the federal and military courts' interpretations of the "constitutionally required" provision. After examination of the historical background, purpose, and scope of Federal Rule 412 and Military Rule 412, followed by a look at the "constitutionally required" exception, the paper focuses on an analysis of the reasoning given by the courts in determining what evidence is "constitutionally required" to be admitted. The analysis leads to a final assessment of the present value of Federal Rule 412 and Military Rule 412 as laws designed to protect rape and/or sexual assault victims who testify at trial from a degrading inquisition about sexual behavior.

Dodson, Ella Wendell

CONSTRAINTS ON CHINESE BANKING AND FINANCIAL POLICY AND THEIR IMPLICATIONS FOR FOREIGN LENDERS

Columbia Law School 1986 M

90 pages

Footnotes

In the last decade, Chinese economic and financial policies have undergone significant changes. Recent reforms in several sectors of the Chinese economy have replaced the "command model" of economic activity with a "quasi-market model." As a result of these economic changes, Chinese banks and financing entities have emerged as potentially powerful regulators of the Chinese economy.

In addition, Chinese banks and financial institutions have become more important to Chinese modernization through their activities in raising foreign capital. Given the growing roles of Chinese banks in China's interaction with the world economy, it is important for foreign attorneys and bankers to recognize some of the constraints on Chinese banks and banking policies.

Some of China's banking systems and financial policies hearken back to their counterparts in capitalist countries. However, the mere use of capitalist techniques does not mean that China is abandoning the socialist road. The contradictions arising from the use of capitalist techniques to achieve socialist ends suggest the parameters of Chinese legal development in the areas of banking and finance. Moreover, as with any legal development, Chinese banking law and policy are constrained by structural factors, ideological factors and political factors.

Currently, there are several excellent English language works describing Chinese banks and banking laws. Instead of covering the same ground, this paper elucidates some of the factors shaping Chinese banking policies and practices. In particular, this paper will suggest some of the structural constraints which hamper the Chinese banks in their roles as "regulators." Then, the paper examines some of the ideological constraints which limit the independence of Chinese banks. The author then focuses on some of the legal constraints on Chinese banking policies and practices. Finally, examined is how these constraints affect the foreign lender or investor. Suggestions are then made for ways a foreign lender or investor might protect itself in light of these constraints.

Duyang, Jehng

THE APPLICATION OF CRIMINAL RULES IN IMPERIAL CHINA: A STUDY ON THE PERIOD OF RESPONSIBILITY

Harvard Law School M

85 pages

Footnotes and appendices

It can be said that the rule of the period of the responsibility is a delicate device to discern the responsibility of the offenders by taking into account the harms of the acts in question. Lying behind this rule is the traditional criminal concept that punishments fit the crime. Such a rule of responsibility period is required from a practical need to make a clear-cut line between the acts of homicide, which must be dealt with extremely carefully by the authority of a society, and other less serious offenses. It can also be seen that accompanying the design of the rule is the Confucian idea to encourage the offenders to make up for their wrongful acts. Though this idea is in fact not enforced completely, it frequently appears in the judicial decisions when the application of the rule of responsibility is in debate.

It is also notable that the rule of the Pao Ku Chih Hsien has been stipulated in a quite consistent way for a long time. Even expanded to a very complicated degree in the Ch'ing dynasty, this rule did not depart from the basic mode defined in the Tang code. This, from a macro-structure perspective, reflects the symbolic implication of the criminal codes as an embodiment of legitimacy, which is subject to less changes. On the other hand, the unchanged substance of the codes indicates that, for a political power newly grasping the power, it would be a wise policy not to impinge upon the established legal order for the purpose of solidifying the control and preserving social stability. It is also possible that without encountering a strong rival in culture, as of the last half of the nineteenth century, radical changes of the long established patterns of legal order can hardly take place.

However, the complication of the rule of the

period of responsibility in the Ch'ing dynasty indeed poses as an obstacle to its smooth application. From the case reports examined in the paper, it is clearly shown that many magistrates could not handle the rule well. The competence of the local-level judicial officials in dealing with complex rules is questionable. In this respect, the criminal sanctions and administrative disciplinary actions prescribed in the Ch'ing code and statutory rules for incompetent judicial officials might be helpful in solving this problem, but how effectively these rules worked is not very clear. However, it is true that the experienced judicial officials of the Board of Punishment played an important role to hammer out the consistency in applying law. Through the delicate and careful use of analogy, they could exclude the aberrant application of legal rules, and finally managed to interpret and enforce the rule of the responsibility period with constancy.

Elkins, Debra Rae

MEDICAL PEER REVIEW: IMMUNITY AND CONFIDENTIALITY UNDER THE LAW

George Washington Law School 1986 M

53 pages

Footnotes

The availability, expense, and quality of health care received by the public has become a major concern in this country. Virtually all individuals in our society are recipients of, or at least come into contact with some aspect of the health care industry. And, as a nation, vast amounts of funds are spent on gaining or preserving our health. Because of the importance and ubiquitous nature of health care, much attention has been focused on the maintenance and improvement of the quality of health care given by health care providers within our health care facilities.

One mechanism by which the quality of health care is monitored is through a process of self-critical analysis commonly termed "peer review." Peer review is a "formal, periodic review of care by the persons providing the care .... use to provide retrospective review of a single case or group of cases, and to provide standards or goals for future care." Inherent in the review of the quality of patient care is the evaluation of the abilities, knowledge and skill of those individuals providing the care.

The process of the administration of health care within our society touches every individual. The pursuit of high quality health care that is available to all is a major concern. In response to the increased demands for quality, the health care profession is continually seeking ways to improve its service to our society. In return for these efforts, legislatures have provided an amount of dispensation to the health care profession, at the expense of some others, in order that the public interest best be served. As has been demonstrated, the issues surrounding the means the legislature chose, immunities and privileges for medical review participants and records, to aid the health care professionals are still controversial, and still the subject of much discussion. The practice of medicine is evolving at an exponential rate. Incorporating the clinical and operational realities of the hospital into the rather utopian atmosphere of the courtroom, while preserving the nature by which each pursues its common objective, will mean a challenge to be mediated by those who are charged with the responsibility to forward the interests of the public. As the role of the health care within our society evinces no signs of diminishing, but instead becomes one of ever-increasing importance, issues surrounding its fair and skillful administration will continue to occupy a place of prominence.

England, William Luke, Jr.

CONSTITUTIONAL ISSUES IN FEDERAL PROCUREMENT LAW

George Washington Law School 1986 M

136 pages

Footnotes

As a subject area of the law, government contracts has not been a prolific source of legal issues that rise to the level of constitutional significance. Although litigation between the federal government and its contractors has produced a large body of case law and federal statutes deal with many of the matters at issue in government contract controversies, constitutional issues do not frequently arise in the government contract context. However, because the federal government now spends billions of dollars in procurement each year, both the Government and its contractors have sufficient high-stakes interests in the procurement process to precipitate controversies that raise constitutional issues. This paper addresses some of the current constitutional issues in federal procurement law.

The paper first deals with the separation of powers issue of what type of cases or controversies must be adjudicated in article III courts. This is a constitutional issue in federal procurement law because of the statutory scheme that now requires litigation of contractual claims against the United States before either an administrative agency or an article I court whose judges do not receive the article III salary and tenure protection.

The author then discusses the fifth amendment as both a safeguard of contractor rights and interests during the procurement process and, under the "state action" doctrine, a basis for potential contractor liability in civil damages for deprivation of constitutionally protected interests of their employees or other individuals.

Finally, the author discusses the impact of the separation of power doctrine on congressional oversight of federal procurement. The Supreme Court's decision in Buckley v. Valeo and Immigration and Naturalization Service v. Chadha reaffirmed the vitality of the separation of powers doctrine as a fundamental principle of our system of government. The implications of both cases have enormous significance in the procurement arena that will be manifested in the role of legislative agencies and the use of statutory mechanisms to control executive branch actions in the procurement process.

Escarameia, Paula V.

THE LIMITATIONS OF INTERNATIONAL LAW: THE CASE OF EAST TIMOR

Harvard Law School M

106 pages

Footnotes and bibliography

Nothing is new in the statement that International Law suffers from serious limitations in its implementing machinery. Nothing is particularly unique about pointing our systematic violations of fundamental human rights that are facing the inability or paralysis of every one of the numerous institutionalized international bodies. However, when a people's desperate plea to the world to put an end to a situation of genocide is answered only by the apathy or self-interested passivity, there is the need to effectively rethink what this abstract concept known as "International Law" really signifies.

Timor is a striking case, perhaps because effective measures could have been taken but were completely absent. The topic is intriguing because of the unforgettable feeling of abandonment, of silent conformation and of terror of the outside world that was apparent in the eyes of the few refugees that arrived in Portugal.

The research for this study was based on books, U.N. materials, newspaper articles and NGOs' journals for little direct source material was available. Nevertheless, it was felt that the East Timor problem was worthwhile researching. Because of its extreme features, it is an interesting case to be confronted with the so-called existing rules of International Law, with the decision-making procedures and with the enforcement of internationally accorded decisions. This study inevitably leads to some thoughts about the role and essence of international norms, to an analysis of the main strands of international legal thought, and to their application in the case presented.

The paper is divided into four major areas: the first one introduces the case in question, presenting the major facts of the problem; the second tries to grasp the minimum possible content of the existing International Law where there exists at least some sort of fundamental consensus; the third analyzes the various international documents and the institutional legal involvement in the Timor case, trying to present the divergent solutions proposed by the antagonistic forces in the case; to conclude, the fourth area attempts to reflect on the concept of International Law, a systemic apparatus obviously in crisis for it fails to provide effective solutions to acute international problems. An effort is made to point out shortcomings of the present constitutional, methodological and substantive aspects of the international legal system. Its focus is on the dissociation between institutional and substantive international life, on the lack of preventive schemes to cope with the generalized absence of consensus and, mostly, on the structural claim for self-survival that perpetrates international arrangements because of the desire to harmonize opposing tendencies at the cost of effective solutions for pressing problems.

Faggi, Fabio Massimo

LIMITS OF THE GENERAL METHODOLOGY OF NEGOTIATION: THE RELATION BETWEEN PREPARATION AND TACTIC

Harvard Law School 1986 M

92 pages

Footnotes

The purpose of this paper is to give a general panorama of the development of the science of negotiation, to present the major theories which have been formulated by the scholars, to underscore the limitations of the all-purpose theories and finally to establish a stronger link between preparation and negotiation in the single negotiation.

Throughout the paper the author does not make any distinction between lawyering negotiation, managerial negotiation and other forms of negotiation. The idea of negotiation dealt with in this paper is the general one, referred to any confrontational approaches of two parties in order to solve a dispute, make a deal, etc. The generality of the kind of negotiation which is discussed leads to generalizations without regard to the particular differences between various types of negotiations.

The paper gives a presentation of the development of the science of negotiation. Negotiation has only recently passed from the stage of unconsciousness to the stage of consciousness, and in this new, and in some aspects, first era of the subject, the main need to satisfy has been to order the variety of ideas that the negotiators have always had during the past. The classification of theories has invited and then produced the discussion to formulate different theories, some of which are supposedly all-purpose theories.

The author then presents the limitations of the "all-purpose theories" with the conclusion that each of the different theories works only when the reality of the negotiation corresponds to what the author of the negotiation strategy expected; when all the assumptions and values which have been imagined are actually found in front of the negotiator. This is a rare and idealistic case, and most of the time, the variety of the factual situations mar the validity of the "all-purpose negotiations".

The author then concludes that the way to elaborate any single negotiation should be faced with the peculiar elements of that single circumstance that lead to the negotiation. This belief imposes a reconsideration of the relation between preparation for the negotiation and negotiation theory. Even if according to some negotiation strategies, the preparation of the negotiation has simply to determine the range and the limits within which to play the real negotiation, the author feels that the preparation should lead to the formulation of the negotiation technique itself.

Fairley, H. Scott
CANADA, EXTERNAL AFFAIRS AND THE CONSTITUTION

Harvard Law School 1987 D

432 pages

Footnotes

Interpretation of the Canadian Constitution, both judicial and academic, have yet to recognize external affairs as a discrete subject of national concern. The material portions of the written Constitution of 1867 do not account for any powers over foreign relations for the obvious reason that these were withheld at Confederation. Nevertheless, the constitutional blueprint was suppose to be an organic creation for an evolving polity. The polity did evolve and Canada subsequently became a nation with full powers to enter into and regulate its relations with co-equal foreign sovereigns. But, as a constitutional matter, this burgeoning field has acquired no identity of its own in terms of legislative jurisdiction and only parenthetical recognition in terms of acquired executive power: that which adhered to the Crown in right of Canada under the enigmatic rubric of the Royal Prerogative. In short, a constitutionalized concept of external affairs has eluded altogether the mainstream of Canadian federalism jurisprudence. Notwithstanding traditional perceptions to the contrary, this is by no means a trivial shortcoming.

In this paper the author develops both substantive and procedural arguments for constitutional revision. The two propositions are interdependent. The substantive claim is that comprehensive federal jurisdiction in relation to external affairs - Canada's foreign relations - ought to be recognized and accommodated within the existing constitutional structure of the Canadian federal state. The complement to this argument is a claim of preference and legitimacy for the process of judicial review to reformulate received constitutional understandings in aid of the desired goal. The second claim carries with it considerable faith in the merits of incremental constitutional revision by judicial processes. It further manifests a basic concern with not selling the

Constitution short on the unrealized potential of flexible language in an organic document.

The choice of means may be more controversial than the end in view. That is perhaps as it should be, since the procedural mechanism is at least as important as the substantive results, especially if one wishes to arrive at a solution that is both flexible and enduring. While the context of the argument is specific to the field of external affairs, the nature of the subject raises broader implications for the general constitutional theory of judicial review in relation to Canadian federalism, portions of which are challenged, but much of which can also be defended.

Common ground for both the form and substance of the argument is the notion that basic principles of the law of nations in relation to the nature and duties of sovereign states merit not only affirmative recognition, but actual accommodation in the structure and interpretation of the Canadian Constitution. Canadian federalism jurisprudence has been overwhelmingly the product of an internalized point of view: one dictated by the weight of history and first principles. Nevertheless, it is argued that it has the potential for self-correction through the appreciation of an external point of view to modify principles of internal order for a federal state that has since become a nation.

Funck-Brentano, Francois

THE U.S. AND E.E.C. EXPERIENCE IN THE APPLICATION OF ANTI-DUMPING LAWS TO NON-MARKET ECONOMIES: A NEED FOR A NEW APPROACH

Harvard Law School 1987 M

106 pages

Footnotes

Nowadays, some still fear that foreign trade is considered by communist states as an essentially political weapon, that low cost exports are used by the Eastern bloc to disrupt capitalist markets. However, although it should be recognized that foreign economic policy in the East cannot be dissociated from social and political considerations, there is little evidence that foreign trade has ever been used by Non-Market Economies (NMEs) for the purpose of political warfare. On the contrary, it is surprising how little advantage NMEs have taken of their unique foreign trade institutional framework to disrupt Western markets.

Not only is there little evidence that NMEs are engaged in premeditated unfair trade practices but there are ample indications that they are often willing to comply with "the rules of the game" followed by market-economies. In the first place, a number of socialist countries are now seeking admission to the GATT. Six of them have been granted membership. This fact reflects a radical change in the NMEs' attitude toward international trade and the West. A number of press articles in the East advocate an extended economic cooperation with Western nations. In order to implement this new orientation, reforms of foreign trade mechanisms have been implemented by many NMEs toward less state direction. Western attitudes toward trade with NMEs have also changed dramatically during the past two decades.

It is believed that a policy that encourages trade with the Eastern bloc would induce trade interdependence and, therefore, increase Western security. Another policy consideration now supporting the normalization of trade relations with

NMEs is the belief that opening trade with the Socialist bloc will induce economic reforms in these countries toward greater decentralization on decisions making and increase market orientation.

This paper studies the application of anti-dumping laws to NMEs by the EEC and the U.S. administering authorities. The paper provides the reader with some general background on dumping. Thereafter, the current practice of the E.C. and U.S. trade authorities with regard to dumping from NMEs is studied in some detail. Finally, taking into account the widespread dissatisfaction with the current situation, the author looks into possible alternative approaches to deal with low-priced imports from NMEs.

Gabriel, Russell

THE POLITICAL QUESTIONS DOCTRINE AND THE POLITICS-LAW DISTINCTION

Harvard Law School 1987 M

55 papes

Footnotes and endnotes

This paper is about the political question doctrine, a United States constitutional law doctrine by which a court supposedly draws a line between politics and law, decides the questions which are legal and refuses to decide those that are political.

The politics-law distinction underlies various discussions in the American legal system. It comes up under the rubric of will-judgment, discretion-administration, politics-law, policy-principle and others. Sometimes it is evident on the face of legal argument, other times it resides beneath the surfaces.

For a century the dichotomy has been attacked as misleading. The attackers have sufficiently illustrated the difficulty in maintaining the distinction to at least warrant the conclusion that the distinction serves no useful purpose. It does more harm than good by maintaining a false impression of the role of the courts.

The political question doctrine is based on the same distinction. There is a long history of the Court refusing to decide cases and explaining its refusal by invoking the doctrine. Because the doctrine is based on the politics-law distinction it is not supportable as an explanation of judicial inaction. The split between politics and law is not necessary to the separation of powers. The court can justify judicial review based on the need to separate power to prevent the over-aggregation of power, and thereby avoid having to legitimate itself through a claim of unique judicial process. Therefore the Court should abandon the political question doctrine completely and refusals to decide should be explained as willful prudential decisions rather than obscured politics-law rhetoric.

The result of all this would not be earth-shaking. However, it would help define the courts and what should be expected of them. It might encourage courts to exercise their part of the power of government more often, or it might not. At the least the role of the court would be clearer.

Clarity is a lost essence in our modern government, and every change helps. At present it is hard to know where power lies; with the Executive, with the Congress, or with the Court. This ambiguity not only discourages citizens from participating in the government, but also encourages those who hold power to exercise it without limit. In the face of many recent executive wanderings from the constitutional and legal tether, a reconstruction of the definition of judicial power seems appropriate.

Gentile, Thomas Augustine

INTERNATIONAL LAW RESTRAINTS ON THE PROLIFERATION AND USE OF NUCLEAR WEAPONS

George Washington Law School 1986 M

132 pages

Footnotes and appendices

While the United States and the Soviet Union continue to argue over the pace and future of the superpower's arms race at Geneva, the long held fear continues that the nuclear arms race will soon include various regional powers who will be less inclined to exercise restraint in using nuclear weapons as have the five nations who currently have the bomb - China, Great Britain and France along with the United States and the Soviet Union.

Indeed, most observers would agree that the most likely scenario for the next use of a nuclear weapon in war would be use by a "new" nuclear power in a regional conflict rather than by a superpower in a global exchange. For this reason, international legal restraints on proliferation and use of nuclear weapons should be rigorously enforced by the international community.

Given the system of restraints on proliferation analyzed in this paper, and the legal restraints on the use of nuclear weapons in many if not most conceivable situations, the question arises whether any manufacture, deployment, or use of a tactical nuclear weapon by a state not now possessing such weapons, would be a violation of international law.

A number of conclusions and presumptions are drawn regarding the legality of the use of tactical nuclear weapons in a variety of circumstances. Through the absence of a multilateral treaty on the subject, the author provides a number of conclusions that were felt to be an expression of the international community on the subject as embodied in the practice of states and in the existing codification of the laws of war.

Beyond specific principles stated by the author it is also concluded by some scholars that a presumption of illegality exists as to any use of nuclear weapons and the user bears a heavy burden of contrary proof at least for any extended or large scale use of nuclear weapons. It is also suggested that a presumption against first use exists.

Protocol I represents the most significant and serious attempt to limit the scourge of war to combatants and to protect civilians from indiscriminate attack. In the nuclear age, non-combatants have never been in greater need of such protection. It is hoped that the would be proliferator would find little incentive in acquiring a tactical nuclear capability if the laws of war limit so severely the use of tactical nuclear weapons.

Girod, Christian G.

THE CLOSE CORPORATION AND THE BUYOUT RIGHT OF MINORITY SHAREHOLDERS IN THE UNITED STATES AND IN SWITZERLAND

Harvard Law School 1986 M

128 pages

Footnotes

The 1936 Act of Swiss Company law provides for two forms of corporate business organizations; the "joint stock company" and the "company with limited liability". The intent of the Swiss Federal Legislature was that the former type would embody the large publicly-held companies, whereas closely-held companies would take the form of the latter. The "company with limited liability" however, has not achieved the expected success. Today, most closely-held companies are registered as "joint stock companies".

Nevertheless, the reform bill on the "joint stock company law" prepared by the Swiss Federal Council and presently discussed by the Swiss Federal Legislature refuses to acknowledge this situation and upholds the principle of the unity of the statute which means that closely-held companies will still be governed by provisions primarily designed for publicaly-held companies.

The situation is the same in most states of the United States, where the rules applicable to closely-held companies are those of the state statute on business corporations.

A close corporation though, differs substantially from a publicly-held corporation. If the legal definition of a "close corporation" is a highly debated issue, its major attributes are undisputed: the number of its shareholders is small (usually less than ten) and the amount of capital invested is limited; its shares are not traded on the stock exchange and are usually not traded at all.

It is obvious that only the law can provide close corporation minority shareholders with the liquidity that their investment lacks. This important issue has received little consideration in Switzerland until recently when a deputy made the proposal during the debates of the Swiss National Council - the Swiss counterpart of the U.S. House of Representatives - on the 1983 Draft Bill that a specific provision dealing with the issue should be enacted. On the other hand, American state legislatures, courts and scholars have become by now pretty familiar with the question, as is witnessed by the number of statutory provisions, judicial decisions and articles by scholars existing on the topic. The various supported solutions however diverge. The purpose of this study was, therefore, to take stock of the issue and to attempt to bring out a workable solution which takes into account the differences existing between the U.S. and Swiss rules governing corporations.

Accordingly, the study first demonstrates why the remedies presently provided by the U.S. and Swiss legal systems are inappropriate as a means for the minority shareholders of close corporations to terminate their business relationships with the majority shareholders. Then analyzed is the feasibility of a statutory buyout right as a future solution to the illiquidity of the minority shareholder's investment in close corporations.

Gmuender, Daniela

A COMPARATIVE STUDY OF THE PRINCIPLES OF LIABILITY IN SWISS AND AMERICAN PRODUCT LIABILITY LAW

Harvard Law School 1986 M

75 pages

Footnotes and bibliography

Under the term product liability, a wave of liability actions of consumers against manufacturers of products is spreading from the United States (US) to the European continent, finally reaching Switzerland. The name product liability, at least in Europe, is relatively new; the situation, however, is as old as the process of manufacturing goods: when a chair falls to pieces because it is badly glued and someone falls and gets hurt, a product damage occurs that entails, other conditions assumed (i.e., causation, fault), product liability on the side of the manufacturer of the chair.

Systematic study of product liability originated in the US with the advent of mass production and consumption of food products in the earlier part of the twentieth century. The concept of product liability results from a market of industrialized production and an extensive consumption. Today, construction defects, to name only one of the possible defects in mass manufacturing, can lead to vast damages earlier unknown. In addition, some products are so complicated that the consumer is unable to recognize inherent dangers. It is thus evident that the balance between consumer and producer is unequal and therefore the legal order should intervene.

This comparative study embraces the principle of liability in Swiss and American product liability law. The principle of liability stands for that element of liability which varies in the different causes of action and which justifies the imposition of damages on either the plaintiff or the defendant. Product liability in general and the principle of liability in particular are defined, and an overview of other elements of product liability are given. After a detailed examination of the current situation in product liability law in Switzerland

and the US, their respective principles of liability are contrasted. Possible explanations for the different principles in Swiss and American product liability law are offered in terms of the two different legal systems, the policies underlying the principles of liability, and how these policies are determined.

The study establishes that American and Swiss jurisprudence have different liability principles underlying product liability law. The reason lies to a certain extent in the fact that the two legal systems are different. At the same time, different policies are also responsible.

Gogek, Daniel

PARALLEL IMPORTATION: HOW TO PROTECT BOTH CONSUMERS AND PRODUCERS

Columbia Law School 1986 M

73 pages

Footnotes and appendices

This paper presents the case for allowing the parallel importation of goods into the United States in such a fashion as to protect both consumers' and producers' interests. All too often the controversial issue of parallel importation has been portrayed as an "either/or" dilemma, suggesting that the choice to be made lies between two radically competing alternatives. Such an all-or nothing choice would be made, based on this kind of reasoning, between producers' interests on the one hand - by prohibiting parallel imports - and consumer interests on the other - by allowing such importation.

Such a characterization of the problem, however, contains a rhetorical fallacy: the false dichotomy. The fallacy is that only the two extremes reflect the available alternatives.

This paper analyzes the arguments for and against the validity of the current Customs regulation, and concludes that arguments on purely legal grounds provide only a tenuous basis upon which either to condemn or uphold the regulation. It is therefore argued that, in order to reach a firm conclusion as to whether the regulation is a sufficiently reasonable interpretation of the statute it purports to interpret, one must examine the policy underpinnings of that regulation. To this end the paper explores the economic and theoretical rationale for the regulation's allowing of parallel importation; a comparative analysis is undertaken with a view to gaining some further insight into the policy footings of the regulation as well as to examine the international treatment of parallel imports generally; and the regulation is lastly considered as a matter of antitrust policy under United States law. Based upon these analysis, the paper concludes that the current Customs regulation does rest on sound policy, but the matter does not end there. The economic analysis of parallel importation suggests that a good deal of the benefits from parallel imports may depend on the quality of the information conveyed to the consumer. On this basis, it must be concluded that gains from parallel importation may be lost unless a disclosure law is passed and enforced.

Grace, Edmond Dermod

PRUDENCE AND LEGAL POSITIVISM: AN ELABORATION OF H.L.A. HART'S CONCEPT OF LAW IN THE LIGHT OF AQUINAS' THEORY OF POLITICAL PRUDENCE

Columbia Law School 1986 M

92 pages

Footnotes and bibliography

The publication in 1961 of H.L.A. Hart's major work, "The Concept of Law," began a debate on the link between law and morality which, until that point, had been out of bounds for theorists of law in the English speaking world. This debate has focused on the validity of legal positivism as a theory of law and on the distinction between law and morality which has been a key element in that theory.

This article is primarily concerned with the question of efficacy and its implications for the relationship between law and morality. It begins by exploring Hart's theory of legal obligations which can only function in the context of an appeal to a perception of justice. Then examined is what are the implications of making such an appeal. This is followed by a discussion on what is involved in speaking about "an enactment" or "a law", given that the rule of law must be specified in particular legal rules. Finally, examined is the relationship between natural law thinking and "the common good", this latter term being understood as the particular set of presuppositions which underlie any given political debate.

While the analysis can and should be judged in its own right, it is largely derived from the philosophical framework of Thomas Aquinas. This may seem incongruous, given Hart's rejection of Aquinas' natural law theory. However, the teleological world view which Hart attributed to Aquinas, while it reflected what was then the prevailing understanding of his theory, would not be accepted by contemporary students of his work. The past thirty years has seen a movement in the thomist natural law tradition away from the arid scholasticism which took hold in the sixteenth and seventeenth centuries. In particular, the central place of prudence, or practical reason, in Aquinas' framework is now more clearly recognized. Aquinas speaks of prudence as "wisdom in human affairs", which can only be acquired through direct experience or by learning from the experiences of others.

Another feature of prudence is the avoidance of evil, understood in the pre-moral sense of harm or damage. A theory of law which is prudent in the thomist sense will make allowances for the possibility of failure at every level. Otherwise, it would simply fail to take account of the practical human realities which are part of every legal system.

Granatstein, Robert

DEPOSIT INSURANCE REFORM IN CANADA

Harvard Law School 1986 M

41 pages

Footnotes

The plight of the deposit insurance system has been obscured by the larger debate surrounding the restructuring of the financial services industry. Yet it is recognized that the integrity of the deposit insurance system is crucial to the future health of that industry.

The paper first outlines and analyzes various proposals for reforming the present system of deposit insurance by reviewing the reports of the Wyman, Senate, Dupre and House of Commons committees, and the role of the Canada Deposit Insurance Corporation. Then the author sets forth changes which must be made if the system is to be satisfactorily rebuilt. The reform of the Deposit Insurance System is related to co-insurance, the limits of coverage, a private market for deposit insurance coverage, uninsured depositors, risk-related premiums, segregated pools, and multiple coverage. The perspective informing the whole of the discussion is that certain features of the deposit insurance system are inherently destabilizing and that only these measures which address these destabilizing influences in a meaningful way are likely to prove useful.

The precise regulatory arrangements under which the deposit insurer functions are far less important to the health of the deposit insurance system than the nature of the economic incentives to which the various actors are subject. Those who would adjust the regulatory arrangements without significantly restructuring the underlying incentives fail to appreciate the sources of the predicament in which the system now finds itself. The measures canvassed in the paper would alter the character of these underlying incentives by ensuring that the participants in the system could no longer shift the adverse financial consequences of their activities onto others.

Grimord, David Leslie

THE IRAN-IRAQ WAR: A JURIDICAL ANALYSIS OF THE ATTACKS ON NEUTRAL SHIPS AND VISIT AND SEARCH OPERATIONS IN THE PERSIAN GULF

George Washington Law School 1986 M

104 pages

Footnotes and appendices

Analyzing the Iranian attacks and visit and search practices under the various contextual criteria does not alter the assessments of Iran's practices under the traditional prescriptions of international law. Iran may have grounds for a reprisal action against Iraq and for retaliatory action to prevent GCC states from assisting Iraq, but engaging in attacks on neutral vessels does not constitute a legitimate means of pursuing these claims. Reasonable visit and search procedures, on the other hand, are a recognized belligerent right and can be utilized to prevent contraband from reaching Iraq.

In the context of limited warfare, the rights of neutral states must be considered and weighed against the belligerent rights. The Iranian attacks threaten neutral interests - to a greater degree than those carried out by Iraq - since they involve interneutral trade and extend to sea-lanes throughout the Persian Gulf. There is no commensurate military need to justify this degree of interference with neutral shipping.

The attacks are also excessive as a means of preventing outside assistance from reaching Iraq. The targets of Iran's attacks are not limited to those engaged in, or reasonably suspected of, being engaged in such activity.

The Iranian attacks, as a military tactic, are not disproportionate to the overall dimensions and intensity of the conflict. However, the attacks are escalatory in terms of geographic scope and in the degree of implication of neutral values.

The international community has rejected Iran's claim to respond to Iraq's attacks by attacking international trade. This is reflected in United Nations Resolution 540, by the defense measures taken by the GCC states, and by the stated intentions and concerns of Western states. On the other hand, states have implicitly conceded the essential lawfulness of Iran's visit and search practices, although reserving the right to respond to any excesses.

These contextual factors, taken both individually and as a whole, suggest that the customary prescriptions of international law pertaining to Iran's practices remain valid under the contemporary circumstances of the Iran-Iraq War. Iran's attacks are unlawful; however, its exercise of reasonable visit and searches are supportable under international law.

Grossman, Antony

THE NEW ENGLISH APPROACH TO TAX AVOIDANCE: JUDICIAL ACTIVISM OR JUDICIAL INERTIA?

Harvard Law School 1987 M

105 pages

Footnotes and appendices

"The law in this area is in an early stage of development. Speeches in your Lordships House are more concerned to chart a way forward between principles accepted and not to be rejected than to attempt anything as ambitious as to determine finally the limit beyond which the safe channel of acceptable tax avoidance shelves into the dangerous waters of unacceptable tax evasion. The law will develop from case to case ..... what has been established with certainty in 'Ramsey's' case is that the determination of what does and what does not constitute unacceptable tax avoidance is a subject suited to development by judicial process."

Since Lord Scarman uttered these words just over three years ago in the case of "Furniss v. Dawson" academic and practitioner alike have been preoccupied with the questions of what limits will eventually be prescribed for tax avoidance and possibly whether there is a future for tax avoidance within the English system at all. This paper aims to examine the origins, causes and consequences of the new judicially created anti-avoidance doctrine. The author first highlights the background to the recent flurry of judicial activities. Secondly, he critically analyzed the House of Lords decision in terms of precedent and constitutional importance; while thirdly, probable "acceptable waters of tax avoidance" is mapped out.

Finally, covered is the important policy questions such as whether the new attitude is consonant with society's needs and indicates what the author thinks are the wider implications of the approach. Throughout the paper, in search of solutions to many of the problems that the House of Lords left unsolved, the author examined the state of the law in several other common law jurisdictions, including the United States, Canada,

Australia and New Zealand. The developments in other countries enabled the author to predict the future development of this area of law and hopefully indicate some of the mistakes to avoid. A summary of the law on tax avoidance in each of these countries is contained in the appendices. Such a summary will place the comments in a fuller context for those unfamiliar with the law in these legal systems.

Guendelsberger, John

THE RIGHT TO FAMILY UNIFICATION IN FRENCH AND UNITED STATES IMMIGRATION LAW

Columbia Law School M

148 pages

Footnotes, appendices and bibliography

This paper examines the problem involved in reconciling the national interests in controlling immigration with the citizen's or resident alien's right to be joined by members of their immediate families. The United States selects immigrants under a preference system which places annual ceilings on the number of entrants from any one nation. As a result, applicants for entry from countries of high immigration demand must wait for long periods before visas become available. While the spouses and minor children of some resident aliens enter immediately, those from countries like Mexico or the Philippines must commonly wait for eight years or longer. The inequities are exacerbated by the recently passed Immigration Reform and Control Act of 1986. Paradoxically, relatives who enter illegally may now become legal residents while those who remained behind waiting for their visas to become available are ignored.

This paper suggests that the right to family unification is a fundamental human right to which permanent resident aliens as well as citizens should be constitutionally entitled. Because of the importance of the individual right at stake, the usual deference of the federal courts to Congress in the immigration area is inappropriate when legislation interferes with family unity. Even should the federal courts continue to exercise only minimal review in this area, Congress should amend current immigration law to give effects to the constitutional right to family unification.

Because family unification has been recently declared a constitutional right in France, this paper compares the French treatment of this issue with that of the United States. The text of the French Constitution explicitly protects the family. Moreover, the French courts have applied protection to individual rights in decisions concerning immigration law.

Amendments are proposed to the current immigration law which would eliminate the numerical ceilings on entry of the spouses and minor children of resident aliens. Finally, assessed is whether the recognition of a constitutional right to family unification should mitigate the application of the qualitative grounds for exclusion or expulsion.

Guillen-LLarena, David

EXCHANGE OF CREDITS: A PROGRAM FOR INVESTMENT IN MEXICO

Harvard Law School 1987 M

104 pages

Footnotes

Mexico has been a major player within the financial community. As an active member of the international community, Mexico has both enjoyed the benefits and suffered the circumstances of changes in the international economy. A few years ago, international economic developments appeared to promise both wealth and growth for Mexico. Unexpected circumstances, however, shifted Mexican expectations and in 1981 to 1982, the nation started to face the worst economic crisis ever experienced in its history.

This disastrous turn of economic events affected not only Mexico. The debt crisis also threatened the stability of the international financial community as well as the solvency of the international financial system itself. Thus, the effects of the Mexican crisis extended far beyond her borders; the shock waves spread from the domestic to the international arena.

At the time of the first signs of crisis, the available solutions were inadequate to the task of ensuring that Mexico would be able to pay off her debt and achieve sustained economic stability and liquidity. The players constructed a feasible solution to overcome the first impact. After these initial steps, structural changes implemented by Mexico, as well as other debtor countries, have also proved to be insufficient long run remedies. The financial community has thus been forced to renegotiate and restructure agreements in order to avoid the disastrous consequences of a default by a major debtor.

The author approaches the debt problem by analyzing the response of Mexico and the financial community to the crisis faced by that nation. The paper examines the nature of sovereign debt in accordance with a developed theoretical approach in order to achieve an accurate understanding of the restructuring process. It further proposes that a long run solution to the debt crisis can be found in an expanded role for foreign direct investment in Mexico. Exchange of credits functions to encourage direct investment and thus can operate to a limited extent to relieve the debt crisis. The ultimate purpose of the paper is to examine the role that exchange of credits has played within Mexico. It concludes that exchange of credits can serve an important, albeit limited, role in remedying the crisis and that Mexican policymakers, therefore, need to encourage utilization of this technique.

Guth, Otto Guevara

NEGOTIATIONS BETWEEN MULTINATIONAL CORPORATIONS AND THIRD WORLD COUNTRIES IN NATURAL RESOURCES: CONFRONTATION WITH THE PRINCIPLED NEGOTIATION

Harvard Law School 1987 M

80 pages

Footnotes

As Roger Fisher and William Ury mentioned at the beginning of their book, negotiation is a fact of life. There are also, without doubt, negotiations with different degrees of complexity. As an example of complex negotiations one can mention those between Multinational Corporations (MNCs) and Third World Countries (TWCs). Normally, these negotiations become complicated because of the interrelation of the multiplicity of parties and their different interests, bargaining powers, or alternatives; the lack of negotiation skills; and so forth. In this paper it is made clear that the complexity of these negotiations and determined whether or not a negotiation based on principles is possible in this content.

It is useful to consider a situation in which there will be just one negotiation between two parties (there is no on-going relationship at stake). In such a situation, the use of the principled negotiation may sometimes require from the party using it to incur in high costs, which may not be reflected on a better outcome, and therefore ending worse off from its use. About the very difficult negotiations it can be mentioned precisely the negotiations between MNCs and TWCs. In some of those, the power; "irrational behaviors" due to political, non ethical or other motivations; and the alternatives available; play a very important role displacing the importance of the merits or principles. Throughout the paper the feasibility of applying the principled negotiation, despite all the difficulties, to the negotiations between MNCs and TWCs in natural resources is explored.

The author indicates that there will be a constant confrontation throughout the paper with the theory of the principled negotiation and the feasibility of its application to the negotiations between MNCs and TWCs. The aim of the study is to make a contribution to the study of topics related with the negotiation theories applicable to the relations between MNCs and TWCs. Some of the topics that are treated in this paper with certain generality could be used in the future as starting points for further and more thorough studies.

Hanessian, Grant

ENFORCING CUSTOMARY INTERNATIONAL LAW AGAINST THE EXECUTIVE IN UNITED STATES COURTS

Columbia Law School 1985 M

105 pages

Footnotes

Is customary international law enforceable against the Executive in United States courts? To date most of the scholarly and judicial discussion of ascertainment and enforcement of customary international law in domestic courts has focused on cases in which private entities have sued foreign states. Actions challenging executive acts of the United States as violating customary international law have not reached the substantive question of executive power to supersede customary international law. Nevertheless, citing the Executive's "foreign affairs power" to "make law" for the United States, and analogizing to Congress's ability to supersede international law and the Executive's supposed authority to terminate treaty obligations, it is argued that the courts will not prohibit the Executive from superseding customary international law.

The extent to which domestic courts will permit the executive branch to supersede customary international law for the United States is essentially a question of separation of powers under the constitutional system of the United States. Where courts in the United States defer to the executive branch, they communicate to the international community a sense of normative content. In limiting application of the act of state doctrine, United States courts seem increasingly willing to apply customary international law against other states.

This paper argues that the Constitution does not commit all customary international law norms to the Executive for determination and compliance; that those norms not within the Executive's exclusive competence may and, in ordinary circumstances where there is no indication of Congressional acquiescence, should be enforced against the Executive in domestic courts; and that to do so would advance "both the national interest and progress towards the goal of establishing the rule of law among nations."

This paper begins by exploring the historical roots of the incorporation of customary international law into United States law and its current status as federal common law. This is followed by a discussion on the power of the Executive to make law for the United States and the limits of that power; the capacity of courts to ascertain and apply customary law against the Executive; and the propriety of the exercise of that capacity, with respect to both the constitutional and international orders.

Harley, James Albert

ECONOMIC DURESS AND UNCONSCIONABILITY: HOW FAIR MUST THE GOVERNMENT BE?

George Washington Law School 1986 M

167 pages

Footnotes

How fair must the Government be when dealing with its contractors? The question has no answer for fairness is and ought to be a subjective standard for measuring conduct. Economic duress, though it may have some objective characteristics, and unconscionability are both subjective standards for insuring the Government does not abuse its vast resources, its "unequal bargaining" power, when contracting with its citizens.

Duress, based on wrongful conduct, has evolved from its "ancient strictness," dealing only with physical duress, by redefining wrongful conduct to include economic wrongs, hence creating the theory of economic duress. Of late, economic duress has advanced beyond defining these wrongs in terms of bare legalities, to bring that which breaches the duty of "good faith and fair dealing under a contract" under a broader umbrella of "improper" conduct.

Unconscionability is, and always has been, a subjective theory to be used by the courts when equity dictates. Fairness, as encompassed by these theories, must thus be measured by the conscience of the society, reflecting through its legal system, which permits these defenses to exist.

At first glance, this might appear to threaten the certainty necessary for our system of contracting. Certainly, such subjective theories have been rightly criticized, here and elsewhere, because they fail to adequately define the type of conduct to be avoided if one seeks to enter enforceable contracts. Yet, in this author's opinion, they are not such a threat as some have made out.

Both theories are disfavored by the courts for

the very reasons they have been criticized. In the cases cited in this paper, those upholding these defenses number less than 25%. Thus, by putting the use of these defenses in proper perspective, one must conclude that both defenses are useful tools to be used by the courts to insure fairness in Government transactions.

Harris, James Dey

TOWARD A CONCEPTUAL THEORY OF MULTIPLE PUNISHMENT

Columbia Law School 1985 M

140 pages

Footnotes

This paper addresses the knotty problem of multiple punishment; that is, cumulative punishment for violations of several overlapping criminal statutes or for several violations of the same criminal statute. The problem arises when the courts impose multiple convictions or sentences in the above situations where such imposition is either unintended by the legislature or, at the least, the legislature's intent is unclear and objectively undiscoverable.

The primary purpose of this paper is to present a conceptual framework for analysis of multiple punishment issues. Toward this goal the paper canvases the present status of multiple punishment, its successes and failures, from the vantage of both the judiciary and the legislature. This tour of the issue's presents status is intended to eradicate the confusion that blocks the growth of a workable solution to the more vexing problems of multiple punishment. The goal is sought by inquiring after a clear understanding of the conceptual underpinnings of the development of a multiple punishment bar.

The paper begins with an overview of Supreme Court decisional law concerning multiple punishment and its constitutional ramifications. This overview illuminates several issues that are necessary to a full understanding of the purpose and evolution of the doctrine of multiple punishment.

The author then explores the state's contribution and intrusion in the area of developing a coherent concept of multiple punishment. Explored are the numerous tests that states have adopted, either judicially or legislatively. These tests are explored in order to illuminate several points essential to the understanding of the concept underlying multiple punishment. Among these important points is the interrelationship between any legislatively or judicially created multiple punishment bar and the individual jurisdiction's substantive penal code and sentencing scheme. In addition, and most important, the general failure of the various state's tests to address the heart of the inquiry which involves no less than an exploration of the essence of the criminal law.

Finally, the paper considers a conceptual approach to the issue of multiple punishment. This final analysis posits the core concept that governs the multiple punishment bar, that is, the presumption that the legislature does not intend to twice punish a defendant for the infringement of a single legally protected interest, even when that single interest is presented in more than one offense. Also presented are various problems that a jurisdiction must face in formulating a workable statutory scheme that alleviates the growing problem of multiple punishment.

Hook, J.

DEBRA P: NEW FACTS AND A NEW LEGAL THEORY

Harvard Law School 1986 M

57 pages

Footnotes

In 1976, the Florida legislature enacted a law which forbid any school district to grant a high school diploma to any otherwise qualified student who had not passed a "competency test" which was to be constructed by the State Department of Education. In the first senior class subject to the diploma sanction, the failure rate of black students was ten times the failure rate of white students. Black students brought suit under federal antidiscrimination laws, and a federal district court granted a four-year injunction against use of the test as a pre-condition for a diploma. The Fifth Circuit affirmed the decision. Four years later, however, the same district court refused to renew the injunction, and the Eleventh Circuit affirmed. The judges agreed that this turnabout was fair play because the fact situation in Florida had changed, eliminating any basis for an injunction under the Fourteenth Amendment and Title VI of the Civil Rights Act of 1964.

The second wave of litigation, unlike the first, was far removed from the 1971 date on which the Florida schools had become a "unitary system" that there was no longer any "vestiges of discrimination" basis for blaming race disparate test performance on school segregation; and a survey of what was actually taught in Florida, conducted between the two waves of litigation, had demonstrated the content validity of the test, thus establishing a rational relationship between the test and a legitimate state purpose.

The second wave of decisions in this Debra P litigation, together with the release of a heavily publicized federal commission report which called for competency tests in every state, unleashed a flood of legislation across the nation, mandating competency tests and other "get tough" requirements. The tests, and the diploma sanction, are now operative in Florida and many other states; however, it is not clear that other state laws will be as immune to challenge as Florida's.

The purpose of this paper is to present a litigation plan for attacks on the discriminatory use of competency tests as a diploma prerequisite. The basic argument is that such attacks can be successful outside Florida, in part because of the different historical backgrounds of other states, in part better strategy. The paper is limited to federal antidiscrimination law; but it includes some novel ideas about what evidence might be relevant and what legal causes of action might be employed.

Hudson, Judith

PROPERTY AND ECLECTIC LIBERALISM: A DIFFERENT VOICE

Harvard Law School 1986 M

58 pages

Footnotes

The subject of theories of property remains fundamental to legal and political discourse, and raises issues of contemporary relevance. The reason for the importance of property theory to legal and political philosophy is that property is deeply and inherently political. Property is political because it is not merely the state of possession but a right, an enforceable claim to exclude others from a thing. An enforceable claim implies that someone will enforce it, and the only body that can enforce it is a whole organized society or the state. Property is, moreover, not a thing, but a political relation between persons.

The view of property as a thing rather than a relation, with the resultant de-emphasis on the politics of economic power, can be seen as a product of capitalism, but also as its victim. When property revolved substantially around land, it was clear that rights to land and to the use of land varied. However, as land became more freely marketable, and many of the old limited rights were bought out or removed by reforming legislation, it became more natural to think of the land itself as the property. Similarly, as wealth began to be measured in terms of money or industrial plant, the things exchanged so readily in the market began increasingly to be viewed as property.

Since property is political it is inevitably controversial. The institution, therefore, requires to be continually justified, at least as to its presently existing form. One of the functions of the essay is to suggest that the laissez-faire view of property, allowing state intervention only to protect property rights and enforce contracts between property owners, cannot be so justified.

But it is not only in the domestic arena that these issues are significant. The predominantly

Western, liberal, democratic conception of rights, particularly human rights, exists in a situation of more or less unstable reflective equilibrium with property notions; property is a right, but a right can be a kind of property, and other rights may conflict with the right to property.

The purpose of this paper is to show that the prevalent Western notions of exclusive property have important repercussions for the way issues of human rights are viewed internationally, as well as for domestic policy in America, and for political debate in general. It investigates the theoretical basis of such notions, to see whether they are rationally coherent. Property theories form something of a continuum from left to right, and Western liberal property theory is a concept wide enough to cover a considerable part of that spectrum. For purposes of this research, it was convenient to consider Robert Nozick's thesis, because it argues most explicitly for the consequences that can be observed to arise from the laissez-faire approach, namely the dislike of positive state duties, and of taxation for purposes of redistribution.

Hyun, Chun Wook

LEGAL ASPECTS OF TECHNOLOGY LICENSING IN THE REPUBLIC OF KOREA

Harvard Law School 1987 M

96 pages

Footnotes and appendices

Over the past two decades Korea has achieved remarkable success in industrialization. During the course of economic development Korea's reliance upon foreign technology has been significant, and it is generally recognized that foreign technology will continue to play an important role during Korea's economic development plans for the 1980's and beyond.

Thus, science and technology have been important national planning instruments since the early 1960's and, as a consequence, science and technology development plans were considered part of consecutive Korean economic plans.

In the 1980's, the growing protectionism and neomerchantilism in OECD countries and the increase in labor cost of scarcity of natural resources frustrated and weakened the competitiveness of the export-oriented Korean economy. Thus, the innovation or upgrading of technology has presently become one of the keys to the continuous success of Korean industries.

There are two sources of commercially useful technology: technology developed domestically, and technology developed in a foreign country which may be transferred.

Although Korea is actively fostering indigenous research and development (R & D) activities, like many other developing countries, it was unable either to afford large capital requirements for investment in domestic R & D sectors or to wait for the lengthy gestation period, especially at the early stage of economic growth. Therefore, transfer of foreign technology has been a major means of industrialization and its upgrading in Korean economy. As with foreign investments, the Korean government encourages more diversification of technology supply sources so that competitive advantages of the special nature of the technology can be strengthened.

The ultimate goals of economic development - elimination of poverty, unemployment and inequality - will be better realized through mutual understanding and cooperation coupled with reasonableness and unselfishness of both parties rather than through exploitation or bargaining between developing countries. Korea cannot think only of inducing foreign technology for its one-sided benefit; rather, it must seek mutual benefits to sustain equally productive relationships. It is of the utmost importance that Korea take an affirmative attitude towards international cooperation and collaboration, be it bilateral or multilateral, in advancing the interdependency of the world.

Imasaki, Yukihiko

EXTRA-JUDICIAL STATEMENTS OFFERED TO PROVE DECLARANT'S THEN EXISTING STATE OF MIND: A STUDY OF LAW OF EVIDENCE IN JAPAN

Harvard Law School 1986 M

73 pages

Footnotes and appendices

It has been often pointed out that the Japanese criminal justice system is a hybrid of the continental legal system and the Anglo-American legal system. The rule against hearsay adopted by the Japanese Code of Criminal Procedure after World War II has its roots in the Anglo-American system. However, not only the criminal justice system but the whole legal system of Japan retains some characteristics like those of Western Europe. Recognizing that the social and cultural background of Japan is different from that of the United States, the Japanese Code of Criminal Procedure adopted the hearsay rule of the US in a modified and abridged form.

Under such conditions, it is natural that the rule against hearsay in Japan has developed in a different manner from that in the US. A theory about extra-judicial statements offered to prove declarant's then existing state of mind is one of the notable examples of such divergent development.

Following an overview of the rules against hearsay in Japan that reveals their unique setting, the paper reviews the legislative development of the law of evidence in Japan.

The concept of hearsay as it is used in the Japanese legal system is presented with particular attention to the use of extra-judicial statements classed as non-hearsay.

Extra-judicial statements offered to prove declarant's then existing state of mind is explored in the context of the theories advanced by Japanese practicioners and scholars. Cases that illustrate these theories are analyzed in detail.

The appendices provide excerpts from the Japanese Code of Criminal Procedure.

Indest III, George Felix

DOES THE MEDICAID STATUTE PERMIT STATES TO RECOVER EXPENDITURES FROM THE CHILDREN OF RECIPIENTS?

George Washington Law School 1986 M

179 pages

Footnotes and appendices

With a continuing increase in the reduction of federal aid to the states over the past several years, rising pressure has been placed on the states to find alternate sources of funding for programs which previously were primarily funded by the federal government. That pressure has been multiplied by skyrocketing medical costs and an increasing elderly population. The Medicaid program, a program which provides health care treatment for the aged and others, is one such program receiving joint funding from both state and federal government.

Prior to 1983, the policy of the Department of Health and Human Services (HHS) was that, consistent with the intent of Congress and the department's own implementing statute, a state could not require the children of an aged Medicaid recipient to reimburse the government for those services. However, in February 1983, the Health Care Financing Administration (HCFA), the agency within HHS which oversees and promulgates guidelines for each state's Medicaid program, issued a Medicaid Manual Transmittal, an administrative interpretation of Medicaid regulations, which reversed that long standing policy. That Transmittal from the Director of HCFA concluded that states which had family responsibility laws of general applicability would be allowed to force children to repay the states for Medicaid funds expended on behalf of their parents, thereby reversing prior policy and seemingly going against the clear wording of the Medicaid Act, the intent of Congress and the existing Federal Regulations. As a result, several states have either passed new legislation or begun using existing statutes to bring civil actions against the children of aged Medicaid recipients to recover the costs of their medical treatment and nursing home care. These suits and actions are typically in the tens of thousands of dollars.

This paper examines the legality of HCFA's Action Transmittal and the state statute which might be used to justify state attempts to force reimbursement. The author reaches the conclusion that the HCFA Action Transmittal is not valid since it is contrary to the existing legislation and the intent of Congress and has not complied with the provisions of the Administrative Procedures Act. Likewise, any state's statutes enacted pursuant to the "new policy" announced in the Transmittal or used to enforce that policy of requiring repayment of Medicaid funds, are likewise invalid. A number of constitutional deficiencies with the Transmittal and state enforcement actions pursuant thereto are also discussed.

Injia, Salamo

THE SYSTEM OF EMERGENCY DECLARATION UNDER THE PAPUA NEW GUINEA CONSTITUTION

Harvard Law School 1987 M

121 pages

Footnotes

During the 11 years since Papua New Guinea (PNG) gained independence, the government has imposed a state of emergency several times. Twice such emergencies were necessitated by what the government claimed to be a serious breakdown in law and order evidenced by a sudden upsurge in criminal activity in certain parts of the country. The first one was imposed in 1979, the second in 1985. A major factor in both situations was the increase in crimes of violence such as group fighting, murder, rape, robbery, and burglary.

The propriety of these two declarations, in particular their constitutionality, has never been the subject of meaningful debate. Thus the citizens of PNG continue to live under the impression that such declarations were a good thing for the country and were also constitutionally valid. Indeed an overwhelming majority of Papua New Guineans probably do not even know what an emergency is all about and what significance it can have for their lives, government, and country.

The paper studies the system of emergency declarations under the PNG constitution, with a view to understanding the problems associated with interpreting and applying the constitutional provisions. Particular emphasis is placed upon the inherent deficiencies and dangers within the legal system which, in turn, threaten the abuse and infringement of the people's constitutional rights. Further discussion concerns the contemporary principles of international human rights law and practice as found in international conventions. Finally, some workable suggestions intended to minimize the abuse of emergency powers and thereby effect maximum protection of the basic rights of the PNG people are made.

Some of the relevant social, economic, political, and legal circumstances of PNG are examined with a view to understanding the particular context in which the emergency provisions operate. An overview of the system of emergency declarations under the Constitution is presented, with a review of the problems associated with defining "emergency." The limitations that are prescribed by the Constitution to prevent or minimize the infringement of constitutional rights are described. The practical implementation of the emergency provisions and its effects on the constitutional rights of the people are analyzed with a special focus on the institutional safeguards which are provided by the Constitution.

The PNG Constitution makes detailed provision for almost every stage or aspect of the emergency process. However, this does not mean that the process is free of defects and problems. Many of the problems discussed here are not confined to PNG but are also of concern to the broader international human rights community. The PNG Constitution does make adequate provisions, especially in the Courts, to utilize the principles of international human rights law in its deliberations.

One of the main problems revealed is the country's almost total reliance on the political institutions to handle all aspects of the emergency process. The Constitution, to a large extent, facilitates this. The silence of the Courts and the Constitutional institutions vested with the duty of safeguarding the people's basic rights and checking and preventing abuse of governmental discretion may be interpreted as indicative of their trust in the political institutions' ability to prevent abuse of and safeguard the basic rights of the people. The public's inaction, in particular the inaction of private organizations having an interest in the protection of basic rights, may be regarded as complementary of the political institutions. This research concludes that such political safeguards are substantially inadequate.

Janoray, Charles M.

INTERIM MEASURES OF PROTECTION IN INTERNATIONAL COMMERCIAL ARBITRATION

Harvard Law School 1986 M

54 pages

Footnotes

There are four reasons for which businessmen value arbitration over other dispute resolution mechanisms, namely: speed, lower expense, more expert decision and greater privacy. At the same time, the parties involved in a commercial dispute want to benefit from the advantages offered by courts; i.e., pre-set rules, fairness of the proceeding and enforceability of the award.

The availability of interim measures of protection is crucial if arbitration is to be a viable alternative to court litigation. One of the core concerns of the parties involved in an arbitration proceeding is to make sure that the assets in existence at the beginning of the arbitration are still available once the arbitrators have rendered their award, so that practical effect can be given to the award. This is an issue of primary practical importance in the business community. One too often sees private persons or companies depleting their available assets in order to neutralize the effects of an award or a judicial decision. It is important that a part have some assurance, before entering arbitration, that they will not be left with a mere piece of paper without any possibility of enforcing it against assets of the losing party.

A plaintiff might also want to prevent a defendant from disposing of the asset in dispute, for instance by selling the goods that are at issue; or a plaintiff may wish simply to secure an attachment, so that he could be sure of receiving the amount awarded in the event the final decision proved him right and the unsuccessful party failed to pay voluntarily.

Discussed are the two broad types of interim measures of protection, namely provisional measures that prevent one of the parties from transferring or disposing certain assets, and interim measures of protection that aim to improve the process of arbitration. Also addressed is the question of who has the authority to grant provisional relief and how such power is distributed between the courts and the arbitrators.

Finally, the paper discusses what will happen when, in the arbitration, one of the parties is a foreign state and the other party seeks interim measures of protection against it. Addresses is the impact of the sovereign immunity doctrine on arbitration, and more specifically on provisional remedies.

Jones, John Thomas, Jr.

CONTRACTING OFFICERS: APPOINTMENT, AUTHORITY, AND DISCRETION

George Washington Law School 1986 M

153 pages

Footnotes

One of the principle methods our federal government employs to carry out its purposes is contracting with the private sector. The federal government simply does not have the resources to carry out all of its constitutional duties. This is the consequences of the national policy that the means of production should be in private hands. In these contractual dealings with the private sector the government, like any corporate body, acts through its agents. The officers properly empowered to contract on behalf of the United States are called contracting officers.

This paper discusses several aspects of contracting officers. The author first describes how specific individuals are selected and appointed as contracting officers. This is followed by a discussion on a contracting officer's authority including the limits placed on that authority, the various doctrines used to mitigate the harsh effects of the "no apparent authority" rule, and when a court or board of contract appeals is likely to so act.

Finally, the paper discusses a contracting officer's discretion to act on behalf of the United States. It will focus on the contracting officer's obligation to act in good faith and his duty to exercise independent judgment in some of his actions.

Contracting officers are shown to be very important individuals within the federal government. They are the focus through which a significant portion of the federal budget is returned to the private sector. However, contracting officers are primarily agents for the government. It is the leaders within the government who remain responsible for the contracting officer's actions.

Kabeberi, Janet Wahito

INTERNATIONAL COMMODITY AGREEMENTS: SUCCESS AND FAILURE IN REGULATION THE WORLD TRADE

Columbia Law School M

98 pages

Footnotes and bibliography

In determining the effectiveness of International Commodity Agreements, one has to consider the content and level or organization regarding commodity policy. The rationale behind international commodity agreements has changed ever since the Paris Sugar Convention of 1864 and together with these changes, the content of international commodity policy has also expanded.

The purpose of this paper is to discuss the various problems and conflicts that have arisen and how they have been solved, regarding international commodity agreements particularly with reference to the Third World countries.

The author first looks into the historical development of international commodity agreements from the Anglo-Dutch era, to the League of Nations era; to the Havana and post-Havana eras. There is a discussion of the role played by international law regarding commodity agreements.

This is followed by a discussion on the various regulatory techniques used by International Commodity Agreements, namely the export quota system and the buffer stock system. Thereafter the author looks into the problems and conflicts that have hindered the effectiveness of these regulatory techniques and thus affecting the effectiveness of the agreement as a whole.

A discussion is then presented, in detail, of the International Coffee Agreement, and the International Tin Agreement. With reference to the former the position of Kenya (whose major export is coffee) is discussed with respect to the International Coffee Agreement. However, reference is made to other coffee producing countries. Also discussed is the International Tea Agreement and

International Cocoa Agreements and the current problems facing these two agreements.

Finally, the author pays attention to the role played by UNCTAD with regard to International Commodity Agreements. This also includes a discussion of the Integrated Programme for Commodities.

Kanai, Michiko

COMMERCIAL ARBITRATION BETWEEN THE US AND JAPAN: WHAT DIFFICULTIES AND CHALLENGES DO JAPANESE COMPANIES FACE?

Harvard Law School 1986 M

68 pages

Footnotes

As international trade has expanded in recent decades, so too has the use of international arbitration to resolve disputes arising in the course of that trade without recourse to the formalities of court proceedings. In the United States, arbitration has already become a part of conflict solution methods. In Japan, arbitration historically has not had a major role compared to conciliation, at least in the domestic area. Now, however, arbitration has begun to assume a greater role especially in an international context, even in Japan. Many Japanese companies that contract with foreign companies insert an arbitration clause in their contracts to secure simple, more informal, and expedient results when they are faced with legal disputes. Commercial arbitration thus has already taken its place in the area of international transactions in Japan before it has become common in the domestic area. These trends, both in the US and Japan, show that in US-Japan trade disputes, having an arbitration clause is routine in contracts, and arbitration has a great role once disputes arise.

This review of selected cases both in the US and Japan arising from or in connection with arbitration sheds light on the problems which Japanese companies face and their practical implications. ("Japanese companies" are intended here to include Japanese subsidiaries in the US.) Cases in the US and Japan are treated separately to delineate the problems and effects of arbitration agreements, the difficulties arising from the waiver of right to arbitrate, and the scope of arbitration agreements.

Even after arbitration comes to an end without any problems and parties are satisfied with the arbitration award, special problems may remain with regard to the recognition and enforcement of the arbitration award which was made in foreign countries. These problems are examined in terms of enforcement under the FCN Treaty and the New York Convention.

The paper concludes that, while many of the pitfalls encountered in international commercial arbitration proceedings could be avoided in advance if the parties prepare for the hypothetical dispute and arbitration, others could not be avoided. As the actual cases reviewed suggest, most of the difficulties that Japanese companies face are avoidable. Accumulation of knowledge of and experience in international commercial arbitration will help to reduce the difficulties. However, considering the domestic context of arbitration in Japan where not only laypersons but lawyers as well are unfamiliar with arbitration, such accumulation is not readily achieved. The development of lawyers or corporate legal staffs well versed in this field is recommended.

That the many difficulties of Japanese companies involved in arbitration between the US and Japan are avoidable has positive implications for arbitration between these two countries. The advantages of international arbitration are available to them if they carefully prepare for arbitration, since these difficulties and challenges are under the control of the parties. The role of arbitration between the US and Japan is to provide the high level of stability and predictability that enhances reliance on arbitration. These factors will continue to reinforce the system of arbitration and increase its use in US-Japan transactions.

Kapanke, Carl Stephen

RIGHTS AND LIABILITIES OF THE PARTIES IN GOVERNMENT COST-TYPE CONTRACTS

George Washington Law School 1986 M

377 pages

Footnotes and appendices

Fixed price contract arrangements have in common an agreement by the contractor to deliver a product or perform a service in accordance with the terms and conditions of the contract, and an agreement by the Government to pay the firm price specified in the contract or, if the contract includes a tentative price subject to later adjustment, at no more than a specified ceiling.

In contrast, cost-type arrangements are agreements by the Government to reimburse contractors for monies expended, subject to certain restrictions and any special understandings negotiated. The parties agree to an estimate of total costs and the Government is not obligated to reimburse the contractor for costs incurred in excess of that estimated amount. The contractor agrees to use its best efforts to complete contract requirements within the estimate, to notify the Government when there is reason to think that the estimated cost will be exceeded, and to give the Government a revised estimate of the cost for performing the contract.

In most situations involving the use of cost-type arrangements, the Government agrees not only to reimburse the contractor for monies expended, but also to pay the contractor a fee for doing the work. Three fee-bearing alternatives are authorized for use. One provides a fixed fee, one provides for a formula determination of fee, and one is an award arrangement.

A major criticism of the cost plus fixed fee arrangement is that the contractor has no incentive to manage its costs under the contract, since allowable costs will be reimbursed and the fee is the same whether the contract is underrun or overrun. A second disadvantage is the high administrative costs for both contractor and Government.

This paper focuses on several aspects of the cost type contract. First, it examines the practical relationship between the parties. Next it examines their legal relationship and liability toward third parties, directly and vicariously. Obligations and liability between the parties are examined by focusing on the nature of the contractor's obligation to complete performance, the manner of performance, and applicable limitations on liability.

Karanja, Minneh M.

OTIENO VERSUS OUGO AND OMOLO: A CASE STUDY OF CONFLICT IN MODERN KENYA

Harvard Law School 1987 M

82 pages

Footnotes

On the 20th December 1986, SM Otieno, a prominent Nairobi advocate died of a heart attack and plunged his family into one of the most publicized legal battles in the history of Independent Kenya. At issue was the right to choose a burial place for his body, and to conduct the burial ceremony. His widow, Wambui Otieno wanted to bury her husband near Nairobi, at one of their properties. His brother and other members of his patrilineal clan insisted that the funeral be held at the deceased's ancestral home in Nyamila Village.

When it became clear that Wambui intended to go ahead with her plans, the clan hired a lawyer, and announced their intention to stop the funeral that Wambui tried to conduct in Nairobi. Wambui reacted by also hiring a lawyer and the legal battle started that was to take the parties twice to the highest court in the land.

Wambui took the case to Justice Shields at the High Court in the form of an ex parte application which was granted. When Shields refused to vary his order upon an interparte application by the clan (now the defendants) they appealed to the Court of Appeal and it ruled that the order of Justice Shields be set aside and a full hearing be held before another judge. The case was taken to Justice Bosire who after a full hearing ruled essentially in favor of the defendants. The plaintiff, Wambui has now appealed the judgment and the case is still pending in the Court of Appeal.

In the authors view, the question of conflict of laws and the distinction between customary law and customary law enforcement should have been dealt with. Discussed are the relevance of these questions, and the theory as to why they where not raised by any of the parties. In so doing the author delves into the question of the status of women in Kenya. It is shown how the attitudes of contempt shown women by the Nyalgunga clansmen, and condoned both by other women in Kenya and publications like the Weekly Review are rooted in the present material conditions of women. Discussed in particular is how women have been reduced to a state of dependency on men by the land registration systems which give legal ownership of land to men in a country where the majority of women depend on the land for their survival. The author proposes that by returning to women their traditional land rights would give to them the material basis to become equal participants in national development and national debate, and would eliminate many of the conflicts that are at present being aired in Kenya in the guise of "burial disputes."

Kawatra, Gagan Kumar

TAXATION OF CAPITAL GAINS: AN INTERNATIONAL COMPARISON

Harvard Law School 1987 M

66 pages

Footnotes, appendices and bibliography

Although the concept of income has been developed at length by Henry Simons and other economists, Professor R.M. Haig's definition of income as 'the money value of the net accretion to economic power between two points of time' may be regarded as very satisfactory theoretical definition of income. India, by including capital gains in income, has come closer to this definition. However, countries like Singapore and Hongkong follow the accounting concept of income which exclude capital gains from taxation.

The position regarding capital gains taxation in various countries is given in the Appendix. The effective legal definition of capital gains varies in different countries. In Hongkong and Singapore capital gains are altogether excluded from taxable income. In Argentina, Brazil, Chile, Peru, Taiwan, Thailand, Uruguay and Venezuela, capital gains are generally taxed as ordinary income. In Australia, New Zealand and South Africa the gains are exempt from tax unless they arise in the ordinary course of business.

This different treatment of capital gains in various countries raises a basic question that whether capital gains should at all be taxed. Some argue to exempt completely the capital gains from taxation on grounds of economic expediency, illusory nature of such gains during inflation, irregular and unexpected nature and stimulating tax avoidance. At the outset these arguments do not seem to have much force. It is true that exemption of capital gains mitigates to some extent the evil effects of taxation of income on savings and investment. But in this manner any device which enables the taxpayer to avoid taxation would have a similar effect. Avoidance of tax can, by no means, be justified.

Capital gains taxation has a stabilizing effect on the economy. With the existence of provisions for carry forward of capital loss such inequity of discrimination against fluctuating income would be avoided to a large extent. That is the reason why most of the countries which tax capital gains have the provision for carrying forward the capital losses. Further, under a progressive tax system without averaging, this tax would substantially enhance the built-in-flexibility of the income-tax system in that it would withdraw into the Exchequer much larger funds from active circulation in a period of upswing than during the recession or depression. This point has also been advocated by J.G. Head who emphasizes not only the contribution of this tax to automatic stability but also the role of such taxation in discretionary stabilization policy in booms sustained by capital gains in real estate and stock values.

Khan, Khizr Muazzam

INTERNATIONAL COMMERCIAL ARBITRATION IN THE LEGAL SYSTEMS OF DEVELOPING COUNTRIES

Harvard Law School 1986 M

39 pages

Footnotes

With the expansion of international commercial activity in today's interdependent world, there is an emerging need for methods to resolve disputes and disagreements in international commercial relations, particularly in light of the growth of commerce between the industrialized nations and the developing countries, coupled with the growing role of state enterprises in commercial transactions. For those who are engaged in international commercial transactions, arbitration is the most efficient, economical, and effective method of dispute resolution.

This paper presents the facts and issues reflecting different world views about international commercial arbitration and advocates a decentralized method of achieving it. That arbitration has become increasingly important as a form of coordination and accommodation in multicultural relations, even to the point of becoming a symbol of internationalism is demonstrated by an examination of the arbitration laws in the legal systems of the countries of Africa, Eastern Europe, Latin American, the Middle East, India, Indonesia, and Pakistan.

The paper discusses the different conceptual and doctrinal approaches to international commercial arbitration in these various developing and industrialized countries. Suggestions for realizing the potential of arbitration for the resolution of disputes are considered. Existing international arbitration institutions are in an excellent position to see that the potential for increased resort to arbitration is more fully realized. The regionalization of traditional arbitration centers, now located principally in Western Europe, would be an important step in enhancing the image of arbitration in developing countries. Regional centers would offer developing countries the opportunity to participate in arbitrations in which the procedural rules would be more familiar to them. This regionalization should be accompanied by full-scale attempts to create a genuine partnership between the national judiciary and the arbitration centers.

The effective use of arbitration for efficient dispute resolution on a consensual basis lies, in part, upon the initial freedom of the parties to choose the substantive and procedural law governing the ultimate proceedings. Careful planning is necessary to avoid many of the pitfalls otherwise associated with international arbitration and to ensure that the conceptual nature of arbitration is preserved while its reputation for impartiality is enhanced.

Khashayar, Kayvon

THE ACT OF STATE DOCTRINE: A SEARCH FOR RELEVANCE

Harvard Law School 1986 M

104 pages

Footnotes

The act-of-state doctrine has been subject to much controversy since the time of the United States Supreme Court's decision in Banco Nacional de Cuba v. Sabbatino, until the American Law Institute's drafting of the Restatement of the Foreign Relations Law of the United States (Revised). The Congressional attempt to repeal the Supreme Court's Sabbatino decision by the passage of an amendment did not put the issue to rest. In the subsequent act-of-state cases decided by the Supreme Court, the close majority and the compelling dissent blurred the boundaries of the doctrine but also reaffirmed its validity and importance. It continues to be cited and discussed.

The study examines the present status of the act-of-state doctrine and the degree to which it is still functional. It demonstrates that the act-of-state doctrine bears relevance to the international legal order and is applicable not only in the US but in the courts of other countries, especially those of Britain. The act-of-state doctrine assumes respect for sovereign states and is grounded in the separation of powers. The study contends that, besides having "constitutional" underpinnings, the doctrine is a principle of international law.

The essay does not treat areas related to the act-of-state doctrine, such as sovereign immunity and the choice-of-law principles. It is limited to the study of the doctrine as a principle of judicial restraint. It explores in particular the present status of the doctrine as applied by the Supreme Court, focusing on the Court's relevant decisions from 1964 to 1985. In addition to the Sabbatino decision, recent developments regarding Citibank and Dunhill are explored. The author identifies the means and ends of the act-of-state doctrine, as well as its logic, by a critical examination of the texts of the cases themselves.

Khattar, Naoum M.

CONFLICT OF LAWS SYSTEMS: HARMONY OR DIFFERENCES

Harvard Law School 1987 M

56 pages

Footnotes

We are in a world today in which, as a result of improved communications, distances are rapidly shrinking. Where it once took months or weeks some decades ago to travel from one side of the globe to the other, this same trip now has become possible in a matter of only a few hours. Nations are drawing closer to each other and businessmen are developing ever-growing contacts with businessmen in other parts of the world. As a result of this evolution, international law has become more involved in day to day operation.

It is important to point out that international law itself does not prevent conflict or injustice, and cannot alone create order. It is, however, a powerful instrument in organizing, rationalizing, consolidating and extending that order. In that sense, trying to reach a quasi-universal level of harmony between the systems of conflict of laws does not necessarily imply the elimination of all conflicts nor the harmonization of all methods. The use of different conflict of laws methods can often be compensated by reaching the same judicial solutions.

Numerous national and international reports clearly show that international lawyers are now beginning to analyze and restate the complementary rights and duties that derive from the new juxtaposition of 'permanent sovereignty' with 'economic interdependence'.

One of the question the author deals with concerns a study of the existing differences in the conflicts of laws methods between various diverse legal systems including the Common Law System, the Civil Law System and the Islamic Law System. It is worthwhile observing that countries that have adopted the same legal system, such as Lebanon and France, do not adopt essentially the same conflict of laws methods. In this instance, both countries have civil law systems but have different conflict of laws approaches and thus exhibit sharp differences.

The author then analyzes the existing and possible techniques that are helpful in creating a harmony in private international law based on the promotion of common interests among states. Finally, the author discusses various practical ways and alternatives already adopted by some legal systems in order to achieve a step towards harmony and perhaps unity in the field of international law.

Kobayashi, Toshio

RES JUDICATA IN PATENT INFRINGEMENT LITIGATION: A COMPARATIVE STUDY OF AMERICAN AND JAPANESE LAW

Harvard Law School 1986 M

65 pages

Footnotes

Historically Japan has been influenced by many foreign legal ideas regarding methods of interpreting laws. First of all, Japan was under a brief influence by French law. Second, Japan was under an overwhelming influence by German law. Thereafter, although it was not until the end of World War II that Japan received a substantial influence by Anglo-American law, the influence by Anglo-American law was far-reaching and drastic. As a result, Japanese method of interpreting laws became such a hybrid of various countries' legal ideas that it cannot simply be generalized as "theoretical" or "dogmatic". Thus, the generalization about the difference between the U.S. and Japanese laws seems to be dubious even as a matter of fact.

However, aside from the hybrid nature of Japanese method of interpreting laws, the generalization seems to be a kind of oversimplification. First of all, when talking about the practicality of law, or about the method of interpreting laws, it should not be forgotten that the laws applied to concrete cases. In Japan, there is a tendency to talk about civil procedure law apart from concrete cases, as is also the case in other areas of laws in Japan. In addition, procedural laws, together with substantive laws to be applied to the case, serve to settle the dispute reasonably and peacefully. Accordingly, it should be impossible to talk about practicability or procedural laws apart from the concrete case, and the substantive laws to be applied.

On the other hand, it should be noted that even in American laws, the role of case law which serves to formulate general rules has been emphasized apart from concrete cases.

When we analyze Japanese court decisions, we frequently find a remarkably flexible application of laws to concrete cases, particularly in lower court decisions. We should not neglect these decisions in talking about the practicability of the Japanese method of interpreting laws.

Attention is called to the fact that in Japan sometimes a "theoretical" interpretation is asserted in order to fulfill a practical purpose. For instance, the very "theoretical" nature of res judicata serves to set a limitation to the court's right and obligation to hear the case and to the parties' scope of right and obligation to prosecute the case. Very frequently, an interpretation is proposed under the disguise of "theory" for a practical purpose.

All in all, what must be noted here is that the dichotomy of "practical" American law and "theoretical" Japanese laws is a dangerous oversimplification. It is easy to ascribe all special attention to its metamorphosis.

Explained is American and Japanese res judicata with specific attention to its phase in patent infringement litigation. Lastly, discussed is Japanese res judicata in patent infringement with an example of legal action, and how the effect of previous judgements affected the suit.

Lashmit, Douglas A.

SECONDARY CONSIDERATIONS AS EVIDENCE OF NONOBVIOUSNESS UNDER 35 U.S.C. SEC. 103: THE TREND AND EFFECT OF DECISIONS OF THE COURT OF APPEALS FOR THE FEDERAL CIRCUIT

George Washington Law School 1986 M

55 pages

Footnotes

The patent system in the United States has its foundation in the Constitution, which grants Congress the power "to promote the Progress of Science and useful Arts, by securing for limited Times to ... Inventors and exclusive Right to their respective ... Discoveries ...." Congress has enacted various patent statutes over the past two centuries to carry out this constitutional mandate and to attempt to meet the needs of a changing society against a background of technological evolution and revolution. However, the interpretation and application of the patent laws by the judiciary, under the guidance of the Supreme Court, have been prone to extreme fluctuations which in the past have made it difficult, if not impossible, for inventors and patent owners to predict with any degree of certainty whether their patents will be held valid.

The first interpretation of Section 103 by the Supreme Court after the 1952 Patent Act was the landmark decision of Graham v. John Deere Co., which was one of three cases decided the same day that were popularly referred to as the Trilogy. The Court in Graham logically and succinctly set forth the criteria to be used in determining whether an invention is nonobvious and therefore patentable. The Court also explicitly recognized "secondary considerations" such as commercial success and long felt but unsolved needs which, "(a)s indicia of obviousness or unobviousness ... may have relevancy." The application of these principles by the lower courts and by the Supreme Court itself has been erratic.

The current trend in the use of secondary considerations as evidence of nonobviousness of an invention is explored by first tracing the historical development of Sec. 103 and its interpretation in Graham. The post-Graham case law is reviewed to determine the effect of this case on subsequent holdings and, finally, recent cases decided by the Court of Appeals for the Federal Circuit are analyzed along with their effects on district court holdings.

Lautjarvi, Kari Juhani

INTERNATIONAL ARBITRATION IN MULTI-PARTY COMMERCIAL DISPUTES

Harvard Law School 1986 M

74 pages

Footnotes

The arbitration agreement engenders rights and duties between parties but it produces no effect with respect to third persons, who as a result can neither rely on it nor be affected by it. A problem therefore arises where there are more than two parties, one of whom is not bound by the same arbitration agreement or by any arbitration agreement at all, and the disputes to be referred to, or pending before, two different arbitrations, or an arbitration and a court, concerning the same or similar subject matter, common questions of fact and law, substantially similar issues and defenses.

The problem of multi-party disputes is especially noticeable in the context of international arbitration in the case of commercial disputes which have a multilateral character. International business transactions usually involve more parties than domestic transactions. In an international case, the national courts will only rarely have jurisdiction over various parties, and even then this jurisdiction may be excluded by the fact that some of the parties have agreed to submit to arbitration. Moreover, in recent years commercial contracts and other legal arrangements have become more and more complex, with growth in the number of parties and the number of ancillary contracts. The realization of major projects in the framework of contemporary trade and economic cooperation usually requires the coordination of different and complimentary skills and performances; technical and financial resources must be pooled, insurance coverage must be secured and specialized services must be combined harmoniously to fulfill contractual obligations which even a sophisticated business concern cannot carry out single handily.

In the United States courts in some states have regarded themselves as empowered to order consolidation of separate arbitration proceedings or joinder of a third party in certain circumstances. Others, on the other hand, believe that multi-party arbitral systems can best be developed by arbitration institutions.

This paper is structured according to the various methods available to solve the problem under consideration. The existing or proposed options to consolidate or harmonize international arbitration proceedings in multi-party commercial disputes are presented. The crucial question in this context is, whether these options are able to effectively regulate multi-party disputes resolved in international commercial arbitration. Because each of these alternatives has shortcomings, the question must be raised which of these solutions would be advisable for cases of multi-party arbitration.

Leahy, John Michael

THE CLARIFICATION AND SIMPLIFICATION OF STATUTES THROUGH USE OF STATEMENTS OF PURPOSE: RENTON REVISITED

Columbia Law School 1986 M

52 pages

Footnotes

In an ideal world statutes would be drafted in clear, simple language readily understandable to the ordinary citizen and would achieve with certainty the legal effects sought by the legislature. It is evident from criticisms made in recent years that there is a widely held view that, in Australia at least, the utopian ideal has not yet been attained. The principle obstacle to achieving the ideal is that, in the practical world in which legislation is prepared, the objective of clarity and simplicity frequently conflicts with the objective of legal certainty. However, that is not to say that the area of conflict could not be reduced through improvements in drafting and interpretation and that we could not get closer to "the perfect Bill".

The connection between drafting and interpretation is a close one. Problems arising from the statute book have been variously attributed to deficiencies in drafting and in the process of interpretation. The reality is that the form of communication and the rules for interpreting the communication interact: drafting influences interpretation and vice versa. If it is true that deficiencies in drafting complicate the process of interpretation, it is also true that an unsatisfactory process of interpretation can lead the drafter to respond with an over refinement in drafting at the cost of the general intelligibility of the law.

It would be well at the outset to put the criticisms that have been made of drafting and interpretation into perspective. There is good reason to believe that the objective of certainty is generally being achieved in Australia.

This paper examines whether, as suggested by

the Renton Committee, statements of purpose provide a useful drafting technique. Such a drafting technique has the potential to directly complement the changed judicial approach to statutory interpretation and lead to the clarification and simplification of statute law.

Levin, Stephanie A.

JUDICIAL OVERSIGHT OF MILITARY POWER

Harvard Law School 1987 M

72 pages

Footnotes

Recent revelations about the Iranian arms sales and military funding for the contras are a reminder of how much military policy, even in this nation "of laws, not of men", operates at the fringes of, or beyond the constraints of, legality. Nor are these revelations an anomaly; the mining of the Nicaraguan harbor, the invasion of Grenada, the unfolding of the war in Southeast Asia, the secret bombings of Cambodia, and the involvement of the American government in various military plots to overthrow the Castro government in Cuba, to name a few examples, all raise serious questions of legality as well as of policy. Since "lawfulness" is such a central value in this country, the author explores the relationship between it and military policy, and even more specifically to investigate the role of the courts in overseeing that relationship.

The paper starts by describing the history of the debates over the military which took place in the period leading up to the American Revolution and in the framing of the Constitution and in the ratification debates. This history suggests the parameters for the debate that could set the essential framework for understanding subsequent legal developments.

The author then looks at a number of United States Supreme Court opinions which have addresses claims of the unconstitutionality of various military policies, or policies justified by a claim of military need.

The final section of the paper attempts to draw some general conclusions from an integration of the historical and case law perspective. Since Supreme Court doctrine has oscillated between one stance which sharply limits military overreaching in the name of constitutional values, and another which is highly deferential to military power, any statement about a "natural" or "proper" role for the court in this area must be viewed with skepticism. Since the constitution incorporates a commitment to democratic and libertarian limits on military power, the courts should feel empowered to play as much of a role in enforcing that commitment as in any other area of constitutional concern.

Lidsky, Michael Alan

THE POTENTIAL CHALLENGES FACING USDA IN REGULATING THE RELEASE OF GENETICALLY ENGINEERED ORGANISMS UNDER THE FEDERAL PLANT PEST ACT

George Washington Law School 1986 M

95 pages

Footnotes

The purpose of this paper is to examine the potential challenges that USDA may encounter in seeking to regulate the deliberate release of genetically engineered organisms under the Federal Plant Pest Act. Because the Federal Plant Pest Act was not intended by its drafters to regulate the deliberate release of genetically engineered organisms, USDA will have to interpret the Act in a novel and expansive manner. Such an interpretation would be subject to challenge by the regulated public, with the public alleging that USDA has exceeded its statutory authority.

In addition, unless USDA adequately complies with the National Environmental Policy Act (NEPA), environmentalists are likely to bring suit under NEPA challenging USDA's compliance with NEPA as a means of thwarting deliberate release. In addition to discussing the potential challenges USDA may encounter, this paper discusses certain cases and theories USDA may wish to rely on in seeking to overcome the challenges that may occur.

In discussing the challenges USDA is likely to encounter under NEPA and by interpreting its authority broadly under the Federal Plant Pest Act, the paper examines the terminology and technology of biotechnology In examining the potential challenges USDA may encounter in attempting to regulate the release of genetically engineered organisms under the broadest of its plant protection statutes, the Federal Plant Pest Act, this paper also discusses the limitations of the Plant Quarantine Act and Federal Noxious Weed Act, in regulating certain genetically engineered organisms.

The paper concludes by indicating that because a reviewing court may not take an expansive view of

USDA's authority to regulate deliberate release under the Federal Plant Pest Act, USDA may wish to have remedial legislation introduced in Congress that would explicitly give USDA the authority to regulate deliberate release. With respect to overcoming challenges from environmentalists brought under NEPA, USDA is advised to prepare thorough and analytical environmental assessments before deliberate releases are allowed to occur.

Linehan, Denis M.

THE MOBILITY OF LAW: THE COMMERCIAL LAW MODEL

Harvard Law School 1987 M

67 pages

Footnotes

The focus of this general essay is on the mobility of law. This concept refers to the potential in law which enables it to be taken from the legal climate wherein it is developed and put into effect in another legal climate.

The potential within law to transfer from one environment into another is perhaps one of its least appreciated characteristics. The primary reason for this lack of appreciation may be psychological. Having surmounted the psychological barrier that may dim our vision of the mobile quality of law, there is then an intellectual objection to be met. Surely, it may be argued, a law developed within the milieu of one society is likely to be inept when placed in the environment of another society. This objection has only partial validity. On reflection, it can be appreciated that the problem arising for legal resolution in different societies will differ in detail and degree rather than in essence.

Whether law can translate from one society into another is not therefore a pertinent question. Further examples of the phenomenon are given in part one of this paper which treats of the means whereby law can transfer between different legal climates. Four types of processes are distinguished, namely, imposition, transplantation, reception and hybrid processes consisting of a combination of some of the other three.

In the paper consideration is given to the relationship between jurisprudence and the mobility of law. Apprehending jurisprudence as "simply law in its most generalized form", the aim is to ascertain how jurisprudence can inform our understanding of the mobility of law. There is an obvious affinity between the mobility of law and comparative law. This affinity is explored with reference to the functions and techniques of comparative law.

Finally, the paper concentrates on commercial law. That branch of law is commonly recognized as the one most readily transfers from one legal climate into another. The factors which give rise to the special mobility of commercial law, and its expansion by means of efforts at unification, harmonization and internationalization, are examined in some detail.

The concept of the mobility of law is a wide one. In this paper, an attempt has been made to define the concept and to examine it in its major aspects. The essential quality indicated by referring to law in terms of its mobility is the potential within law to be transferred to a climate other than the one in which it has been developed. The climates between which such transfers occur may be, and usually are, different countries. It has been seen, however, that legal translations may also occur between different legal cultures in the same country.

Lowell, Dorian M.B.

A SELECTIVE SURVEY ON INDEMNIFICATION OF DIRECTORS UNDER SECTION 145 OF THE DELAWARE GENERAL CORPORATION ACT

Harvard Law School 1987 M

61 pages

Footnotes

This paper is a critical survey of the rights to indemnification of directors and officers under the Delaware General Corporation law. It is not an exhaustive survey and only those provisions which raise particular points of interest are considered. The main thrust of the paper is that the law has reached the point where it would now make sense to grant automatically rights to indemnification against expenses and liabilities in all cases where a director has acted in good faith. Along the way an attempt has been made to highlight certain anomalies and problematic areas in the statute, its history and the surrounding case law.

The author first looks at the need for indemnification in light of the litigation to which directors are now subject, the corresponding difficulties in obtaining insurance coverage and the need for an effective system of corporate governance. This is then followed by a brief look at indemnification at common law.

The author then looks at the main indemnification provisions of the Delaware General Corporation law. There is a discussion on problems of construction with respect to the standard of conduct required by the permissive section of the statute. A major attack is made on the public policy reasoning which prohibits indemnification against settlement and judgment sums paid in derivative suits. The operation of the mandatory section of the statute is briefly considered. The ambit and operation of the non-exclusive section which entitles a director to draw on extra-statutory rights of indemnification for his protection is subject to close scrutiny. Particular attention is paid to the case law and the more liberal attitude that the courts now appear to be taking with respect to authorizing indemnification under extra-statutory provisions arising out of the non-exclusive section. Finally, the author looks at how far corporations could go beyond the statute in providing for extra-statutory rights to indemnification and in what instruments they should be embodied.

The author concludes that in the final analysis it is perhaps ironic that corporations on the one hand rely on the words "to the fullest extent permitted by law" to bring themselves within the constraints of public policy while the courts on the other hand refer to public policy without ever precisely determining its limits. It is further concluded that it would make sense to follow the approach adopted recently in Missouri which now permits charter provisions and by-laws approved by shareholders to provide for indemnification in all cases as long as it is not authorized in any case which "was finally adjudged to have been knowingly fraudulent, deliberately dishonest or willful misconduct".

Lyndon, Mary L.

THE TRADE SECRET EXEMPTION IN ENVIRONMENTAL AND WORKER HAZARD COMMUNICATION LAWS

Columbia Law School M

87 pages

Footnotes

Since World War II, commercial production and use of chemicals has increased dramatically. This change has brought both benefits and concerns. Chief among the latter are the human health effects of exposure to chemicals in food and the environment.

The society currently has a relatively small, but growing, base of information concerning chemical toxicity. Similarly, a framework for policy formation exists, but is still rudimentary in nature. Information and policy tools have developed slowly, in part because of the idiosyncratic characteristics of chemical health effects. First, the medical dynamics of commercial chemicals' known effects vary tremendously. Second, toxicological and epidemiological methodologies used to study these effects are subject to severe criticism. Perhaps, the most basic difficulties accounting for the deficiencies in study of chemical effects are the facts that many diseases which may result from chemical exposure - notably cancer - have latency periods of twenty to forty years and, isolating a particular chemical as a cause of a disease is difficult when multiple exposures have occurred and there are other disease fostering conditions, such as smoking and poor diet.

Recently a new and innovative regulatory approach has emerged. Many states and the federal government have enacted laws which require businesses using chemicals to establish programs of information exchange. These programs may together develop into a system which will foster better, more widespread use of data of chemical health effects.

The laws are currently a patchwork of "hazard communication" regulations promulgated by the federal Occupational Safety and Health

Administration (OSHA) and state "right to know laws," which mandate disclosure of chemical hazards to those who handle them in the workplace. In addition, a number of the state laws direct firms handling chemicals to confer with local emergency response agencies, such as fire departments; several states provide for general public access to hazard information. Finally, Congress has recently directed the Environmental Protection Agency (EPA) to issue federal rules providing for state and local governments and public access to chemical hazard information, in the Emergency Planning and Community Right to Know Law.

This paper describes the history of the laws, discusses their economic rationale and questions some aspects of their design, for the new laws do have several problematic aspects. The generation of new information is a dynamic which has not been addressed as such in the literature on the economics of information. This paper suggests several basic prerequisites for the success of this function in the hazard communication context, including the need for consistency in the rules' coverage. The paper also explores in detail one aspect of the hazard communication laws: the general exemption granted to certain trade secret information.

Ma, Hongjiang

INTERNATIONAL COMMERCIAL ARBITRATION IN THE PEOPLE'S REPUBLIC OF CHINA

Harvard Law School 1986 M

58 pages

Footnotes

Since the People's Republic of China adopted the "open door" policy, it has made impressive efforts to create and implement the legal structure and environment for foreign business activity. Up to now, there have been thousands of Chinese-foreign equity joint ventures, cooperative joint ventures, and foreign wholly-owned enterprises operating in China. China has economic and trade relations with more than 170 countries and regions. In terms of the value of imports and exports, China had become by 1985 the 16th largest country in the world. Thus the outlook for trade and business with China remains, at the very least, cautiously optimistic. Increased trade and business with China, therefore, heightens the importance of international commercial arbitration.

The paper examines the practical aspéct of international commercial arbitration, the method of foreign trade and economic dispute settlement in the People's Republic of China. Following an examination of the influence of historical experience and ideology upon the Chinese conception of arbitration, the practical aspect of international commercial arbitration in China is considered, as well as conciliation - a uniquely Chinese concept which is one of the main mechanisms of foreign trade and economic dispute settlement in China. Finally, the fundamental principles of and recent developments in the applicable law in international commercial arbitration in China and the enforcement of arbitral awards in China are analyzed.

A method of "joint conciliation" has been developed to resolve disputes between the Chinese and foreign trading partners (including foreign investors). While the customary reliance on negotiation and conciliation is becoming incompatible with the needs of increasing foreign trade and foreign business activity in China, as well as the expectation of China's foreign trade partners, the current practice integrates Chinese culture with the Western legal tradition, as no country can escape the influence of its own culture and tradition.

As Chinese economic philosophy becomes more pragmatic and as foreign trade increases, it can be anticipated that the cultural, historical, and ideological factors fueling a reluctance to arbitrate and impeding development of the legal system will subside. In the context of its new policy of welcoming foreign investment, loans, and other forms of cooperation with business firms that generally are privately owned, the People's Republic has recently taken steps to facilitate the resolution of the disputes that will inevitably arise. The major Chinese foreign trade arbitration institution has been renamed, wider jurisdiction granted, and a branch office set up in the Special Economic Zone.

China has begun to establish an arbitral system and is in the process of accepting the Western style international commercial arbitration as a consequence of its efforts to modernize and develop. As a result, China should make arbitration in China attractive not only for disputes between Chinese and foreign nationals, but also for disputes involving only foreign nationals. China's increasing participation in such neutral forms of dispute settlement is a logical extension of its participation in world trade, and the promotion of its position in the economic community. As its position improves, the author argues, China should make arbitration in China attractive not only for disputes between Chinese and foreign nationals, but also for the disputes involving only foreign nationals.

Mabinton, Loretta Inei

THE UBERRIMA FIDES (UTMOST GOOD FAITH) DOCTRINE UNDER NIGERIAN INSURANCE LAW: THE UNANSWERED QUESTION AND THE INCOMPLETE ANSWER

Harvard Law School 1986 M

90 pages

Footnotes

The law of Nigeria as it is today is a combination of the received laws, statutory enactments, and native law and custom. By the received laws is meant the English rules of common law, doctrines of equity and statutes of general application which were in force in England on certain dates. The received laws were statutorily adopted and so form part of the applicable law.

In this examination of the law of insurance not only is case law in Nigeria considered, but case law in England as well. With regard to the application of English cases and judicial precedent in Nigeria, the courts say that English decisions are only of persuasive authority. In actual fact they act as if they are bound firmly by English decisions, especially those of the House of Lords. The courts' attitude explains why English decisions are cited and approved religiously to this date. The idea of importing English law wholesale without regard to societal differences leaves much to be desired. The result is that laws operate in a locality which is ill-equiped to deal with such laws. The rules of marine insurance are governed by the Marine Insurance Act of 1961 which is largely copied from the British Marine Insurance Act of 1906. The 1976 Insurance Act and the Motor Vehicle Act of 1958 are both adaptations of English statutes. The result of these adaptations are antiquated and unsuitable statutes.

The rules of insurance law and more particularly the doctrine of utmost good faith, which is the subject of the paper, evolved during the 16th century in England. At that time communication was poor and neither effective nor efficient. As a result, insurers, especially marine insurers, had to rely on the insured to give them all relevant information. Common law therefore evolved the doctrine of utmost good faith to protect insurers. One of the questions addressed is whether there is still need for common law protection of insurers today and, if there is, how much protection is necessary.

On the basis of these considerations, the paper discusses the duty imposed by the uberrima fides doctrine in the law of insurance as urged by insurers and applied by the courts. Non-disclosure, particularly in terms of marine insurance, is reviewed. Other topics examined are misrepresentation and the basis of the contract clause. Specific suggestions for reform are offered in addition to a model statute.

Madigan, Michael

ADMINISTRATIVE RULEMAKING IN SWEDEN AND THE UNITED STATES: WHAT CAN BE LEARNED FROM THE AMERICAN EXPERIENCE?

Harvard Law School 1986 M

45 pages

Footnotes

Swedish administrative law has up to the last decade for the most part adhered to what in the United States has been termed the "traditional model".

Under the traditional model of administrative law, policy decisions are made by a legislative body which is democratically elected and political accountable. The function of an administrative agency is limited to the implementation of specific policy decisions. The agency's duty is to apply a regulation on a given case in an accurate, impartial and rational way. The traditional model conceives "the agency as a mere transmission belt for implementing legislative directives in particular cases. It legitimates intrusions into private liberties by agency officials not subject to electoral control by ensuring that such intrusions are commanded by a legitimate source of authority - the legislature".

The continuous expansion of the public sector and the increased complexity in administering a highly industrialized welfare society has brought about changes in the classical Swedish administrative model starting in the beginning of the 1970's. New regulatory program - the most important in the area of occupational safety and health and environment protection - have delegated substantial lawmaking power to government agencies. The regulatory statutes, passes by the Parliament, only state the basic regulatory objective and authorize administrative agencies to formulate substantive regulations through rulemaking.

The shift to this new legislative technique was motivated by a belief that agencies were better equipped to set detailed standards and that the model would allow more flexible and efficient adjustment for rapidly changing conditions in society.

The new lawmaking function of administrative agencies has been virtually unbound by any procedural constraints on the decisionmaking process. In sharp contrast to the American rulemaking process, the Swedish administrator - not bound by any requirements for notice, comment or hearing - can in theory write a regulation in the morning and adopt it in the afternoon.

Although there are no signs of abuse of this new regulatory power there is a growing concern over this new model of public administration. Members of the Parliament have recently started to express their worry over policymaking by unelected officials and there have been accusations that the new powerful bureaucracy lacks political control. Some of the problems involved with administrative lawmaking have also been discussed briefly by two Government committees and scholars have questioned the constitutionality of some delegations.

The objective of this paper is to undertake a comparative study of how administrative law governs the lawmaking process carried out by administrative agencies in Sweden and in the United States. The focus will be on policymaking through promulgation of general rules. This is the method implemented in Sweden and a shift to rulemaking procedures instead of adjudication has also gained popularity in the United States during the last fifteen years. A comparison of two legal systems usually serves the purpose of providing a perspective from which one can see the legal system more clearly. The aim is to provide greater self-understanding of the Swedish regulatory process by observing the American experience.

Martin, Scott M.

MARCHING IN PLACE: STATE LEGISLATIVE ATTEMPTS TO CODIFY THE RIGHT OF PUBLICITY

Columbia Law School 1986 M

108 pages

Footnotes

The right of publicity, which has been defined as the right to control the commercial exploitation of an individual's name, likeness, or personality, has in the United States been almost entirely a creation of the judiciary. Where state courts have not acted, the federal courts have stepped in to create a right of publicity under the state law.

The right of publicity is in many ways analogous to copyright and patent rights: it is widely regarded as a property right, which may be assigned and enforced by an assignee. Unlike copyright and patent rights, however, there is no federal scheme of protection covering the right of publicity. The result is a patchwork of state case law of such variety that one court has concluded that "(t)he state of the law is still that of a haystack in a hurricane."

Within the past few years, however, a new stage in the evolution of the right publicity has begun as states have begun to enact right of publicity statutes. To date eleven states have adopted statutes establishing various forms of a right of publicity. Although these statutes do not resolve the conflict among the laws of the various states and do not settle the debate over federal preemption of the right, they do have the advantage of clarifying (with varying degrees of success) the parameters of the right of publicity within that state. The statutes vary from several sentences to several pages, from complete right of publicity statutes to slightly expanded right of privacy statutes, and from comprehensive regulatory schemes to barely useful pronouncements of state policy.

This paper examines all of the state right of publicity statutes, as well as the issues which they raise, including the questions of preemption and choice of law. Also included in the examination are state right of privacy statutes creating rights similar to the right of publicity. The paper also considers the elements of a model state statutory scheme, and concludes with an argument that the adoption of a federal statute regulating the right publicity is the only effective means of resolving the problems created by the establishment of a right of publicity.

Martinez, Maria Alejandra

BIOTECHNOLOGY: ITS PATENTABILITY AND COMMERCIALIZATION IN THE PHARMACEUTICAL INDUSTRY (THE CASE OF ARGENTINA)

Harvard Law School 1986 M

105 pages

Footnotes and appendices

The world is facing the "biotechnological revolution". It is considered to be the second of the late twentieth century revolutions - the first being microelectronics. Although it started in industrialized countries, its impacts will reach the Third World very soon.

Biotechnology has a broad range of applications, some of them related to some of the most essential human needs such as food, health, shelter and energy. Its potential cannot be ignored for very much longer. For many cultures it could be a phenomenon difficult to understand that gives rise, because of its nature, to many ethical problems. In particular, it poses significant challenges to legal systems and processes and to the role of law in contemporary society.

This paper deals with the application of biotechnology to the pharmaceutical industry: its development, its commercialization, its patentability and its future both in an industrialized and in a developing country. To carry out this objective, the United States and Argentina are used as examples. The reasons for this choice are the leading position of the U.S. in the field of biotechnology and the particular strength of the domestic pharmaceutical industry in Argentina, which is relatively advanced as compared with other industries of the Third World.

The impact of biotechnology will soon reach the Third World. The analysis in this study is principally on two issues: the protection of intellectual property and the commercialization of biotech pharmaceutical products.

As Argentina has a very large domestic market

of pharmaceuticals and a good indigenous production of these products, it was considered an excellent place to commercialize biotech pharmaceuticals. Since intellectual property issues are closely connected with marketing and foreign investments, it was very relevant to try to establish the possibility of patenting biotechnology in Argentina under the present legislation, and, in particular, to clarify which is the specific protection given to pharmaceutical compositions.

When considering the principal producers of biotechnology today, it was then observed that the "leaders of the biotech boom" are the NBF's which, although licensing their products to establish companies at the moment, are planned to market these by themselves in the near future.

The purpose of this paper is to present several issues, very broad but very connected and to offer different possibilities for their interrelation. It also aimed at stimulating the NBF's to produce and help to produce biotechnology in Argentina.

Marzano, Rodrigo Rosenberg

A JOINT VENTURE OF COFFEE IN GUATEMALA

Harvard Law School M

35 pages

Footnotes

The purpose of this paper is to explore the possibilities of a foreign investment in the agricultural sector of Guatemala.

The general idea is to take advantage of the high coffee prices by improving the future productions of coffee plantations in the country, but with a diversification plan to mitigating the loss of profits that will occur when the prices fall.

In order to examine this idea, it is first necessary to look at the background of coffee growing, the role of the International Coffee Organization, its development, and why this organization works so well, and the Guatemalan relationship with the organization.

Then analyzed is the actual situation and what may happen in the near future, based on situations that have happened in the past, as well as how diversification plan would be a good measure in an oversupply market situation.

This is followed by looking into the present situation in Guatemala and how everything indicates that the economy and the political situation of the country are improving rapidly. Guatemalan economy is mainly based on an agricultural production and, as coffee is the country's first exporting product, its role is extremely important. Nevertheless, since the coffee prices change constantly, it is necessary to find a diversification plan that will make the national economy less dependable on the coffee industry and, therefore, more stable.

Examined also is how a joint venture can be created in both the private and public sectors, the diversification plan, and some of the most important elements that are likely to appear in a negotiation of a joint venture.

It was concluded that there is a good possibility of foreign investment in coffee because its market situation makes it very profitable. Nevertheless, a diversification plan is needed to ensure the success of the operation because of the fluctuation of the coffee market. The problem of the regional conflicts that are happening in Central American should not be a decisive factor for not investing in the country, because Guatemala is not directly involved in this conflict.

Mbu, Patrick B.

THE ROLE OF AGRICULTURE IN NIGERIA'S ECONOMIC DEVELOPMENT: THE EFFECT OF FOREIGN AND FEDERAL GOVERNMENT INVESTMENT IN THE SECTOR

Harvard Law School 1987 M

59 pages

Footnotes

Although this paper does not attempt to assert the contention, there is indeed a feasible case for saying that no substantial development has in fact occurred in Nigeria since its independence in 1960. At best it can be argued that the development that did occur was extremely unbalanced with astonishing urban growth going hand in hand with stark rural stagnation. One of the major reasons for this lack of balance or agriculture stagnation was as Olatunbosun puts it, "(central government's) regressive pattern of distribution of public expenditures in favor of urban communities that ... created inequality and social injustice (on a scale) that never existed before".

As great as the contributory factor of the government policy was to the dramatic decline of agricultural output, it was by no means the only major factor. Others include the chronic depletion of the agricultural workforce caused by massive rural-urban migration and indeed the colonial legacy that manifested itself in the structural underdevelopment of the country, the hallmark of which was excessive emphasis on the exportation of primary products coupled with limited industrialization.

During the course of discussing the role of agriculture in Nigeria's economic development, this paper traces agricultural development from its colonial days (1880-1960) up to and including the 'Green Revolution' scheme which officially was introduced in Nigeria in February 1980.

This paper also discusses the nature, effect and role of both foreign investment and Central Government investment in the agricultural sector. In connection with foreign investment, the major emphasis was on foreign direct investment. Similarly, though domestic investment was seen primarily from the viewpoint of Federal Government investment, limited mention was made of private local investment as well as that of the 19 state governments that now exist. In all events the paper deals purely with investment in agriculture 'per se' but also compares investment with trends in other sectors. From this comparative approach it is shown that agriculture was not deserted overnight in the wake of the huge OPEC instigated oil price hikes of 1973-74 but in fact had for quite some time been a relatively unpopular target for investment; indeed it is probably because of the strength and resilience of this sector that it took some 10-15 years of neglect before the damage really began to show through in the early 1970's.

Finally, this paper attempts to answer the question "did Nigeria handle its economic development well, unavoidably or badly?" As is so often the case when a squandering of riches on the scale that occurred in Nigeria is carried out, there are no few, convenient culprits at whom all the blame can be directed. Nevertheless, in spite of the existence of other major actors whose share in the blame cannot be underplayed, it is the assertion in this paper that the question of how the Nigerian government handled the country's economic development should be answered "badly".

McCullough, Larry Andrew

INTERNATIONAL AND DOMESTIC CRIMINAL LAW ISSUES IN THE ACHILLE LAURO INCIDENT: A FUNCTIONAL ANALYSIS

George Washington Law School 1986 M

153 pages

Footnotes and appendices

Ultimately, the problem of terrorism must be addressed through "political accommodation and compromise," with recognition that historically, governmental attempts to suppress terrorism through military means do not appear to have succeeded, and that law enforcement methods of prosecution and punishment of terrorists will not, of course, eliminate the problem.

So long as there are individuals willing to engage in discriminate murder to advance a belief they personally hold to be just, absent a fundamental change in human nature, terrorism, like common domestic crime, will pose a continuing problem. However, adherence to the rule of law and resort to international enforcement mechanisms can contribute greatly to control of terrorism and possibly reduce its frequency.

Individual states within the international community owe certain obligations to all members of that community. Among those obligations are the protection of innocent people from violations of basic human rights. The expectation that this obligation will be met is widely shared, and governed by universal standards.

The rule of Law and successful operation of international legal norms requires states to divorce politics from the decision to bring an alleged international criminal to justice. Making terrorist acts a crime under United States domestic law is an important first step in any response to international terrorism. Nevertheless, without international cooperation, the existence of appropriate United States jurisdiction will have little impact. International terrorism cannot be combated effectively by the United States acting alone. To counter terrorists on a global basis will require the cooperation and assistance of foreign law enforcement authorities.

A consequence of state action similar to that observed in the Achille Lauro incident may be a future unwillingness of the United States and other militarily powerful states to rely on the criminal enforcement mechanism and other peaceful procedures as a means of controlling terrorism. The alternative is an increasing use of force. Although this alternative may be required if cooperative efforts to judicially enforce are lacking, it carries the obvious potential for further loss of innocent civilian life, and a perpetuation of a violent cycle of further acts of terrorism.

Medina, Jose Nicolas

IN SEARCH FOR CHANGE IN CLINICAL LEGAL EDUCATION AT THE SCHOOL OF LAW OF THE UNIVERSITY OF PUERTO RICO: A PROPOSED MODEL OF INSTRUCTION IN THE CRIMINAL LAW FIELD AND OTHER RELATED MATTERS

Harvard Law School 1987 M

63 pages

Footnotes

This paper describes and deals with three main dimensions that shape the clinical legal education of Puerto Rico. The first dimension deals with a broad societal context as a way of examining long range goal orientation in legal education. A second dimension involves reviewing some considerations for curriculum reform, and thirdly, a pedagogical dimension is proposed as a model for a clinical course in the criminal law field. The picture is one that runs from the general social overview and moral and political discourse to the more concrete dynamics of the teaching-learning process.

Clinical methodology should be separately understood from any legal subject matter of instruction. The method can be used as an exceptional device since it involves the students in active, direct nonvicarious experiences that enhance learning in superior ways. The method encompasses the interaction of student's lawyering role playing, the teacher's use of that experience as a focal basis for inquiry and understanding, and the tensions generated in the interaction of the teaching, learning process. This process assumes identifiable dynamics that can vary according to the area of instruction. In the criminal area (defense function) constitutional, professional responsibility and practical considerations shape and condition the dynamics of student's practice and supervision. Clinical methodology should be integrated to further the broad and simple goals of legal education.

The role of the clinical professor is not to act as a practitioner when the teaching device used is active lawyering. They should act as facilitators who identify the dynamics, skills and ethical dilemmas when a role is performed. The teachers need to build their own pedagogical models adapted to the particular clinical setting. An adequate number of cases must be provided and institutional arrangements must be made to deal with the problems of overburdening, among them, changes in the curriculum. One possible solution would be to offer two lawyering process courses - one civil and the other criminal - the latter with classroom and practice sections.

Particular attention is given to the process by which the clinic culturally impacts the faculty, the courses, legal institutions, agents and their practices. The inhouse clinic is the best radar to capture the process in the lawyering world. Adequate channels of communication, interchange of faculty and information about the daily work of the clinic is important to strengthen the whole educational project of the law school.

Medjad, Karim

MINING THE BUSINESS OF HUMANKIND: FINANCING SEABED MINING UNDER THE LAW OF THE SEA CONVENTION

Harvard Law School 1986 M

53 pages

Footnotes

When the third Conference on the Law of the Sea started, the deep seabed was expected to become the Eldorado of the twenty-first century, despite the fact that its mineral bonanza had not been precisely assessed.

Led by other concerns, the negotiators, more interested in modalities than in figures, have underestimated the importance of these data which, even if they were constantly modified, were always changing in the same direction. This explains why the Law of the Sea Treaty of December 10, 1982, the first attempt in the history to set the law before the occurrence of the facts, indicated certain weak points, hardly compatible with its vocation of "prospective treaty."

Such a scenario is based on a double postulate: first, the adhesion to the treaty of a majority of states, including the richest; second, the affordability of the costs involved. Yet, the present situation hardly reflects such an ideal outcome. Since the L.O.S. Treaty retains the U.N. scale, France and the Soviet Union are the only major contributors which have signed the treaty, while states representing more than 60% of the total financial contribution have as yet not done so. Moreover, current estimates indicate that the cost of the first mining operation would amount to over $2 billion dollars. As regards the financial capacity of the States Members, such a figure is simply out of proportion, and it would be unrealistic to image that their loans or contributions could finance the bulk of the undertaking.

Beyond the controversy over the "over politicization" of the L.O.S. Treaty which, as a result would have - or would not have - shattered the future of the international exploitation of the common heritage of mankind, the purpose of this paper is to demonstrate that the enterprise can, within the legal and philosophical scope of the L.O.S. Treaty, adapt itself to the present situation. The following developments are an attempt to prove that if brakes upon its application do exist, current analysis tends to dislocate them. The opposition of most of the OECD countries is a parameter which has been over estimated, and the financial scarcity can and should be overcome even if the reasons to do so would not really help implementing the L.O.S. Treaty's genuine objectives. In the view of the treaty, the Enterprise is allowed to borrow in order to complete its financial resources, and to get involved in some specific kinds of joint undertakings.

Mei, Shan

HUMANITARIAN INTERVENTION UNDER INTERNATIONAL LAW

Harvard Law School 1986 M

49 pages

Footnotes

International law is created by states to govern relations among them and for the purpose of maintaining international peace and order. International law use to deal solely with external relations between states. What occurs within the state between the "sovereign" and his "subjects" has, by definition, no effect on external inter-state relations.

In the past, acts which violate basic human rights and oppressed freedom occurred repeatedly throughout human history. With the increased spread of the idea of human rights, and the gradual transformation of human rights from ideas and rhetoric into international as well as national law, those acts which were ignored and are continuing to occur are considered as an intolerable affront to basic human dignity and to the collective conscience of mankind in the contemporary world.

Besides the effort of the international community, many forms of intervention - economic, diplomatic, social, cultural and military - have been used by individual states to interfere with other states' internal affairs in the name of humanity. While most of these are generally considered as normal state conducts and therefore, are legal under international law, the issue on the legality of military intervention for humanitarian purpose by an individual state or a group of states has caused sharp differences among governments, politicians and international lawyers.

Thus, in many crisis, two important objectives of international law appear to be in conflict: That of peace and that of justice. The former objective is set out in the rules of the United Nations Charter against the use of force by states except in self-defense against armed attack. The latter is found in the provisions of the Charter and in various resolutions, declarations, and covenants pertaining to fundamental human rights and self-determination.

It is concluded that the argument that intervention is justifiable on humanitarian grounds is quite simply not true. It is not so in terms of the black letter rules of the United Nations and relevant international documents: it is not so in terms of state practice; and it is not so because it is a bad policy. Therefore, no military intervention by individual state or a group of states, in the name of humanity, in another state is permissible under the current international law, except in an extreme emergency requiring instant response and subject to immediate termination of such emergency action on the request of the United Nations or an appropriate regional organization.

Meyer, Hans-Juergen K.

DRUG REGULATION AND THE ANTAGONISTIC ECONOMIC INTERESTS OF RESEARCH-BASED AND GENERIC MANUFACTURERS: A SURVEY OF THE SITUATION IN THE UNITED STATES OF AMERICA AND THE FEDERAL REPUBLIC OF GERMANY

Harvard Law School 1986 M

68 pages

Footnotes and bibliography

In recent years, the pharmaceutical market in the United States (US) and West Germany (FRG), as in many other countries, has become the arena for increasingly intense competition between research-oriented brand name producers and generic drug companies. The two industries differ fundamentally in their competitive strategies. To reduce public spending on pharmaceuticals, both the US and the FRG have taken various steps designed to make doctors and patients aware of drug prices and to foster the prescription of less expensive drugs.

The shaping of certain legal mobility barriers in the pharmaceutical market in the US and the FRG is the topic of this paper. The most important market entry barrier is the patent protection that a pioneer drug usually enjoys. Patent law constitutes a mobility barrier that has been deliberately designed to protect the economic interests of inventors. This distinguishes patent law from de facto mobility barriers which actually serve a non-economic objective, but at the same time in a reflex-like manner establish a shelter from competition. Such is the case with the requirement of pre-market approval of new drugs under the American Food, Drug, and Cosmetics Act (FDC Act) and the German Arzneimittelgesetz (AMC, Drug Act). Even though the only purpose of the regulatory scheme is to prevent hazards to public health, it has in fact become the most important market mobility barrier next to patent law. The design of this scheme receives special attention here.

An overview is presented of the methods that both countries have used to consider pre-market approval of generic (or copycat or me too) drugs.

After a discussion of the interdependence between the regulatory scheme and the rival industry's standing in the market, the way in which the Food and Drug Agency and its equivalent, the Bundesgesundheitsamt have dealt with the issue is explored.

The discussion reveals more than a specific problem in drug regulation. Rather it presents a paradigm for most situations in which government regulation simultaneously affects antagonistic economic interests. Rival industries, because of a different business structure, have colliding expectations for the best shape of the regulatory scheme. In the case of a regulated market a company's competitive position depends on the terms of regulation as much as on market forces. This is particularly so when regulation establishes market entry barriers. Consequently, under these conditions regulation ceases to be a merely bilateral concern of government and individual. Instead it becomes a concern involving the government and two individuals (companies). Hence it follows that the government which distorts the conditions of a free market in favor of implementing a certain regulatory scheme should not only pursue the objective which is the actual justification for regulation - such as protecting the public health - but also take into account the economic impact of regulation on rival industries.

Mikhail, Henry Jad

ISRAELI POLICIES AND PRACTICES IN OCCUPIED ARAB TERRITORY: AN APPRAISAL UNDER INTERNATIONAL HUMANITARIAN LAW

George Washington Law School 1986 M

178 pages

Footnotes

Palestine is the area of land in between the Golan Heights and the Sea of Galilee to the north, the Negev and Sinai deserts to the south, the Mediterranean Sea to the west and the Jordan River to the east. Palestinians are the descendants of Abraham, Semites by race, who have continuously inhabited Palestine for thousands of years. In 1948, upon the creation of the State of Israel, hundreds of thousands of Palestinians were forced into exile as refugees.

Territories acquired by Israel it its conflicts were acquired by force, contrary to the well established international legal principle which declares inadmissible the acquisition of territory by use of force, a principle embodied in Article 2(4) of the United Nations Charter. Acquisition of territory as a consequence of an exercise of the right of self-defense is also prohibited. Thus, the fact that subsequent events posed an obstacle to its implementation does not detract from the legal validity and binding nature of General Assembly Resolution 181 of 1947. Distinguished international lawyer, Henry Cattan, insists that Israel is "especially obligated to respect and to implement Resolution 181(II), owing to the formal assurances it gave to the United Nations in 1949 as a condition of its admission to the organization's membership."

Belligerent occupation is distinguished from an invasion in that an invasion does not require or demand the establishment by the occupying power of complete and effective control over a territory. And an invasion does not necessitate the assumption by the invader of the governmental and administrative functions of the area penetrated. Furthermore, in a state of invasion war can still be in progress.

What is important to remember is that neither Israeli occupation nor annexation can deprive the Palestinians Arab population of Palestine of national sovereignty over their lands, for "sovereignty is inalienable and survives aggression, occupation, and annexation." Palestinians are at present only temporarily deprived of the enjoyment and full exercise of their sovereignty over Palestine, a sovereignty no party can legally withhold from them. Neither in 1948, nor in 1967, did Israel challenge Jordan's assumption of sovereignty over the West Bank region. In fact, Israel sought to conclude a peace treaty with Jordan in which only minor border modifications would be made along the Israeli-Jordanian border of 1948. Gerson maintains that "these facts negate any claim that Israel's rights to sovereignty over the West Bank are superior to those of either Jordan or the indigenous population. Nonetheless, pending the ultimate determination of the legal status of the occupied territories, Israel continues to make lasting geographic and demographic changes in this territory at an alarming rate.

Mirabel, Eric-Paul

PRODUCT-BY-PROCESS CLAIMS: A PRACTICAL PERSPECTIVE

George Washington Law School 1986 M

66 pages

Footnotes

In a product-by-process claim, perhaps as its terms imply, a product is defined by setting forth the process by which it is made. It is important to bear in mind that "the invention so defined is a product and not a process." Thus, a more descriptive expression than "product-by-process claim" defines the product as "claimed in product-by-process terms."

Use of product-by-process claims raises a number of problems and issues, the answers to which are by no means settled. The major issues discussed in this paper involve defining these claims, deciding when they can properly be made and determining their relationship with the provisions of Title 35 of the United States Code. The scope of the problems which can be encountered suggests what is perhaps the most descriptive definition for these claims - a trap for the unwary.

Throughout this paper a view is kept towards the practical consequences of employing this claim format. While it will be seen as disadvantageous in many respects, it is nonetheless necessary where a product cannot be adequately defined in other terms. These disadvantages only arise, however, if product-by-process principles are applicable to the claim in question. Therefore the fundamental inquiry is always: into what category does a particular claim fit?

If both conventional claims and product-by-process claims are submitted, the applicant risks invalidity of the latter as there is no "necessity" for them, which would also leave the unnamed products unprotected, The CCPA never did overrule the "rule of necessity."

The solution to this dilemma is to simply eliminate the notion that product-by-process claims are somehow a "peculiar" or "exceptional" claim format. The concept of "necessity" is simply not relevant. Compliance with the requirement of 35 U.S.C. 112, second paragraph - that there be claims particularly pointing out and distinctly claiming the invention - should be the only issue. Inventors should be safe in the knowledge that the limitations of the English language and of known technology to adequately define their inventions do not deprive them of protection, irrespective of the format of their claims.

Morgan, Edward M.

CONSTITUTIONAL DISCONTINUITY AND INTERNATIONAL RECOGNITION IN ZIMBABWE: A THEORETICAL PERSPECTIVE

Harvard Law School 1986 M

115 pages

Footnotes

The year 1985 marked twenty years since the occurrence of a political act of rebellion which has come to be seen as a paradigm of international illegality: the Unilateral Declaration of Independence (U.D.I.) from the United Kingdom by the white settler government of Southern Rhodesia. That this rebellious act, though clothed in the verbiage on inalienable rights, was contrary to the accepted norms of international conduct has been well documented. Nevertheless, the legal analysis of the position occupied by the now defunct regime during its more that fourteen years of existence has left constitutional and international legal theorists in something of a quandry.

Any evaluation of the juridical status of the settler regime must commence with an acknowledgment that U.D.I. itself embodied an avowed rebellion against the authority of the Imperial Government and a conscious violation of Southern Rhodesia's pre-existing 1961 Constitution. While this fact alone is not, of course, conclusive of the insurmountably illegitimate nature of such a regime in international law, it must be perceived in combination with the universal refusal of states to extend the crucial act of recognition to the government of Ian Smith or to deal with it in any terms other than as an "international outlaw" at large in the world community. While some courts attributed acts of the U.D.I. regime and its agencies with uncontrovertible validity, others denied enforcement of Rhodesian acts and judicial rulings on the basis of international non-recognition rather than intrinsic unconstitutionality.

It is something of a historical irony, therefore, that the jurisprudential dilemma embodied by the renegade settler regime may be rekindled by the present Zimbabwe Government, whose existence has been legitimized by widespread recognition in the international community and whose independence has been perceived as having validly devolved from the British Crown. As is evident, the issues entail an exploration of the generally accepted approach to constitutional discontinuity, in which abrupt annihilation and efficacious transformation of a state's constitutional order are perceived as providing a necessarily legitimate base on which to prop the newly emerged regime.

Morningstar, Joan Catherine

THE UNITED STATES STRATEGIC DEFENSE INITIATIVE AND ITS EFFECT ON THE ANTI-BALLISTIC MISSILE TREATY

George Washington Law School 1986 M

96 pages

Footnotes and appendices

Outer space, accessible only since 1957, has been added to the arena of arms competition. Unfortunately, it was realized soon after the first space launching that as long as the world community was divided into sovereign states, each with special national interests, military competition in space was as inevitable in outer space as it had been on land, sea and air.

In 1983, President Ronald Reagan challenged the scientists, engineers and industrialists of this country to find the way to remove the threat posed by strategic nuclear missiles, to render these nuclear weapons impotent and obsolete. That announcement was the introduction to the world of the establishment of the Strategic Defense Initiative (SDI), whose purpose is to develop an operational space-based ballistic missile defense system. The SDI contemplates a complete reversal of the deterrence to nuclear war based on mutual assured destruction, which for more than 20 years has prevented the nuclear Armageddon so feared for so long.

SDI presents a new arms control policy which seeks "greatly reduced levels of nuclear arms and an enhanced ability to deter war based on an increasing contribution of non-nuclear defenses against offensive nuclear arms."

Criticism of the SDI has grown since its introduction in 1983. Some critics of the SDI have seriously questioned the technological feasibility of a space-based ballistic missile defense system. More importantly, others fear that existing arms control agreements and world stability will be threatened by the Strategic Defense Initiative.

The Anti-Ballistic Missile Treaty (ABM), which

is considered in detail, has been the subject of so many divergent interpretations that its very existence is jeopardized. The collapse of the ABM Treaty will assuredly signal the end of the limited goal of reducing the offensive threat and the ultimate goal of preserving world peace through arms control agreements.

The task of making space a peaceful environment is clear but the methods unsure. The object of this study is to detail the proposed Ballistic Missile Defense Systems, analyze their inadequacies in view of present technologies, and most significantly demonstrate the deleterious effect that the SDI could have on the ABM Treaty.

Motloli, Santo A.

THE SOUTH AFRICAN JUDICIAL SYSTEM AND POSITIVISM

Harvard Law School 1987 M

72 pages

Footnotes and appendices

The authors concern throughout this paper is positivism as employed by South African lawyers. There were reservations about entering into a study of positivism as a legal theory. Such a study and also the question of whether unjust laws can compose what may be called a "legal system" is beyond the scope of this paper. There is also an argument that a judge faced with the application of unjust laws should resign. Though the author does not dispute that assertion, it was found not to be relevant to the contents of this study.

The South African legal order is in a state of crisis. The majority of the South African population see it as a discriminatory and repressive instrument of white rule. Foreign critics, even some of moderate standing, equate it with that of Nazi Germany. The legal profession and the judiciary are an extricable part of the legal order and cannot escape responsibility for it by invoking vulgar positivism or any jurisprudential creed. South African judges should examine their consciences. They have only two courses left open to them; resignation or judicial activism in the cause of human rights. The Natal judges have already become aware of the options left to them and now are reacting strongly against the view of taking laws as simply the commands of the legislature. The course they have taken can be described in jurisprudential terms as the rejection of positivism as a legal creed and the adoption of an idealist approach to the judicial process and civil liberties.

Adherence to legal positivism has reduced the South African legal profession to the status of a technical trade in the eyes of the public. It has undermined the profession's claim to leadership in the South African society. A new creed is called for based upon the scepticism infusing legal realism and the idealism inherent in natural law. South

African judiciary should not be content to be merely bricklayers - its judges should be architects.

It is shown in this paper that the strict adherence by the South African judges to the formal rules and the distinction of law from legal values lies in their acceptance of legal positivism as a jurisprudential guide.

Mudd, John O.

THE PLACE OF PERSPECTIVE IN LAW AND LEGAL EDUCATION

Columbia Law School 1986 M

66 pages

Footnotes and bibliography

In recent years American lawyers and the education they receive have come under intense scrutiny and criticism. Whether lasting change will result from this concern and rhetoric remains to be seen. A frequently proposed direction for change calls for combining the teaching of traditional legal subjects with instruction in the skills needed to perform as a lawyer. To make progress in this direction it is important to have a clear picture of the elements of effective lawyer performance and how they relate to each other. This paper attempts a further step in that direction by examining a particular dimension of lawyering that has thus far received little attention.

Among the many abilities needed to practice law is the capacity to view legal problems within a frame of reference; to be able to describe matters, not just in legal terms, but also taking account of the many non-legal factors that bear upon them. This ability to grasp the larger meaning of a legal problem, to position or fix it within the context of forces relevant to its solution, and to assess accurately the impact of the lawyer's activity regarding the problem is what the author calls "perspective."

Perspective is not merely a desirable ability. It is essential for the lawyer. Unfortunately it has been largely overlooked in much of the recent discussion about lawyer competency and legal education. Attention has been focused rather on other practice skills like writing, counseling, negotiating, and litigation. But neither traditional legal education nor the contemporary correctives offer adequate in understanding and developing perspective.

The paper first describes perspective by relating it to other aspects of professional performance, by showing how it operates in concrete situations, and by tracing its relationship with different kinds of lawyer tasks. This is followed by analyzing the roots of perspective in cognition and its relationship to judgment. From this analysis of what perspective is and how it operates in lawyering, the author offers preliminary suggestions about how perspective may be developed in an educational setting.

Murthy, Sleela

THE NON-GOVERNMENTAL ORGANIZATION ROLE: A CASE STUDY OF DOWRY IN INDIA

Harvard Law School 1987 M

110 pages

Footnotes

Non-governmental organizations (NGO) are a modern concept in international human rights law. The term NGO has become fashionable, and in India, organizations of all sorts term themselves NGO's. Women's NGO's are no exception.

There is at present no means of quantifying the nature and degree of human rights violations. While it will probably remain impossible to rank situations, given the inherent difficulty in comparing, for example, torture with starvation, social statistical techniques could well be applied to a phenomenon such as torture to identify those factors which affect and determine reporting and so influence the preconceived incidence in a particular situation. The torture of women in India on the pretext of dowry may or may not have been as prevalent in historical times, but the increased publicity and coverage that the dowry issue is generating could be regarded as a sign of the relatively higher legal awareness among the Indians of today than the Indians of yesteryear. All current endeavors at quantification have attempted to identify indicators which could be used globally and in all situations. This task may not be that simple, since each country has its own idiosyncrasies and cultural differences. Moreover, it is unlikely that valid measures can better be found by examining very specific problems in a country and only then attempting a generalized approach.

In this paper the author discusses, and critically analyzes, the role of women's NGO's in solving the problem of dowry. In India, dowry is associated with the extortion of money by the bridegroom's family from the bride's family, not only during the wedding, but even thereafter. If the dowry is inadequate the wife/daughter-in-law is harassed, tortured, and often either murdered or driven to suicide.

By focusing on the narrow problems of women's NGO's and the dowry issue the author exposes the defects in the NGO's approach and their neglect of broader social considerations, making it impossible for them to tackle problems at the level which they are now being dealt. These women's NGO's are a hopeful sign for Indian democracy but they have to "struggle against the tide", and the author explains why they have not been successful so far. Indeed, what may be essential in the Indian context is some sort of radical restructuring of the society.

Muys, Jr., Jerome Christian

MORTGAGE-BACKED SECURITIES: TAX, ACCOUNTING, AND SECURITIES LAW CONSIDERATIONS

George Washington Law School 1986 M

92 pages

Footnotes

This paper considers various aspects of Federal income tax, securities law, and accounting treatment of "mortgage-backed securities." The term "mortgage-backed securities" is used to refer generically to the various investment instruments which are backed by pools of residential (and, recently, commercial) mortgages. These instruments include, among others, mortgage pass-through certificates, mortgage-backed bonds, and mortgage pay-through certificates.

The author concludes that the secondary mortgage market has emerged as a primary source of housing credit. Recent legislative and regulatory initiatives have helped transform mortgage-backed securities into widely accepted investments that are competitive with other traditional securities. As a result, other types of assets, such as automobile loans, are now targeted for use as collateral backing securities.

In the short run, the major players in the secondary mortgage market will continue to be the three quasi-governmental agencies - GNMA, FNMA, and FHLMC. However, with the enactment of the SMMEA, it appears that future growth in the secondary mortgage market will be concentrated in the private sector.

Although the focus of federal policy in recent years has been to encourage the development of the secondary mortgage market, there is a continuing need to reform the federal tax laws to provide greater flexibility in the structuring of mortgage-backed securities issuances. In addition, other regulatory encumbrances, resulting from state regulation of real estate and securities, need to be removed to reduce complexity and expense of issuing mortgage-backed securities.

It seems likely that the increasing demand for mortgage credit will foster efforts to further reduce the regulatory burdens on issuers and holders of mortgage-backed securities. Less likely if further expansion of the federal role in the secondary mortgage market. The present trend is to reduce the advantages held by the quasi-governmental corporations and to place them on more equal footing with private issuers of mortgage backed securities. However, no one is predicting an end to the federal presence in the secondary mortgage market.

Narus, Harold

LEGAL ASPECTS OF DOING BUSINESS IN CHINA

George Washington Law School 1986 M

133 pages

Footnotes and appendices

This paper considered the more important provisions of the Laws of the Peoples Republic of China concerning, special economic zones, the attractive opportunities for compensation in trade and joint ventures, the protection of intellectual property, taxation, United States import and export regulations, Chinese contractual policy, and arbitration, for the purpose of giving a party, interested in the opportunities of investing in China an overview of some of the requirements and attendant problems related thereto.

It is obvious from the laws that as a result of the "simplicity" of the drafting, that there exists the possibility and probability of a variety of problems arising, many of which may be serious if not specifically addressed in the contractual documents. When one takes into consideration the way business is conducted in the United States compared to a communist country's conduct of business, such as China, and the cultural differences that exist, it can be safely assumed and anticipated that there will be problems that will not be resolved without one side or both agreeing to a settlement which is contrary to its business philosophy, experience, politics, and cultural values.

Aside from any criticism of the laws, the related risks can be overcome or at least the risk reduced by the foreign investor. The vehicle by which this reduction of risk can be achieved is a contract. Any areas of concern that are not covered under the law will require an adequate contractual provision to address this deficiency. Where a deviation from the law is necessary, it must be stated clearly, concisely and with sufficient detail to accomplish the purposes desired of the parties concerned. Regardless of the final agreement between the foreign investor and the Chinese, a long term deal must be evaluated in light of the political, legal, economic and social environments in which the joint venture must operate.

Because of China's history over the last forty years it is prudent to be cautious; there is no guarantee that China will become predictable and stable in its development. If the new laws and other business arrangements help China to begin to achieve its goal of modernization without jeopardizing its political, cultural, and social system, it is almost certain that the economic policies and related laws and regulations will develop further and strengthen the interest of foreign investors to invest in China.

On the other side, as China's economy improves and the country acquires the skills and technology necessary to continue and maintain growth, the open-door policy may again become restrictive as foreign investment and know-how becomes less necessary for growth. In any event, a real opportunity exists which could lead to a new long term and possibly permanent market.

Nishimura, Itsuo

EXTRADITION: THEORY AND PRACTICE IN JAPAN AND THE UNITED STATES

Harvard Law School M

54 pages

Footnotes

The remarkable development of international public transportation and international communication systems has had a great impact on criminality. The number of international crimes which require cooperation among states to suppress has increased rapidly. In this situation, extradition has assumed a more important role in improving world public order. On the other hand, recent development of international human rights demands protection, even for fugitives, based on humanitarian considerations. These recent trends have influenced the scope and the notion of extradition, bringing about difficult problems in the field of the political offense exception in particular. This paper examines the development of extradition by comparing Japanese extradition practices with those in the United States.

The courts' denial of extradition of terrorists in the McMullen and Mackin cases shocked the United States government, which prompted the movement to revise the law so that terrorists can be excluded from protection by the political offense exception. But reform efforts to stipulate the clear definition of political offense are facing rough going. Current reform efforts are criticized in two ways. On the one hand, too much curtailment of the scope of political offense by law is criticized as inflexible since it makes the court's discretion very narrow. On the other hand, efforts to revise the domestic law are insufficient to suppress terrorism because even if the United States extradites terrorists based on its reformed extradition law, there may not be an assurance that the requesting state will extradite terrorists to the United States in future cases. In order to assure reciprocity, priority must be given to revising treaties so that terrorism cannot be protected by the political offense exception.

Extradition can be effective measures to suppress international crimes. Particularly, it can be a tool to bring terrorists to justice. For the maintenance of world public order, further efforts must be made by states to improve both treaties and domestic laws related to extradition so that they can cope with international crime effectively.

Nivens, Norman Francis

LEGAL PRINCIPLES AND STANDARDS INVOLVED IN THE GRIEVANCE AND ARBITRATION OF ADVERSE ACTION CASES IN THE FEDERAL SECTOR

George Washington Law School 1986 M

130 pages

Footnotes and appendices

This paper deals generally with the rules of law and administrative regulation which apply to arbitration of misconduct and other adverse action cases in the arena of federal sector employment. The standards and principles applied in federal grievance arbitration of adverse actions provide the main focus. However, in order to provide a more complete perspective on this area of administrative litigation, materials regarding other areas of significant interest to practitioners is included.

The definition of grievance provided by the government is sweeping and intended to include virtually any type of dispute which may arise involving complaints by employees, unions or agencies regarding employment, the collective bargaining agreement or the impact of laws, rules or regulations on employment conditions.

Grievances may arise from many causes. Some causes may be deep seated, and systemic in nature, while others are the product of a single event which impacts a single employee. Each grievance, irrespective of its cause is important to the employee and agency involved. The employee who grieves an adverse action depends upon the negotiated grievance procedure to right a perceived wrong.

Most government employees have access to a negotiated grievance procedure which contains a provision for binding arbitration. Grievances will arise which cannot be resolved short of arbitration. As federal employees are asked once again to "do more with less" by recent legislatively mandated budget cuts, job satisfaction is likely to decrease. Although arbitration is only one avenue available to federal employees for venting feelings of frustration and dissatisfaction, practitioners may well see increased activity in this area. There are many similarities between private sector and federal sector arbitration, even though significant differences exist. Arbitration in the federal sector is regulated to a somewhat greater extent than private sector arbitration by law and regulation.

This paper has focused on the principles and standards which govern federal sector arbitration, beginning with the negotiated grievance and followed through to the enforcement of the arbiter's award. Although it is somewhat more structured by statute and regulation and less by agreement than its private sector cousin, arbitration in the federal sector appears clearly to provide an equitable forum for speedy resolution of disputes in adverse action cases.

Nwabueze, Jessie

STATUS OF WOMEN IN NIGERIA

Harvard Law School M

86 pages

Footnotes

The major premise of the theses is that there is a sixth dimension to the generally known status of women which the author calls "natural status". This natural status is generally confused with the biological function of women. But the author submits that it is more than a biological phenomenon. This is more so when it is considered in conjunction with the nurturing instinct of women. It is argued that the term 'natural status of women' would be better appreciated if treated as a special role assigned to women by nature, without giving women any option of choice. Thus it is submitted that the role having been assigned to women without their own choosing by nature should be better called "natural status".

The nurturing instinct of women which makes them play the role of wife, and mother makes them different in many respects from men. This has nothing to do with intellectual ability. However, the argument that women are created differently from men because of their different roles, does not underscore any argument that women should not be treated equally as men. The discrimination against women all over the world and consequent exploitation of their natural role is due to a basic weakness in human nature.

The minor premise of the theses is that women and men should be aware of the differences in their natural roles and accept them as complementary to each other's role. Such a positive approach to women's role will go a long way in correcting the negative social norms that have arisen as a result of men's perception of women's natural status.

It is noted in the theses that the complex nature of the Nigerian society was compounded by its received English Laws and customs which have not blended with the existing traditional customary laws. This in discussing the status of women or the rural and urban women must be noted and taken into account. The interest of the 80% rural illiterate women should not be overlooked. Any policy geared towards them should take into consideration, their level of illiteracy, unenlightenment, unexposure and general ignorance. Unlike their 20% urban counterpart who are generally off.

All the same, there is need to enhance the status of women in Nigeria. However, law per se cannot achieve the desired goal. Whereas education will go a long way in enhancing the status of women. It is noted too that improvement of women's economic power will in turn improve women's status.

Obuchi, Tetsuya

INTERNATIONAL LIS PENDENS AND CONFLICT OF JUDGEMENTS

Harvard Law School 1987 M

127 pages

The conflict of the lis pendens in the international situation is conflict of two actions between the same parties involving the same subject-matter initiated in two states. This situation (double action) involves positive conflict of taking jurisdiction and can result in the problem of contradictory judgments, vexation to the defendant due to the second action, or uneconomical litigation.

The domestic lis pendens rule, which gives priority to the first-initiated proceeding in many legal systems, does not necessarily apply to the international situation. The plaintiff in the second action can have a legitimate interest in initiating it because of the peculiarity of the international setting. Some policies which rationalize the domestic lis pendens rule do not necessarily apply, or at least they are not always strong enough to defeat the plaintiff's legitimate interest in the second proceeding.

Recognizing foreign judgment is similar to considering foreign lis pendens in that both of them consider the effect of foreign judicial proceeding. However, they are different in the stage and thus in reliability of the content or quality of a foreign judgment and in the strength of requirement of repose.

In conflict of judgments, foreign and domestic, two actions are maintained and two decisions are issued and contradictory judgments may result. If the judgment of one state (the foreign state) is recognized in the other state (the domestic state), there may be a conflict between the two judgments in the same jurisdiction. This is the problem of the conflict of judgments in the domestic sense in the international situation. This problem is very serious, because there is a very serious conflict between the international interest and the domestic interest. In this paper the author also discusses the problem of conflict of foreign and domestic lis pendens.

If recognition of otherwise recognizable foreign judgment is sought, despite the existence of the first-concluded domestic judgment, such recognition should be refused because of the existence of such domestic judgment. And if foreign judgment is concluded first and it is recognizable in the domestic state, the domestic pending action which would conflict should be dismissed. However, the existence of such foreign judgment is not raised in the domestic action and thus it is continued and the domestic judgment is rendered, this domestic judgment should prevail, because, at this stage, there would be much concern about the domestic legal stability and the domestic integrity of decisional effect, even though theoretically the foreign judgment had a binding effect before a domestic judgment is concluded as long as the former is otherwise recognizable.

Odagiri, Yasuko

CONFLICT OF LAWS IN U.S.-JAPAN PRODUCTS LIABILITY CASES

Harvard Law School M

80 pages

Footnotes

The ultimate goal of this study is to develop a theory of law on how societies may best deal with products liability cases with international elements. The study involves comparison of the respective societies' approaches to the problem of injury and damages arising from "defect" in a product, especially in the realm of law, and discussion of conflict-of-law rules in such products liability cases.

Law of products liability has developed and is developing in all industrialized nations with advanced technology and modern, complicated networks of product distribution, because of the following two factors which industrialized nations share; the relatively helpless position of the consumer, and the ambiguity of the locus of liability and economical responsibility of a problem arising from a product.

Because it heavily reflects a society's economic and political policies, product liability law is more policy-oriented than justice-oriented, or at least is on the border of justice on one hand and political and economical policy on the other. A society's approach depends upon the particular situations and seriousness of the product defect problem and the social, political, legal, and economic background of that particular society, such as the expected role of private law and civil litigation in the whole dispute resolution system - and particularly in the resolution of disputes involving a corporation as a party, manufacturers' attitude towards safety control of their products, the expected role of the government and its relationship with the private sector, and a line between civil remedies and criminal sanctions. Availability and effectiveness of other means of compensation and deterrence besides civil litigation is another important factor which must be taken into consideration. And all these factors above are inseparably interrelated. Japan and the United States, the two nations which are the subject of this paper, have their own respective approaches.

Assuming these approaches work well within a society, it is not easy to decide what approach to take when a case has a transnational element. Policies about and approaches to a particular type of problem differ among nations. A solution which is fair and appropriate in light of one culture may look unfair in light of another. A solution seems efficient and effective in one society may be meaningless in another. Because a tremendous amount of trade takes place between nations worldwide and the possibility of products liability problems involving transnational elements is abundant, it is important to develop approaches and rules to secure transnational fairness and decisional harmony in solutions for such transnational cases, even though they do not come together easily.

There is a more promising approach to the problem. Since there are features of legal systems which are not only unique to the American system but also regarded by other jurisdictions as unfair to foreign defendants which have no office in the United States, lawsuits brought by an American plaintiff against a foreign defendant in an American court causes is the most problematic. The author calls for an international convention or treaty to be developed which allows an American forum to apply its own products liability law to a case in which a foreign corporation is the defendant, in exchange for the exclusion of jury trial, punitive damages, and the American-style discovery system.

Oh, Yoon Kyung

THE MARITIME BOUNDARIES OF THE REPUBLIC OF KOREA

Harvard Law School 1987 M

99 pages

Footnotes

This study reviews the maritime jurisdiction of the Republic of Korea, focusing on the legal issues concerning the maritime boundaries. It deals with the outer limits of maritime zones of the Republic of Korea, as well as with the delimitation of maritime zones between the Republic of Korea and its neighbors with opposite and adjacent coasts. The study is but a starting point for the necessary analysis of the evolution of the new maritime order in Northeast Asia.

Maritime boundary, like territorial or land boundary, is a politically sensitive subject, because it affects the coastal state's jurisdiction concerning the fishery, petroleum and other resources of the sea as well as concerning the other uses of the sea. Therefore, a durable boundary agreement must establish or lead to the establishment of a boundary which is fair and equitable to the parties. Although it would be desirable for all littoral states of the Sea of Japan, the Yellow Sea, and the East China Sea to conclude a multilateral agreement, their current political relations prevent them from doing so in the near future.

The question for the Republic of Korea is not whether to settle its maritime boundary issues, but how and when. As for the delimitation question between the Republic of Korea and Japan, a mutually beneficial solution could probably be worked out in light of the past record of mutual consultation and amicable negotiation between the two neighbors. The area of potential conflict, however, is the Japanese challenge to Korea sovereignty over Tokdo in the Sea of Japan.

A negotiated settlement of the controversy between the Republic of Korea and the People's Republic of China does not seem impossible, in spite of the absence of diplomatic relations between the two countries. An arrangement concerning fisheries relationship is not a completely unreasonable prospect, given the PRC's previous precedent of dealing with 'private parties' and the fact that the People's Republic of China has never insisted upon formal diplomatic relations as a prerequisite for entering a negotiation and concluding an agreement.

Any problem of delimitation of maritime boundaries between the Republic of Korea and North Korea is being held in abeyance until an overall solution to the problem of the relationship between the two parts of Korea is obtained.

It may be in the interest of all parties to defer a final boundary delimitation and to exercise restraint until the region as a whole has assembled an equitable and effective strategy for ocean development and management on a regional scale, with careful thought given to the implications of bilateral and multilateral boundary-making in the area.

Ohara, Kazuhiko

SECURITY INTERESTS IN PERSONAL PROPERTY UNDER THE LAWS OF JAPAN

Harvard Law School 1987 M

37 pages

Footnotes

The paper describes, with reference to Article 9 of the Uniform Commercial Code (1978), the laws of Japan in the area of security interests in personal property which create ostensible ownership problems. The major security devices, title-transfer security and reservation of title, are explored in some detail to explain how ostensible ownership problems that arise under them are treated under Japanese law. After an overview of special legislation which enables creations of hypothecs in movables of some sort, some perspectives of Japanese law in the area of security interests in personal property are discussed.

The Civil Code of Japan, one of the major laws which govern personal and real security interests, explicitly recognizes only two security devices as consensual security interests, pledge and hypothec. Under the former device, the debtor must transfer the possession of the collateral to the secured party, while under the latter the collateral remains in the possession of the debtor.

Parties to secured transactions find this difference decisive when they choose between the two. In general, they use pledge when the collateral is personal and hypothec when real. The hypothec allows the debtor to continue to use the collateral, and this enables him to hypothecate his business property to get credit necessary for this business. In the current Japanese business world, however, various other forms of security devices have been used, each tailored to the needs and circumstances involved in the particular transaction.

The paper explores two major security devices. (The discussion is limited to personal property transactions.) These devices function as security by creating, at the stage where the proposed transfer of ownership (title) of the collateral from the debtor to the secured party has not been substantially completed yet, a tension between the debtor's ability to regain the ownership of the collateral if and when he performs his obligation and the secured party's ability to finalize his formal or tentative retainment of its ownership to satisfy his claim against the debtor if and when the debtor fails to fulfill the obligation, thereby creating the ostensible ownership problem. Under these devices, the collateral is usually personal property. These devices are known as title-transfer security and reservation of title. Although the Civil code has no provisions for security interests of these sorts, they were introduced as a practice and are recognized as enforceable security interests by both courts and commentators. These devices are sometimes referred to as atypical securities.

Okawa, Masatoshi

LEGAL PROBLEMS IN WIRE TRANSFER SYSTEMS: TOWARD THE STABILITY OF FINANCIAL SYSTEMS...

Harvard Law School 1986 M

72 pages

Footnotes

Payment methods with negotiable instruments, such as checks, bills of exchange, and so forth, are in such common use that they are taken for granted. Historically, payment methods which prevail in today's business practices have their origins in the medieval trade fairs of Western Europe. A contract to transport the money of one country and to exchange it for the money of another country is recognized as the predecessor of the bill of exchange which evolved into the modern draft or check, still a convenient payment method for debtors and creditors who are often located at a distance from one another.

From the rather primitive methods for making payments in medieval Europe have come various types of methods. This evolution owes much to the development of technology. Today, for instance, most international funds transfers are made through a correspondent network between individual banks which use a cable for sending instructions.

This paper focuses on the legal aspects of payment systems, especially those that are called wire transfer systems. First, the author briefly describes the major wire transfer systems of the United States, the United Kingdom, France, West Germany, and Japan; and the legal environments surrounding their wire transfer systems. Second, some legal issues which are the most problematic within existing legal structures in those countries and the most crucial to achieve the stability of the financial systems are considered. Third, the roles of the monetary authorities which are deemed to shoulder the responsibility of maintaining the stability of payment systems are examined, specifically focusing on their regulatory roles. Finally, the author makes some proposals for attaining the stability of wire transfer systems and points out the complicated issues which have been brought about by the internationalization of banking activities.

The need for international cooperation for the study of wire transfers is stressed. There are some specific legal issues in international wire transfers which cannot be seen in domestic wire transfer systems, such as jurisdiction, time-lag risks, sovereignty on currency, and so forth. Some form of international cooperation would be necessary to cope with the risks which potentially exist in international wire transfer systems. The United States, as the nation whose currency is most frequently used in international business transactions, should make an effort to lead this effort in accordance with domestic developments of wire transfer systems.

Ono, Mitsuru

SECURITY ACTIVITIES BY BANKS: A COMPARATIVE STUDY OF THE SEPARATION POLICY IN JAPAN AND THE UNITED STATES

Harvard Law School 1987 M

97 pages

Foortnotes

In both Japan and the United States, commercial banks are generally prohibited from engaging in securities business by article 65 of the Japanese Securities and Exchange Law, and the Banking Act of 1933, commonly known as the Glass-Steagall Act. This legal compartmentalization of these two major financial services has conferred special benefits, protection and obligations to each industry. Particularly in Japan, it is the general view that article 65 of the Securities and Exchange Law was intended to contribute to the development of the securities industry.

Article 65 of the Securities and Exchange Law is called Japan's version of the Glass-Steagall Act. However, the legislative purposes of these two laws are different. Such a difference is not unnatural because each country has an individual history, policy, and law. In Japan, as long as one looks at Japanese securities firms' successful business results, it seems that the initial purpose of article 65, to nurture securities firms in order to help democratize the nation's economy, has already been achieved. However, repeal of article 65 could not be readily justified because it is likely that the separation policy has been, and will be expected to contribute to the protection of depositors to some extent. Nevertheless, it seems odd as a legal framework that the Securities and Exchange Law is expected to protect depositors. Furthermore, as demonstrated in the controversy on foreign commercial paper, the role of article 65 in separating banking from securities business might distort or weaken the protection of investors, the main purpose of the Securities and Exchange Law

In the recent significant and rapid changes in the financial world, banks are struggling to go beyond the legal barrier, insisting that the separation policy is already outmoded. Although separation might have been a reasonable policy from the viewpoint of the economic and social situation forty years ago, it is questionable at the present time whether a flat prohibition is desirable in the drastically changed economic and social climate of Japan.

Indeed, it is necessary to examine to what extent securities activities by banks are permissible based on constructive policy goals and theoretical analysis, rather than the patchwork of political compromise. In such an examination, the safety and soundness of banks, which leads to the protection of depositors, should be given primary consideration.

The possible benefits from securities activities by banks include the diversification of risks, a stable flow of bank revenue, the maintaining of an international competitive edge, the reduction of costs, increased competition, and greater convenience. On the other side of the ledger, the possible adverse effects include a concentration of resources, decreased and unfair competition, and conflicts of interest. When re-evaluating Japan's separation policy, all these possible effects must be carefully considered in light of the main policy goal of maintaining the safety and soundness of banks while protecting depositors.

Ospina-Lara, Adriana and Luz Patricia Toro A.

PROFESSIONAL WOMEN AND SEXUAL DISCRIMINATION IN COLOMBIA

Harvard Law School 1986 M

108 pages

Footnotes

This examination of the current situation of women in Colombia reveals that the Colombian legislature has carried out for the last thirty years an extensive reform in most areas of the legal system. This reform, instituted in an attempt to battle gender inequality and discrimination, gave women the same rights men have always enjoyed. The new statutes have not, however, brought equality to Colombian women.

Not only are there many imperfections in this legal reform, but the existing social system reveals that the central problem women face in Colombia is not the absence of legal equality, but rather the implementation of this principle. Economic, psychological, social, and cultural factors interact to produce manifold patterns of discrimination. Even though legal equality is a basic foundation for real equality, discrimination cannot be eliminated until these factors and how they contribute to the discrimination of women in our society are understood.

These economic, psychological, social, and cultural factors are studied in terms of how they hinder the implementation of a principle of legal equality. The existing legal system is examined with a view to providing alternatives for the establishment of a legal equality that can be translated into a real equality, within the context of Colombian society. The study presents the social aspects of sex discrimination and provides a picture of the society in which the legal reforms must be implemented. The laws in the Colombian legal system which affect the current situation of women are analyzed with respect to political rights, education, family law, and labor law.

The socialization of Colombian women has been

translated into wage, promotion, and hiring differentiation based on gender. To battle the static condition of women, studies of the actual situation of women in Colombia should be launched so that their problems can be identified. On the basis of these studies, an educational campaign should be initiated. Colombians should realize that women's current inferior condition is neither an individual problem nor a natural nor unmodifiable situation, but rather the product of economic and socio-cultural factors that should disappear as the society progresses and develops. Moreover, a separation between Church and State should be sought in educational matters.

Only after the society understands that rights are not concessions will employers be ready to take advantage of financial incentives stemming from hiring women. In this way, labor laws guaranteeing equal access to jobs, wages, and fair promotions would actually work. Furthermore, all the norms aimed at guaranteeing real equality for women should be strictly enforced. Greater control over the enforcement of these rules could be achieved by a reassignment of the personnel of the Ministry of Labor and the decentralization of enforcement control. With a society that values the real status of women, and a government that is committed to the promotion and enforcement of norms guaranteeing this status, the professional women in Colombia may be able to achieve equality.

Otero, Miguel A.

FOREIGN DEBT EQUITY SWAPS: CHILEAN EXPERIENCE

Harvard Law School 1987 M

62 pages

Footnotes

Latin America is a continent characterized by its heterogeneity. Latin American countries differ from each other, each country has its own idiosyncrasy. Nevertheless, they have some common elements, as the Spanish tradition and common problems. Among the problems, a common disease, is the enormous outstanding foreign debts.

Although foreign debt equity swaps is not a solution for the Latin America's foreign debt, Chilean experience has shown that it is a clever and useful mechanism for those developing countries that are facing the same problem of an excessive foreign debt. It allows the reduction of the foreign debt, or at least to control its growth. At the same time it stimulates the return of flight capitals and foreign investment. It changes debt for productive investment. All this, without having to impose new burdens on the already diminished standard of living of their nationals. It is a mechanism that deserves to be considered and studied by debtor countries.

The Chilean mechanism may well be taken as a model, but the usefulness of debt swapping does not lay only in a coherent and clever set of regulations. As important as the latter, is the host government's attitude towards the foreign investment, and the investor's towards the development of the host country.

Developing country's government must realize that they need foreign investment as a means for their development. Through it, they can develop their economic and resources without risking their own capital, which, at this time, they do not have. The usefulness of foreign investment for a developing country lays within the host country. When coherent and clear developing policies are drawn and effective supervision is implemented, foreign investment should produce the benefits expected from it.

It must be noted that without an effective supervision, a liberal debt equity swaps mechanism, like the Chilean one, may turn out to be a facilitator and stimulator of speculative investment, which may produce more damage than benefits.

Pardinas, Claudia M.

THE DILEMMA OF THE LEGAL LIABILITY OF MULTINATIONAL ENTERPRISES

Harvard Law School 1987 M

79 pages

Footnotes

An analysis of the functioning of the legal liability of multinational corporations would encompass the survey of countless areas: bankruptcy, contracts, labor relations, etc. In some of these fields the developments are richer, as for example, the ones previously listed. In other areas, as for example the tort liability field, the dilemma of the legal liability of multinational enterprises are much more pronounced. Events such as the Bhopal tragedy sporadically revive the vacuum of a regime to guaranty voluntary and involuntary creditors.

The abandonment of the principle of limited liability is being forced by the great clash of limited liability with the critical economic reality that shows that the entities within the multinationals "are so linked that one or more of them may be able to exercise a significant influence over the activities of others." The multinationals are a cluster of corporations in which the parent unit generally takes the leading role in defining the purpose and allocating the collective resources.

Experience demonstrates that up to now, the departure from the limited liability rule has been justified under notions such as "economic reality", "worldwide financial responsibility for multinationals", "multinationals' duty to manage responsibility", that ultimately do not transcend the equity concept of piercing the corporate veil. The special feature of the concept is that it "has been the most discussed problem of corporation law concerning large combines and multinationals in the century."

The description of the empirical and normative data existing on the topic of liability of multinationals may sound discouraging: codes of conduct that have no binding characters; insurance that has been considered as functioning in the sense of reducing the management duty of overseeing, already too low because of the existence of limited liability; lack of intrinsic concepts; customary international law that has not developed specific norms applicable to MNE's; the utopia-like aspirations of an international regulatory agency to control MNE's above the national level. Multinational corporations are a recent and modern phenomenon. It has taken centuries for scholars and jurists to polish and accommodate the law to old institutions, until they were modeled to meet social and equitable, and even moral, needs. Legal liability of multinational corporations is today one of the fields where time will bring definite responses and conformations implemented by mankind's creativity and conceptualism.

A fertile road to pursue is the one that recognizes the primacy of the control factor and that transit towards the adoption of the business organizational concept of enterprise unit.

Patel, Niranjan D.

THE STRUCTURE OF LEGAL EDUCATIONAL REFORM IN COMMONWEALTH AFRICA

Harvard Law School 1987 D

606 pages

Footnotes

More than a quarter of a century has passed since the first institutions for legal education were established in Commonwealth Africa. The subject of legal education in Commonwealth Africa is a topic which generated much interest in the 1950s and 1960s, an interest inspired by the newly independent nations' desire for their own systems of legal education, as well as the colonial power's belated concern with establishing liberal constitutional government in its African territories. Although this was not a period during which there was significant innovation or even overhaul of legal education in England, there was a simmering debate continuing in England, which influenced and informed the new nations' legal education projects. This debate in England culminated in the report and recommendations of the Ormrod Committee which was to have some impact on Commonwealth African efforts in this area. The first real expressions of concern about legal education in Commonwealth Africa was born in the 1950s and 1960s when many Commonwealth African countries were about to, or had just, secured formal independence.

The focus of the thesis is primarily on legal education. To establish the proposition that there is cause for concern, the major tendencies of the reforms so far undertaken in the realm of legal education in the Commonwealth African countries of Zambia, Nigeria, Ghana, Ethiopia, Tanzania, Kenya, and Uganda are reviewed and appraised. The term "reforms" applies to both the movement to institutionalize legal education in these countries, responsive to the peculiar needs of each, as well as to criticisms and proposals to improve legal education in local institutions.

As projects for the reform of legal education

are examined, the first striking feature observed is the overall lack of diversity in the six different countries. Even given the commonality they share, namely, common law legal systems introduced early in the colonial period, it is surprising that there should be so much similarity in what were thought to be appropriate policies of legal education for the circumstances of each new nation. Similarity is by far the greater part of the story of legal education in Commonwealth Africa. The questions addressed here are therefore not only why the systems of legal education introduced into these countries are so similar but also whey this similarity has occurred.

An examination of legal education during the pre-Independence ere of the African Commonwealth nations must, of necessity, begin with a review of the trends and reforms in English legal education. After a summary of reforms prior to 1935 and after the Second World War, the education of solicitors and barristers is reviewed. English efforts to reform legal education for Commonwealth Africa is discussed in terms of the Denning committee report. Attempts at reform in the pre-Independence era in the colonies is appraised with respect to Northern Rhodesia and Nigeria.

The approaches to the reform of legal education taken by Commonwealth Africa are discussed in detail. Curricular changes are surveyed as are the foundations for reform, faculty law, governmental reactions, the dichotomies between the academic and the practical, the relationship of the law syllabus and local law, and the influence of ideology.

Pechewlys, Charles

EXTRINSIC EVIDENCE IN CONTRACT INTERPRETATION

George Washington Law School 1986 M

140 pages

Footnotes

A contract is suppose to be individual and self contained, with the contract documents representing the agreement of the parties. Actually, a contract will carry some extra baggage in the form of evidence from outside the documents that may have an effect on the rights and responsibilities of the parties.

This extrinsic evidence can play an important part in interpreting exactly what the agreement of the parties is. During a disagreement over contract provisions, the purpose of interpretation is to determine the intent of the parties from their objective manifestations of that intent.

The use of extrinsic evidence in this interpretation of a Government contract is especially important, because interpretation controversies are frequent in the complex world of Government contracting. The purpose of the expressed contract language is to specify requirements, but artful expression is not a famous characteristic of the Government contract community.

This paper examines the role of extrinsic evidence in the interpretation of Government contracts. Each of the following types of evidence is discussed in turn: custom and trade usage; prior course of dealing; and, discussions and concurrent actions. The discussion of each begins with the nature and sources of the evidence. Qualifications to the use of that type of evidence is explained. Then, the uses of the evidence in the interpretation process is examined. Each type of evidence has its own discussion, because there are some differences in use and authority that can be more clearly treated separately. Included in the examination is the relationship between extrinsic evidence and the expressed words of the documents. Restrictions on the use of this evidence is also discussed.

There is a wealth of decisional law in this area of Government contracting. The cases that have value as precedent as well as all the other cases that are otherwise of interest are discussed. Other additional authority is cited for reference in footnotes.

Perez-Luna B., Manuel A.

THE TAXATION OF DIVIDENDS IN THE VENEZUELAN LEGISLATION

Harvard Law School 1987 M

61 pages

Footnotes

On the sixteenth of October 1986 the Venezuela's eleventh Income Tax Law came into effect. In spite of the public expectation, the Income Tax Law did not introduce substantial changes to the abrogated Income Tax Law, thus carrying forward all deficiencies and defects of the Income Tax Law of 1978, as amended by the Income Tax Law of 1981. This circumstance is even more troublesome when we consider that only a few of the recommendations of the "Comision de Estudios y Reform Fiscal" were taken into account.

In this sense, excepting some minor changes made by the 1986 Act, all the provisions concerning dividend taxation are from the Income Tax Law of 1978. It is important to state that the taxation of dividends has been an important issue in Venezuela Income Tax history. In this respect, it can be pointed out, that it took twenty-four years for Congress, after the enactment of Venezuela's first Income Tax, to approve a tax law that considered dividends as taxable income. This law, approved in 1966, contained many of the provisions concerning dividend taxation that are still present in the 1986 Act. The author presents an analysis of the 1986 Act and a comparative study of Venezuela's most important Income Tax Law.

Presented is a brief explanation of the Venezuelan Income Tax Law according to taxpayer classification. The Income Tax Law classifies taxpayers into three groups. These are (1) Individuals, (2) Corporations, and (3) Taxpayers engaged in oil, mining and related activities. Dividends are only paid by taxpayers treated for income tax purposes as corporations.

Dividends are only paid by corporations and joint stock companies where shareholder ownership is evidenced by a stock certificate. In the case of limited liability partnership and civil, irregular or de facto partnerships treated for income tax purposes as corporations, evidence of ownership is not by stock but by a quota of participation. Partners or owners are generally referred to as quotaholders, and dividends are referred as participations. Disregarding this semantic difference for purposes of this paper, the word dividend is used to designate any kind of payment made by corporations and taxpayers treated alike.

Poirier, Joseph Martin

THE COMPARABLE WORTH THEORY AND SEX-BASED WAGE DISCRIMINATION

George Washington Law School 1986 M

137 pages

Footnotes

The "comparable worth" theory is perhaps the most controversial issue emanating from Title VII of the 1964 Civil Rights Act. Although this theory has been given many names with various definitions, it has come to embrace the concept that men and women should be paid equally for work of equal value. The controversy that surrounds this theory stems from the fact that its application goes substantially beyond the reach of the Equal Pay Act.

The Equal Pay Act requires the plaintiff to demonstrate the equality of jobs within an establishment before a comparison can be made between wages earned by women and wages earned by men. Further, the plaintiff is required to prove that the jobs being compared require equal skill, effort, and responsibility, and also requires proof that they are performed under similar working conditions. The term "equal" has since come to mean "substantially equal."

The thesis of this paper is simply that Title VII does not embrace the theory of comparable worth. Title VII was enacted for the purpose of guaranteeing minorities and women the right to nondiscriminatory treatment in all aspects of employment which includes the right to nondiscriminatory compensation within the context of our free market system. The thesis begins by providing a review from a historical perspective of women's role in the labor market touching upon the political, social and economic aspects of the women's movement from colonial times to the years just prior to World War II. This is followed by a discussion on the modern equal pay movement beginning in the war years and culminating with the passage of the Equal Pay Act and Title VII of the Civil Rights Act of 1964.

Finally, the author discusses the development of these laws in courts from the time of their enactment to the present focusing on the development and eventual rejection of the comparable worth theory. In this regard, it is noted that the Supreme Court to date has not addresses head-on a comparable worth case and, therefore, the issue is still alive. However, in light of the growing body of law in this area coupled with the legislative histories of the Equal Pay Act and Title VII, it is concluded that the comparable worth theory is beyond the intended scope of Title VII.

Pollarolo, Pierina

STATE-OWNED ENTERPRISES AND GOVERNMENTAL CONTROL: THE CASE OF PERU

Harvard Law School 1986 M

73 pages

Footnotes

Until 1968, the role of the state in the Peruvian economy was limited to the provision of public services and the stimulation and support of private initiative. The military regime led by General Juan Velasco, aiming to transform radically the Peruvian society, promoted an unprecedented expansion of the state's activities. State Owned Enterprises (SOEs) were to be a key instrument of the government's policies. As a result, SOEs grew dramatically in number and importance in a short period of time.

Currently, SOEs have a pervasive role in the Peruvian economy. They are responsible for 15% of the GDP and 50% of the public investment expenditures. They control important productive sectors and give employment to approximately 18% of the non-agricultural sector. They are also responsible for one-quarter of the fiscal deficit of the last three years.

The performance of SOEs has become one of the most important issues in the political and economic debates. Conservative sectors claim that SOEs are a burden for the state which should be privatized because they are "essentially inefficient entities," when compared to private corporations. Proposals to sell or liquidate SOEs have been rejected by more liberal groups, which denounce the "looting of national assets."

The paper argues that the causes of SOEs' problems are not derived exclusively from internal deficiencies. Rather, it contends, the SOEs' relationship with the government is the most important factor in their performance. As the Peruvian experience shows, the successive governments have not set clear and consistent objectives for SOEs and have not established adequate systems of interaction with them. As a result, SOEs have to operate in an uncertain, disorganized, and troublesome environment.

The theoretical background needed to understand the relation between SOEs and the government is presented with an emphasis on the double identity of SOEs. They incorporate characteristics of both public and private entities. Their unique nature, therefore, requires a set of clear goals for their activities. The paper looks into the Peruvian SOEs' development to focus on the issue of control and evaluation. It examines the relevant national legislation and discusses the political context which produced or thwarted the application of these norms.

Uncertainty and disorder have characterized the state entrepreneurial activity in its different stages. The ideal balance between autonomy and control was impossible to accomplish for several reasons: vagueness in the government's attitude towards the role of the state in the economy; lack of clear objectives for SOEs; and an inadequate system of interaction between SOEs themselves and with the state.

The government that replaced President Belaunde's administration in 1985 should define the role of the state in the economy. Then it should define the scope and limits of state intervention in SOEs. Once the government has decided the role of SOEs in the economy, it should develop a system of channels to allow the setting of measurable objectives, first for the entrepreneurial activity as a whole, and then for each SOE.

Ponnambalam, Tabitha D.

WOMEN, THE LAW AND THE DEVELOPMENT PROCESS IN ZAMBIA

Harvard Law School 1986 M

75 pages

Footnotes

In a male-dominated society such as the one that exists in Zambia, any attempt to change the traditional status of women may be perceived as a threat to the dominant position of the male species. Instead of focusing on the western concept of equal rights, the discussion concentrates on women as catalysts to economic development.

In the context of the international scene, the ideal status of women is identified as it is manifested in international conventions and conferences. The relative position of Zambia at an international level is placed in this context of international law.

The status of women in Zambia is reviewed through an analysis of the socio-economic position and the role of women in traditional society and during the colonial era. The position of women in present day Zambia and the opportunities available to them, particularly in areas of education and employment, are discussed.

In considering Zambia's legislative enactments, those which either discriminate against women or permit discriminatory treatment of women are examined. The particular enactments examined are the Constitution of Zambia, the act pertaining to Employment of Women, Young Persons and Children, the Mines & Minerals Act, the Employment Act, the Income Tax Act, the Education Act, the Building Societies Act, and other relevant statutes.

An evaluation is made of the extent to which Zambia has compiled with the provisions of the international conventions that she has ratified. The role of law and lawyers in a developing country and the prospects of the future of a woman's movement is also discussed. Finally, suggestions for reform are made in terms of the legislative amendments necessary to end discrimination against women in the development process are presented. The economic development of Zambia, it is argued, is closely correlated with and related to the emancipation of women.

Quaye, Christopher O.

LEGAL SIGNIFICANCE OF LIBERATION MOVEMENTS IN CONTEMPORARY INTERNATIONAL RELATIONS: AN AFRICAN PERSPECTIVE

Harvard Law School 1986 D

832 pages

Footnotes

Innumerable books and articles have been written on international relations, focussing generally on the legal ramifications of the use of force and its concomitant effect of the commitment to maintain international peace and security. However, liberation struggles - phenomena which are often pursued through violence and are so susceptible to escalation by foreign intervention as to warrant their treatment as one of the most serious challenges to international peace and security - have received only casual attention. Apart from isolated studies of aspects of liberation struggles - self-determination, human rights, use of force, and intervention, particularly in the context of colonial situations - other areas which are undeniably germane to the time-honored concept of "liberation" seem to be almost entirely neglected. While this paper does not seek to depart from the tradition of scrutinizing the main issues in liberation struggles, it nonetheless provides a new outlook on the subject by studying the issues beyond the colonial scenario. It investigates critically the relevance of secessionist struggles and struggles against established governments to "liberation movements"; examines the relationship between "liberation movements" and the phenomena represented by such terms as "terrorism", "communism", and "rebellion"; explores the issue of whether the term "international law" is a misnomer; assesses the various tools for ascertaining the content and status of norms of international law; and exposes the occasional cleavage between the law as stipulated and pronounced in theory and the law as practiced by those representing the conscience of the international community, notably the United Nations.

The author concedes that as a human construct,

the paper does not provide a panacea for all conceivable difficulties arising from the relationship between the international legal order and the phenomena dubbed "liberation struggles". It focuses mainly on contemporary issues and thus pays little or no regard to events of historical vintage. Moreover, by the complex nature of the international system and its law, the exposition provides only partial solutions for the problems encountered in this endeavor. Of particular significance in this respect is the definition of "liberation movements", which, because of the inherent subjectivity of the term "liberty", receives only a tentative analysis.

It is concluded that, if the international community really bases international peace and security on freedom and faith in human rights, as stipulated in the Preamble to the United Nations Charter, then it necessarily must follow the maim that justice must not only be done but must be manifestly and undoubtedly be seen to be done. The United Nations, then, must use this jurisprudential stricture as the basis for making its presence felt in any conflict by deeds rather than the mere words that have so far characterized the United Nations practice. It is conceded that in a world where the distinction between politics and law is blurred, there may be questions as to whose standards should be used in meting out this all-important justice. But it does not seem logical to entertain this difficulty for long, at least not on the present issue. For, so long as the international community is fortunate enough to have an overwhelming majority of its members supporting the principle of self-determination and the dogmas which go with it, there should be little problem with the soundness of any action undertaken against a state which is found by the majority to have violated, or be in the process of violating, the rights of another.

Reeza, Shahul

MASS EXPULSION OF ALIENS IN INTERNATIONAL LAW

Harvard Law School 1986 M

114 pages

Footnotes and bibliography

This paper is about aliens and their protection in international law. More specifically, this deals with their protection against mass expulsion. The purpose of this study is to ascertain the underlying bases of the power to expel aliens which states claim they have, and to determine the scope and extent of such power. The thesis that will be advanced here is that while states have the power to expel aliens, it is one that is governed by limitations that are inherent in the norms of international law, recognizing this right. These norms are to be found only in traditional international law but also in international human rights law. By traditional international law, the author means those principles which have been recognized as such prior to 1945, and by international human rights law those principles which have received recognition after 1945 through the activities of the United Nations and other regional organizations devoted to the advancement of human rights in international relations. International human rights norms could take the form of treaty provisions as well as customary law. Apart from creating new law, treaty provisions may constitute evidence of customary practice as well as crystallize customary international law norms.

It must be stated that the body of rules pertaining to expulsion in general and mass expulsion in particular is still in its embryonic state just as many other rules of international law are. The author, therefore, sought to draw analogies from those areas of international law having a bearing on aliens and their treatment and ascertain how far they lend themselves to protecting aliens against mass expulsion.

Mass expulsion in many ways encounters the same conceptual and legal problems that are encountered by expulsion of individuals. Nevertheless, they cannot be placed on the same footing since mass expulsions give rise to many different kinds of problems. Mass expulsion, it is suggested, are per se arbitrary and also discriminatory. The assumption is that it will affect the specific category of aliens such as race. Besides, membership in the group is taken into account rather than individual behavior.

Rendon, Santiago J.

THE REUNIFICATION OF COLOMBIA, ECUADOR, PANAMA AND VENEZUELA UNDER A NEW NATION

Harvard Law School 1986 M

108 pages

Footnotes

The topic of Latin American brotherhood has elicited the attention of the region's intelligentsia for many years. Simon Bolivar, the liberator of five countries, envisioned the consolidation of one country covering all Hispanic America. Ever since the independence from Spain, those who have shared his ideal have watched only timid attempts of integration. They have all failed.

The causes for failure are multiple, and Latin Americans tend to scoff when they are confronted with integration proposals. Although they may agree that it is a good idea, it seems to them virtually impossible to execute.

The paper presents practical advice on how to go about realizing the reintegration of the former Gran Colombia.

The paper proposes the total unification of Panama, Colombia, Venezuela, and Ecuador into one new nation. The reasons for integrating these four independent countries are analyzed, together with a discussion on the present state of integration in the area and its recognized stages.

Necessary considerations to start implementing the process of reunification are examined. Closer attention is given to three important issues the process must overcome: the foremost legal order of each country, the constitution; the strongest psychological hurdle, nationalism; and man's motivator and constant preoccupation, the economy. An analysis of both theory and regional reality reveals the true proportion of the problems facing reunification. Federalism is proposed as the more desirable system of governing the new nation.

The term reintegration is used in the same context as reunification. The process is that of reintegration, including its inception, its formalization, and the first years of the new nation.

The reunification of Colombia, Ecuador, Panama, and Venezuela faces many obstacles. Seldom have these four nations enjoyed democratic regimes at the same time to facilitate the implementation of a federation. Panama still remains under military rule to the point where its inclusion in the new nation may be imperiled. Hurdles such as the economy, the legal system, and nationalism can be overcome. These apparent barriers against unification can be overturned and used to the advantage of the process. The federative proposal set forth would guarantee the maximum degree of unity while leaving the regions with as much autonomy and power as possible.

Renner, Shirliy

CONTRACTS DURING TIMES OF INFLATION

Harvard Law School 1986 M

151 pages

Footnotes

The impact of inflation upon a legal system is not limited to a specific part of a legal system, but influences private, commercial, and public law. Thus, in criminal law, fixed fines may take on totally different meanings during various rates of inflation. An example may be a fine that is calculated by way of multiplying the original sum achieved by illegal means. Assuming even a moderate rate of inflation, if the offense was committed a long time before trial, the effect of the punishment is modified. In another field of public law like taxation, without adjustment of the scale of incomes which are subject to the statutory arrangement, the progressive system may turn out to be a regressive system. In the field of administrative law, during times of inflation, compensation payments may turn out to be inadequate to achieve the purpose of compensation, in the absence of additional adjustment. Inflation has a similar effect in private law fields. In the area of unjust enrichment, ignoring the impact of inflation can benefit the party who was unjustifiably enriched, and fail to afford full recovery to the party who was unjustifiably impoverished. In contract law, the impact of inflation varies depending on the type of pecuniary obligation involved. Thus, one may describe the effect of inflation upon the obligation included in the contract as potentially frustrating the real intention of the parties. As to damages for breach of contract, the impact of inflation is quite similar to the effect on damages in tort law. In criminal law, the real issue at stake is that of the decrease in the deterrent effect of the punishments, while adjusting the monetary sums can raise serious problems of retroactivity and uncertainty. Different problems arise in administrative law. The impact of inflation in this area may result in actual confiscation of property by the public authority without giving meaningful compensation. In this context, questions like the constitutional validity of the administrative action may arise. In private law fields, some tend to describe the result of inflation as redistributing wealth among individuals. This description ignores the more specific consequences which are particular to each area.

Legal systems all over the world, common law as well as civil law, have had to confront inflation during different periods in their history.

This analysis of the roles of the parties to an agreement, the judiciary and the legislature of a hypothetical legal system, in providing solutions for inflationary problems is made on three different levels. The first level concentrates on whether the system should choose affirmative intervention or passive non-intervention. On this preliminary level of analysis, examining the full meaning of the impact of inflation upon different institutions entails an examination of the cost of that intervention.

A second level of consideration focuses on the kind of solution that should be adopted, whether a general solution or specific solutions suitable for each area independently. The consideration of specific solutions brings to the forefront the necessity of coordination among these specific solutions. Many situations may give rise to several causes of action in different fields. Sometimes the division is not clear at all. Similar legal problems should be given similar treatment in order to avoid arbitrary results.

The third level of analysis examines each specific area independently with respect to the special problems of that field, the relevant considerations, and the available solutions.

A mutual relationship exists among these three levels of analysis. Thus, the question of whether to adopt a general solution or specific solutions suitable for each particular area depends, among other things, on the available solutions in each field.

The attitude of the legal system can depend on

various characteristics of the inflationary period. The attitude may change depending on the rate of inflation, that is, whether it is a moderate or extreme one. It may vary depending on whether the inflationary situation is temporary or chronic, sudden, unexpected, reasonably foreseeable, and so forth.

Inflation can modify some important legal arrangements. Consequently, a legal system cannot ignore the impact of inflation upon its various institutions. No specific solution is recommended for adoption. Whatever the solution may be, it should be a conscientious one, made after considering and giving appropriate weight to all of the various interests involved.

Ruiz, Carmen Marques

STATE RESPONSIBILITY AND LIABILITY FOR MARINE POLLUTION

Harvard Law School 1986 M

74 pages

Footnotes

Adequate protection of the marine environment requires the establishment of preventive rules to minimize pollution due either to voluntary discharge or to accidents. On the other hand, if damage to the marine environment has actually occurred, provision must be made for an effective system of compensation. This paper discusses the role of a State's responsibility and liability in order to achieve these two basic goals of any environmental law.

The definition of the rules on the breach by the States of their obligation concerning the marine environment is essential to ensure its protection. However, the application of the general rules of responsibility to the marine pollution, presents problems of attribution and of ascertainment of a breach of an obligation.

The State's liability for marine pollution did not receive in UNCLOS 1982 the treatment it deserved. The international disputes on marine pollution do not give much guidance since the legal issues of liability have been traditionally avoided.

There are still important uncertainties, like the issue whether a State should be liable for the damage to the marine environment in the absence of a breach of an international obligation. It seems, however, that an adequate protection of the victims, as well as of the marine environment, requires recognition of the State's strict liability for damage to the marine environment produced by an "ultrahazardous activity" carried out under its jurisdiction.

The term responsibility can be understood in a very broad sense. Responsibility in its widest meaning refers to the duties imposed on States concerning the marine environment. In a narrower sense, responsibility concerns only the legal consequences of a breach of an international obligation. International responsibility, in this stricter sense is a way of guaranteeing international obligations and ensuring their fulfillment.

From the point of view of the victims of marine pollution, the compensation of damages suffered is sometimes more important than the legal aspects of responsibility. Although liability may be considered as a consequence of responsibility, it may sometimes arise from the occurrence of damage.

Ruiz del Rio, Oscar A.

ARBITRATION AND INTERNATIONAL BANKING: ARBITRATION CLAUSES IN INTERNATIONAL LOANS

Harvard Law School 1986 M

50 pages

Footnotes

International commercial arbitration has grown significantly in the past years, and it has done so in practically all kinds of transactions conducted across national boundaries. Private institutions from more countries use it, and more nations, as active participants in world trade, resort to it as well.

This growth has as much to do with the deficiencies of the national court systems as with the intrinsic advantages of arbitration itself. It has affected practically all major industries and operations involved in international commerce. Nowadays the number of transnational freight, construction, sales, insurance, and securities contracts with arbitration provisions in them is remarkable, and this trend is likely to continue in the coming years.

However, there is one basic aspect of international trade and economic relations that seems to remain alien to this tendency and uses international arbitration only marginally. This is in banking and particularly in international loans.

In most instances, the lack of arbitration clauses in international loans contracts or the failure to resort to arbitration when problems arise is simply a matter of long standing practice, and the lawyers in charge of designing such documents do not think about the possibility of using arbitration clauses. That the absence of such provisions is the logical consequence of the banking business structure and the limitations of the arbitration process as applied to financial operations is demonstrated and explained in the paper.

The lenders (and lending constitutes the overwhelming majority of banking transactions) think that, because default is the main cause for litigation, the advantages of arbitration could not compensate for the tendency of arbitrators to split the difference on controversies arising out of specific amounts of money. This seems to be a valid concern of the lenders and their counsel.

The technical analysis of the current state of arbitration shows that there are available systems that could serve the goals of the lenders. However, there are no systems specifically designed to address the concerns of the banking community. ICSID arbitration has a great many advantages but it also has a considerable number of drawbacks which take away from what otherwise could be considered a perfect system.

That the position of borrowers and their role in international arbitration is usually weak skews the arbitration process towards the lender. But one of the rules of arbitration is to provide a fair method of dispute resolution, and the borrowers' interests, even though considerably vaguer than those of the lenders, cannot be ignored. It is not surprising that the majority of the arbitration clauses found in international loans have been usually suggested by the borrower.

Sabbath, Michael D.

CLASSICAL CONTRACT THEORY AND JUDICIAL CONCERN FOR FAIRNESS

Columbia Law School 1985 M

111 pages

Footnotes

It has become fashionable in recent years to discuss the various shortcomings of the classical model of contract law. Contract scholars have criticized such things as its inability to deal with questions of unbargained-for reliance, and the model's failure to provide a meaningful approach for resolving the many problems raised by standardized contracts. It has been argued that the classical model failed to adequately protect third parties to agreements, and contributed little to resolving problems caused by monopolies and restrictive agreements. These critics point to the great volume of statutory interference with freedom of contract as evidence that "the classical model of contract, notwithstanding its formal perpetuation to the present day as a body of general principles, was a failure."

This paper examines the effect that classical contract theory had on the courts' role in "policing" agreements. Courts long have recognized the need to place limits on the enforceability of contracts in order to prevent unfairness. They generally have viewed their task of policing agreements from three different perspectives: status, behavior and substance. Thus, courts have recognized the need to protect certain persons, such as infants, who lack the intellect and judgment to protect themselves. In addition, they have always been ready to intervene where a party to the agreement has engaged in some unsavory conduct, such as fraud, misrepresentation or duress. In the absence of some defect in the bargaining procedure, though, courts have been more hesitant to step in solely because of some perceived unfairness in the contractual terms. In recent years, however, this hesitancy appears to be breaking down.

This article shows that classical contract

theory, with its emphasis on the formation process, had a very positive effect on the courts' ability to police contracts effectively. Without the flexible approach that a formation-centered analysis provided, courts tended to concentrate on specific-type situations. This tended to inhibit the growth and development of certain doctrines, and sometimes led to overly-rigid rules that did little to promote fairness. Particularly from the perspectives of status and behavior, classical contract theory aided in the expansion of existing doctrines, and helped to promote contractual fairness. Moreover, this article shows that, even prior to classical contract theory, no overt principle of fairness ever existed.

Schiessl, Maximilian

ON THE ROAD TO A NEW GERMAN REORGANIZATION LAW - A COMPARATIVE ANALYSIS OF THE DRAFT PROPOSED BY THE INSOLVENZRECHTSKOMMISSION AND CHAPTER 11 OF THE BANKRUPTCY CODE

Harvard Law School 1986 M

65 pages

Footnotes

The economy of the industrialized Western societies is based on the free enterprise system, which in theory enables anyone to become an entrepreneur and gain entrepreneurial profits. The flip side of the coin is entrepreneurial risk of going out of business. It causes harm to the economy as a whole if enterprises which might operate profitably are forced to liquidate. The liquidation destroys economic values, since the firms are worth more as "going concerns" than they are if liquidated. That is the reason why the laws of many countries provide a reorganization proceeding in order to save such enterprises from liquidation.

In the United States a "receivership proceeding" was created in the nineteenth century to deal with the insolvencies of large railroad companies. Today the reorganization is regulated in Chapter 11 of the Bankruptcy Code of 1978. In the German law of bankruptcy there is no comparable reorganization proceeding. In the last ten year, however, this omission has been recognized as one of the main shortcomings of existing bankruptcy law.

In 1978 the Secretary of Justice installed the Insolvenzrechtskommission (Commission for the Law of Bankruptcy) with the mandate to work out a draft for a complete reform of the Bankruptcy Code. The Commission consists of experts from all interested groups - law professors, attorneys, bankruptcy judges, trustees and representatives of business and trade unions. In the following years the considerations of the Commission were accompanied by discussions among legal scholars. In 1982 the reform was one of the topics of the meeting of the Deutscher Juristentag (German Law Association).

In the spring of 1985 the members of the Commission published their reform proposals. They suggest a fundamental change of the entire law of insolvency. The deliberations were much influenced by a comparative analysis of the law of other countries. Several German and American scholars reported on the American law which served as a model, especially for the reorganization proceeding contained in the draft.

This comparative analysis of the draft and the American Bankruptcy Code gives an account of the present German law, its development over the last 100 years, and the weaknesses of the statutes which have led to the need of a change. Also analyzed are the draft proposed by the Insolvenzrechtskommission and the features which distinguish it from the Bankruptcy Code.

Schmid, Hans-Rudolf

CHOICE OF LAW BY THE ARBITRATOR: THE ARBITRATOR'S DISCRETION IN THE ABSENCE OF A PARTY STIPULATION AS TO THE LAW APPLICABLE TO THE SUBSTANCE OF THE DISPUTE. . .

Harvard Law School 1986 M

82 pages

Footnotes

The Model Law on International Commercial Arbitration, adopted by UNCITRAL on June 21, 1985, contains rules applicable to the substance of the dispute. Article 28 paragraph 2 reads: "Failing any designation by the parties, the arbitral tribunal shall apply the law determined by the conflict of laws rules which it considers applicable." In December, 1985, the General Assembly adopted a resolution recommending that "all States give due consideration to the Model Law on International Commercial Arbitration...."

Given this setting, two groups of addressees may be distinguished, the arbitrators and the States. An arbitrator may ask how free he is in choosing the applicable law to the substance of the dispute if the parties did not choose themselves. A State may ask whether it shall follow the recommendation of the United Nations and incorporate the suggested conflict of laws provision in its national body of law. This paper examines each of these points of view.

The discussion concerns the limits of the arbitrator's freedom, on the hypothesis that the arbitrator did a bad job in choosing the applicable law. Only on this assumption, the author argues, is the search for probable excess of power on the side of the arbitrator of any interest.

The growing popularity of arbitration implies an increasing demand for arbitrators which cannot be satisfied any longer by a small group of the best qualified experts. Therefore, the limits of the arbitrator's discretion are considered in detail.

The paper deals exclusively with the choice of law problem in the absence of a party stipulation and concludes that "freedom of the arbitrator" is illusory. It advises that States should neither incorporate Article 28(2) UNCITRAL Model Law nor enact another special conflict of laws rule for the arbitrator. Predictability cannot be achieved so long as there is no choice of law by the parties or no conflict rule established on the level of international law. Every attempt of rule-making on a lower level only adds another eligible conflict rule to the already existing variety and thus increases confusion.

Shaikh, Mumtaz Ahmed

PAKISTAN: INCOME TAXATION OF NON-RESIDENT INDIVIDUALS AND FOREIGN CORPORATIONS

Harvard Law School 1987 M

60 pages

Footnotes, appendices and bibliography

Foreign collaboration has played a major role in the economic development of Pakistan. Foreign corporations and financial institutions participated in the completion of gigantic projects like Tarbela and Mangla Dams, steel mills, heavy mechanical complexes, new seaport and airports, oil and gas explorations and refineries, and are continuously actively participating in the projects for development of the country.

Various factors influence the decision of foreign persons to do business. The tax system undoubtedly is one of the important determinants. A number of tax exemption rebates have, therefore, been provided to foreign persons on their income earned in Pakistan.

On the other hand, about 1 million Pakistanis working abroad, repatriate over 2,000 million dollars annually. Pakistani persons doing trade and business abroad have foreign source of income, and therefore pay foreign taxes.

To avoid international juridical double taxation, Pakistan takes unilateral measures, and has also entered into tax treaties with 27 countries. The treaties have been signed with major trading partners, and with the countries providing economic assistance.

Main provisions contained in the 1979 Income Tax Ordinance are not substantiated by comprehensive rules to properly tax income arising from International business transactions. It is generally left to the discretion and understanding of the assessing officers mainly to determine and allocate income in the absence of comprehensive rules and regulations. Proper research need be conducted to reform the provisions of law applicable to the International Business transactions. It has been stated that no change is engraved in stone, and policy makers must stand ready to alter and adjust their policies to suit changing needs and circumstances. Pakistan may also consider changes in the rules.

Sherwin, Richard K.

PUBLICS, EXPERTS AND THE LANGUAGE OF DEMOCRACY: THREE DIALECTS OF CRIMINAL PROCEDURE

Columbia Law School 1986 M

285 pages

Footnotes

In this paper the author explores the different ways in which individual accountability is accounted for in the criminal process. He suggests that in this area of the law three discrete forms of legal argumentation are used to resolve disputes. Each form is singular. That is, each describes and assesses events and individuals in different ways. These are called discrete forms of argumentation the dialects of criminal procedure. Like dialects, they embody discrete ways of talking and thinking. Also like dialects, each tends to engage and affect different social groups (or dialogical communities) in different ways. Notwithstanding their singularity, however, each dialect of criminal procedure subsists within a common language.

The aim of this paper is to show the ramifications of adopting one or another of these discrete ways of talking and thinking about criminal procedure. The author argues that the consequences of a court's endorsement of a discrete dialect are significant. Using a particular dialect tends not only to pre-shape the way events and individuals are characterized, but also to inform the judgments that are subsequently made about them. It is maintained that because adopting a particular way of thinking and speaking about criminal procedure carries such significant descriptive and normative consequences, the choice of dialects should be deliberate, not unwitting. That is, the choice should be preceded by careful, self-conscious deliberation and followed by persuasive explanation and justification. Put simply, how one chooses to speak about certain events and individuals is no less important than what one chooses to say about them. Indeed, the author claims that these two aspects of judicial decision-making are inextricably linked: the one cannot adequately be understood apart from the other.

In this paper the author argues that dialogical choices in the criminal process engage and affect publics and experts in different ways. In the course of the analysis, it is shown that each criminal procedure dialect also embodies discrete benefits of virtues and that, as a result, each dialect plays an essential role in the criminal justice system.

Simien, Eulis Jr.

THE INTERRELATIONSHIP OF THE SCOPE OF THE FOURTH AMENDMENT AND THE ISSUES OF STANDING

Columbia Law School M

164 pages

Footnotes and bibliography

The purpose of the provisions of our Constitution guaranteeing individual rights and liberties is to guard against the "excesses of popular government." Accordingly, when the judiciary directs its attention to litigation involving individual rights, it is the "instrument by which a free society imposes on itself the seldom welcome, sometimes dangerous, always indispensable restraints that keep it free."

Of particular importance among these provisions is the fourth amendment. It is believed by many that the abuses associated with the writs of assistance issued in the colonies to curb illegal smuggling was a direct and proximate cause of the American Revolution. And that colonial distaste for these writs in turn led to the inclusion of the fourth amendment in the Bill of Rights. However, the fourth amendment has more than just historical importance. Today, "the limits of American society's effective control over the largest part of the spectrum of police powers and potential abuses depend upon the scope given to the fourth amendment."

Unfortunately, the fact that fourth amendment issues are generally presented in the context of criminal prosecutions, tends to obscure the true nature of the right to be enforced. In this context, it is often forgotten that the fourth amendment is a broad statement about our entire legal system and method of government and serves the function of preserving limited and free government.

One of the areas of Supreme Court fourth amendment jurisprudence that has been the subject of much of the attack on the Court is its interpretation of standing requirements under the provision. Standing rules under the fourth amendment have a direct bearing on who will be allowed to assert a violation of this very important right. If standing is artificially restricted, the role that the fourth amendment plays and its ability to serve its important objectives is diminished. Because standing rules play the part of "the gatekeeper" to the important rights and governmental limitation that lay beyond, this paper again visits the highly controversial subject of fourth amendment standing.

As the Supreme Court jurisprudence of the extant era is the one under which fourth amendment standing is currently judged, it is reviewed in detail. Finally, the author presents an alternative method for determining fourth amendment standing. It is submitted that the suggested method is more in keeping with the original purposes of the fourth amendment than the method employed by the Court under either of these eras.

Snipes, William J.

AN EXAMINATION OF THE UNITED STATES POLICY ON THE EXPORTATION OF HAZARDOUS DRUGS

Harvard Law School 1986 M

80 pages

Footnotes

Since 1938, the United States has maintained a policy of prohibiting the export of drugs not approved for domestic use. No other nation has such a policy. But today the rest of the world is seeking to tighten international drug standards. Although the United States is powerless to dictate international policy, it exercises considerable influence in the international market place. Ironically, the United States has no uniform national policy on the exportation of hazardous substances.

The paper proposes that, without a normative hazardous export policy, the subtle and complex intersections between world health concerns and multinationals' commercial interests will continue to frustrate effective regulatory initiatives. The current Congressional initiative on pharmaceutical export controls serves as a useful case study on the formulation of the United States export control policy.

This survey covers the evolving history of the United States export control policies and the domestic and international frameworks for the regulation of hazardous substances. Recent legislative initiatives by the U.S. Congress to control the exportation of hazardous substances are examined. Finally, the assumptions animating Congressional efforts to regulate hazardous exports are described. The failure of Congress to formulate and adopt a hazardous export policy rationale stands as an insurmountable barrier to its efforts to regulate the exportation of hazardous substances consistent with its goals to promote world health.

Allowing American companies to compete in the world market for unapproved drugs may increase their international competitiveness, increase the number of domestic drug production facilities, stimulate capital investment, provide more jobs, and decrease the transfer of technology. The evidence suggest, however, that the economic impact of removing the ban on exports would be relatively minor. But these speculative economic benefits must be weighed against the clear and certain dangers of exporting unapproved American drugs throughout the world.

The legislative initiative to remove the ban on the export of unapproved drugs is a misguided effort. Contrary to its sponsors' claims, it does not promote world health or increase research and development for tropical disease drugs. It is not a jobs bill. Nor will it rectify the trade deficit or stem the flow of overseas operations. The proposed Senate bill misses the mark because Congress has not formulated, and consequently is not guided by, a normative policy on the exportation of hazardous products.

To embrace a rigid non-export policy truncates detailed analysis no less so than an unrestrained policy on exportation. The formulation and articulation of a national policy should serve as the analytical framework for both normative and descriptive assessments. Aside from which drugs are used, world health also concerns the system of distributing drugs to rural and poor areas and removing drugs from the market when they have expired.

It is true that the United States has neither the authority or the influence to set world standards of health and safety. Nor does it have the machinery to stem the abuses that multinational pharmaceutical companies have engaged in worldwide. But only its continuing efforts, in conjunction with other nations and the United Nations, to surmount poverty, ignorance, and corruption will lead to the realization of the United Nation's declaration to achieve world health by the year 2000.

Sperling, Johanna

THE SENSOR CASE AND THE LEGAL IMPLICATIONS OF THE PIPELINE AFFAIR

Harvard Law School 1987 M

75 pages

Footnotes

The Sensor case was a small part of an international controversy that affected not only East-West trade relations, but East-West relations generally, and severely strained relations in the Western alliance. The political issues involved in the pipeline affair were not really subject to judicial resolution, and the political resolution of the affair in fact left its legal outcome in doubt.

The Reagan Administration withdrew the 1982 Regulation in November 1982, two months after the Dutch court rendered its decision and before Sensor's appeal could be heard. Sensor claimed, in its appeal, that if the lower court's decision was allowed to stand, it might be forced into bankruptcy. Sensor was adamant in its refusal to perform, since it feared that performance might subject its employees to jail sentences and that all of its U.S. export licenses might have been revoked. If the United States had in fact imposed sanctions on Sensor, it could have challenged them in U.S. courts, but its chance of success in the United States was also open to question.

In Sensor, a more careful analysis of the regulation might have allowed the court to conclude that Sensor had no defense because it was not subject to the regulation in the first place. Having assumed that the regulation applied, however, the court should not have made the outcome depend on the validity of the regulation in the light of uncertain principles of international law. In another case, with a more carefully drafted regulation and a stronger case for the exercise of jurisdiction under international law, the court would apparently have decided in favor of the defendant. But the legal defects of the 1982 Regulation were irrelevant to Sensor; the sanctions threatened by the United States were real regardless of whether or not their application would be a valid exercise of extraterritorial jurisdiction.

One conclusion that emerged clearly from the pipeline affair and the Sensor case in particular was that the 1982 Regulation, had it been allowed to stand, would have done substantially more damage to Western corporations and Western relations than to the Soviet Union or the construction of the pipeline. The Soviet Union had progressed far enough on the pipeline before the regulation was adopted to complete construction with its own technology. The political benefits reaped by the Soviets through the rift between the United States and Western European countries, on the other hand, were substantial. The pipeline affair provides as object lesson on the hazards of limiting East-West trade as a means of affecting East-West relations.

Stewart, M. LeSueur

CONSIDERATION OF THE GLOBAL DIMENSION IN THE REVISION OF THE PRINCIPLES GOVERNING THE USE BY STATES OF ARTIFICIAL EARTH SATELLITES FOR INTERNATIONAL DIRECT TELEVISION BROADCASTING

Harvard Law School 1986 D

643 pages

Footnotes and appendices

Analysis of the evolving international law of international direct television broadcasting by satellite requires first an identification of that law. The development of a body of international law in the area of satellite broadcasting is taking place in a fragmented manner through the adoption of a variety of legal instruments elaborated in different forums within and outside the United Nations system.

The study focuses on one of the most basic and fundamental legal instruments which has been adopted by the United Nations in the area of international broadcasting by satellite and the most basic and fundamental legal instrument in the area of international direct television broadcasting by satellite: the Principles Governing the Use by States of Artificial Earth Satellites for International Direct Television Broadcasting (IDTBS).

Although the IDTBS Principles were adopted by the United Nations General Assembly in 1982, the controversy surrounding the Principles still continues. The controversy is attributable to the inability of the Working Group on Direct Broadcast Satellites, the Legal Sub-committee (LSC) of the Committee on the Peaceful Uses of Outer Space, and various other committees of the United Nations to reach an agreement on the provisions of three key principles in the IDTBS Principles: Consent and Participation, Program Content, and Unlawful/Inadmissible Broadcasts. The lack of agreement on these principles prevented the adoption of the full set of IDTBS Principles by consensus.

Although Program Content and

Unlawful/Inadmissible Broadcasts were identified along with Consent and Participation as the three most difficult Articles remaining to be agreed upon, the subsequent sessions of the LSC, during the time the elaboration of IDTBS Principles remained on the agenda of the LSC, focused attention primarily on only one of the aforesaid three Articles, the Article on Consent and Participation. It was surmised that if agreement could be reached on the Article on Consent and Participation the Articles on Program Content, and Unlawful/Inadmissible Broadcasts would be unnecessary.

Although the LSC adopted the aforesaid approach of focusing on the Consent and Participation Article, the study argues that the fundamental obstacle to the progressive development of the international principles governing international direct television broadcasting by satellite was the lack of agreement on the question of elaborating principles for the Article on Program Content in the IDTBS Principles.

This analysis of the major remaining legal issues preventing the reaching of a consensus on international legal principles governing IDTBS treats the issue within an overall legal framework which offers the possibility of progress in overcoming the obstacles to the development and implementation of international law in a vital area of international interaction.

In addition to recommendations for revision of the IDTBS Principles, there are nine appendices containing United Nations documentation in the area of peaceful uses of outer space and IDTBS from 1958 to 1985, annexes to Committee reports, working papers, and the specific Articles of the IDTBS Principles.

Strzelecka, Jolanta

THE TRANSITION FROM A PARTY STATE TO A MILITARY STATE

Harvard Law School M

122 pages

Footnotes

The paper deals with the recent changes in Poland and argues that the bounds of its sovereignty have been overstepped. Martial law, imposed on December 13, 1981 in order to silence the Solidarity trade movement came as a big surprise. This study points out that although Poland has always been a very special Soviet satellite, the changes which have occurred since December 13, 1981, albeit directly caused by Solidarity, were possible in part by the reformations of the Warsaw Pact during the seventies and are consequences of these reformations.

The paper reviews the fundamental principles of the Party State and points out how they were dismantled during Solidarity. It discusses the preparations for the introduction of martial law in Poland, the role of the USSR/Warsaw Pact and the Polish Army in these preparations, and changes in the Warsaw Pact and the Polish Army during the seventies. It argues that the situation in 1956 in Hungary and Poland, when divisions of Hungarian and Polish armies faced Soviet intervention, would not have happened in 1981 since the "Polish Army" is not able to defend the country; the army is "Polish" in name only. Changes in the Polish legal system which have been promulgated since the imposition of martial law are discussed. The paper demonstrates the transformation of citizens into citizen-soldiers and the building of a new state structure which affords permanent military supervision over all state agencies, the party, industry, the educational system and social organizations. This military superstructure is ruled directly by Moscow.

The transition from the Party State to the Military State in Poland demonstrates that Moscow secured its capability to intervene in internal Polish matters in order to preclude any future rebellions in Poland. The use of force in its classical sense is no longer necessary in the case of suppression of Eastern European countries. Internal Polish law secured Moscow the right to intervene.

After the changes of 1981 - 1985, the Part State in Poland no longer existed as it had existed before Solidarity. The party powers were based on the reliability of its members. The structure of the Party State was built in order to allow for the leading role of the Party. But the Party without followers was not able to rule. In 1956 in Hungary, and in 1968 in Czechoslovakia, Moscow was able to find reliable groups of party members which helped pro-Moscow groups to gain the party leadership. This was impossible in Poland after Solidarity.

To build the military state in Poland, Moscow had to have been assured that the army would be reliable and under Moscow's direct control. Otherwise to give power to the Polish soldiers could have endangered Moscow's position in Poland. The fundamental changes in the political system of Poland which followed the coup are the best proof of Polish Army subordination to Moscow.

The "integration" of the Armed Forces of the Warsaw Pact in the case of Poland meant an integration of the total social-economic structure. In compliance with the internal legal system of Poland promulgated by the Sejm, Poland is ruled by the USSR/Warsaw Pact. The Soviet/Warsaw Pact intervention was not necessary on December 13, 1981 and will not occur in the future, since Poland has become an incorporated part of the Soviet commonwealth.

Stuesser, Lee

ACTIVE DEFENSE: STATE MILITARY RESPONSE TO INTERNATIONAL TERRORISM

Harvard Law School 1986 M

79 pages

Footnotes

The legality of "active defense" is examined against the international norms represented in the Charter of the United Nations. Moreover, since the United Nations provides the forum for international debate on the propriety of any military response, reliance is placed on United Nations practice. General Assembly resolutions and Security Council decisions are reviewed as sources for interpretation and clarification of the original articles of the United Nations Charter.

In the final decision to use military force considerations of international law may not be determinative, giving way to political and public pressures. Nevertheless, legality is important particularly for the United States, a nation that prides itself as being governed by the rule of law and a nation that has striven to create an international order based upon the rule of law. The battle against terrorism presents no exception; it too must be waged within the rules of international law. And if respect for international norms is to be preserved, the United States must lead by example. For it to resort to illegal means to combat terrorism sets an undesirable precedent. Unlawful use of force only encourages further illegal force. Breach invites counterbreach.

Legality also impacts upon the morality of the cause. Moral righteousness of the action will be enhanced or be diminished according to its perceived legality. The United States argues that it has a moral right to act against terrorism. But moral imperatives will not sway the world community sufficiently to ignore a breach of international law. Action in accord with international norms, on the other hand, is a powerful molder of world opinion.

Subiotto, Romano Francesco

DEVELOPMENTS UNDER THE DECREE OF 12TH MAY 1981 REGULATING INTERNATIONAL COMMERCIAL ARBITRATION

Harvard Law School 1986 M

70 pages

Footnotes

The decree of 12 May 1981 contains provisions of the decree of 14 May 1980 which are grouped under title I-IV relating to domestic arbitration. The 1981 decree also adds provisions covering international arbitration, and recognition, enforcement, and remedies with respect to arbitral awards made abroad or in an international arbitration.

Some heated arguments had taken place on the wisdom of legislating in the field of international arbitration. It was an accepted fact in France that the field of private international law was deemed to be the prerogative of the courts and international conventions. However, the promulgation of the decree of 14 May 1980 generated additional pressure towards regulating international arbitration by decree.

Although various solutions to the shortcomings of the traditional institutions might have been found by the courts, the state of affairs was ripe for a new legislative intervention. It had been clear that it was unsatisfactory to proceed by extending domestic provisions to international arbitration. The new decree had to take account the specific nature of the foundations of international commercial relations based on contractual agreements, the only element which parties, more often than not belonging to different legal systems, could have in common. It was thus clear that a decree providing a framework for international commercial arbitration had to be especially respectful of the will of the parties.

The decree reflects two fundamental ideas: it frees the parties of the restrictions applying to domestic arbitrations and those that might be imposed by foreign laws. Moreover, it reinforces this by giving the parties an almost unrestrained contractual freedom within the confines of international public policy as it is understood on France.

The main objectives of the drafters of the decree, besides preserving prior case law, were two-fold: to provide the most favorable framework for the development of international commercial arbitration on French territory and, in order to make the outcome feasible, to simplify as far as possible the proposed framework.

The last decades have seen a realization by traditional institutions that the arbitration process is reliable and better adapted to the solving of international commercial disputes. It has been realized that protagonists are responsible and not intent on exploiting the system, even in the absence of any restraining influence. The decree thus sets a minimum framework within which the parties can freely develop their relations. The role of the traditional institutions has been reduced to give arbitration its full potential and keep their controlling influence to a minimum.

The second objective has been obtained by excluding, so far as possible, any mechanism of conflicts of laws. It would have been a hard and complicated task to include them in the decree because of the large number of different circumstances and phases of each arbitration. Their significance was also reduced by the fact that one of the objectives was to allow maximum freedom to the parties, providing for a control only at the stage of recognition and enforcement. This could be achieved without a mechanism of conflict of laws.

Subpaisarn, Dumnern

THAI PETROLEUM CONCESSION ARRANGEMENT: A COMPARATIVE STUDY

Harvard Law School 1986 M

82 pages

Footnotes

The pattern of agreements between Governments and transnational corporations in the petroleum sector appears to have undergone considerable qualitative change in recent years. Changing world market conditions, combined with more effective negotiation and better bargaining power on the part of host countries, have led to more favorable agreements from the point of view of the host country.

The benefits that accrue to the developing countries are currently more extensive and substantial than those realized under the traditional concession arrangement. However, these countries, including Thailand, have not wholly attained the multiple goal of permanent sovereignty over their natural resources and the exploitation of their petroleum wealth, in the most efficient manner for the fulfillment of their overall and specific objectives.

Even though the Thai concession agreement has been improved over the traditional concession form, the present concession is not wholly satisfactory. Operational control of petroleum operation remains in the domain of the transnational oil companies. Thailand is still dependent upon these corporations for the provision of vital services and the procurement of finance capital. Thailand should continue to improve her negotiating position in order to attain more favorable terms in future agreements and to amend existing ones.

The petroleum investment business is risky and the cost of mistake is high. Thailand should learn from the mistakes of other countries and avoid such mistakes itself. It should take advantage of the services available from the United Nations, the World Bank, and other oil producing countries to improve its position in dealing with the transnational oil companies.

Thailand has been proved to be one of the most attractive countries in South East Asia for business. Many of the basic factors making for sustained economic growth are positive: a strong sector; a large and low cost working labor force; good internal and international communications; and, a conservative government. Yet in the petroleum sector, in order to attract more foreign investments, Thailand must strengthen her national petroleum policy and improve the political stability and overall investment climate.

Sucher, Mark Laurence

NOTICE REQUIREMENTS IN FEDERAL ACQUISITION CONTRACTS

George Washington Law School 1986 M

151 pages

Footnotes

The United States Government has a pervasive impact in the nation's economy not just as a regulator but also as a massive consumer. As the size and complexity of the federal government has expanded explosively over the last half century, so has its demand for goods and services skyrocketed. A large share of these requirements is filled through contracts with private parties. Those who wish to understand or to participate in this process (or, preferably, both) must realize first that contracting with the United States Government is not at all the same as typical contracting between private parties.

Virtually all aspects of the government procurement process are prescribed in excruciating detail in a number of government regulations.

Since the regulations provide such detailed guidance and mandate much of the contract language, the neophyte might assume that interpreting government contracts would be an easy task. Unfortunately, the truth is quite the opposite.

An excellent example of this potential interpretation trap is the application of the various notice provisions sprinkled throughout the typical government contract. Where sovereign immunity once reigned, the government now shields itself from breach of contract liability with a wide variety of clauses providing for administrative resolution of claims and disputes.

The purpose of this paper is to analyze the notice provisions of several major clauses. Primary emphasis will be given to the Disputes Clause, the Changes Clause, and the Differing Site Conditions Clause. A discussion of the clause provisions will demonstrate that the interpretation and application of the notice requirements by the courts and agency boards of contract appeals often deviate substantially from the apparent literal meaning. In some cases, it seems that the plain language of the clause is totally ignored, often without explanation. Finally, the paper analyzes these deviations to devote a rationale for the approach taken by the boards and courts and discusses whether there is any substantial detrimental impact to the government resulting from their approach.

Suwanmongkol, Ruenvadee

THE THAI MINERALS ACT REFORM AND THE THAI TIN INDUSTRY

Harvard Law School 1987 M

107 pages

Footnotes, appendices and bibliography

It has been remarked that "mankind's progress is measured in minerals" and "minerals can be regarded as man's principal physical material in the development of industrial civilization". From these two quotations, mineral development can be considered to be the key to overall development and the foundation upon which modern societies are built. Moreover, mining can generate remarkable contributions to economic development, such as national income, expansion of fiscal resources, foreign exchange earnings, labor creation, transfer of technology,infrastructure and the development of downstream operations (resource-based industrialization), in the countries that are fortunate enough to have rich mineral deposits. In order to achieve this economic development, mining law is an important factor. Thailand is a country which is extremely fortunate to have a wide range of minerals in commercial quantities. This consists of 36 different kinds of minerals and 3 fossil fuels.

Tin has been the most important mineral produced among Thailand's 36 kinds of mineral for many decades. The tin mining industry is responsible for approximately 80% of Thailand's mineral export value, which brings in a large amount of income to the country. In addition, on the world level, Thailand ranks third as a producer of tin after Malaysia and Indonesia, accounting for 14% of all world production.

This paper deals with the situation of the tin industry in Thailand and compares it with other countries. However, the most important objective of this paper is to analyze the Thai Minerals Act. Hence, the question which is presented is whether this minerals act is efficient in controlling mining activities in order to achieve economic development. This is the major area of inquiry explored in this paper. Moreover, from this study, conclusions are drawn about the main flaws in the current minerals act, and some viable reforms are proposed that are believed to improve existing shortcomings. The author also presents a discussion on the legal aspects of foreign participation in mining activities.

Suzuki, Masabumi

COMPARATIVE STUDY OF THE AMERICAN AND JAPANESE POLICIES CONCERNING COOPERATIVE R&d

Harvard Law School 1986 M

63 pages

Footnotes

American and Japanese policies are examined in terms of their approaches to cooperative research and development (R&D) activities. This comparison reveals the differences in their approaches, not only in R&D policy, but also in so called industrial policy.

In developed countries, governments are, to varying degrees, playing an important role in the field of R&D. Recently, many economists have analyzed the mechanism of technological innovation, and their theories, though varied, all support the role of government in R&D.

The United States antitrust laws are discussed with respect to reactions by the government and the current state of cooperative R&D. Japan's experience is similarly reviewed in the context of Japanese anti-monopoly law and the government's tools to encourage cooperative R&D.

The American and Japanese governments' approaches to cooperative R&D is viewed as an example of their industrial policies. The American approach is regulatory and the laws play an important role as an expression of the government's intention. In Japan, the government acts more actively toward the private sector's behavior (cautiously avoiding harming competition) and not only the statutes but also other governmental tools collectively worked for the same purpose to encourage cooperative R&D. These approaches seem to be fundamentally different, and not variations on each other. But mutual understanding of the experiences would be useful for establishing better policies in both countries. The Japanese experience of many years of encouragement of cooperative R&D under an antitrust law similar to the American law offers many suggestions that the United States would find illuminating.

Takasaki, Hideo

FAIR TRIAL/FREE PRESS PROBLEM: A CHOICE OF DEMOCRACY

Harvard Law School 1986 M

58 pages

Footnotes

In the United States, the problem posed by the sometimes conflicting values of fair trial and free press is "almost as old as the Republic". The dispute in the earlier stage put much stress on the dignity of the judiciary. In the 20th century this problem came to draw more and more attention with special emphasis on the effect that mass media had on the jury system. Two accidents of the century, the kidnap of Charles Lindbergh Jr. and the assassination of President Kennedy, reminded people of the seriousness of this problem. Changes in the nature of mass media during the modern age also added to the Fair Trial/Free Press problem. When the Bill of Rights was ratified in 1791, the press as a whole represented a wide range of opinions at large, although many of the newspapers were narrow in their view. But newspapers have become big business, and there are far fewer of them to serve a larger literate population. Today, established chains of national news services are the dominant feature of mass media.

Mass media must have their own independent newsgathering activities in order to have true freedom of the press. However, these newsgathering activities increasingly impair the privacy of people, especially those who are involved in trials, because of the growing power of mass media.

The Fair Trial/Free Press problem is quite new in Japan, even though Japan borrowed from the U.S. constitutional doctrine and criminal procedure when it set up a new judicial system after World War II. No jury trials are held in Japan. Nevertheless, the peculiar standing and nature of mass media in Japan makes both its newsgathering and newsreporting activities more prone to abuse than in the United States.

In Japan, people ranked mass media as the

second greatest infringement on individual rights, and only the seventh greatest protection of individual rights, according to the poll held by N.H.K. (semi-national broadcasting station of Japan) in 1974. Moreover, 46% of the people answered No to the question "Do you think that newsreports by the mass media fairly reflect the opinion of the whole nation?" in the poll held by N.H.K. in 1975.

Overreactiveness of Japanese people to the activities of mass media influences Japanese people's view of the fairness of courts. Traditionally, Japanese people do not trust the impartiality of judges as much as Anglo-Saxon people do. Such distrust was strongly expressed when the Diet tried to confer statutory contempt power to the courts in 1951. Such criticism as "Japanese judges are subject to the atmosphere of society in deciding respective cases" derives from the distrust. If a judge decides a notorious case against the atmosphere, or the opinion of mass media, he may risk the harm of being criticized by the media. From such distrust derives another view that pre-judicial reports are harmful to bench trials as well as to jury trials.

Taylor, M. M.

A REVIEW OF FOREIGN INVESTMENT POLICY IN PAPUA NEW GUINEA: THE FIRST DECADE

Harvard Law School 1986 M

102 pages

Footnotes

Papua New Guinea, located in the Southwest Pacific basin between Australia and Indonesia, became an independent nation on September 16, 1975. Though politically prepared for nationhood, the country had a small economy, basically reliant on Australian aid. (Until independence, Papua New Guinea was the Australian Territory of Papua and the UN Trust Territory of New Guinea.)

Papua New Guinea's small open economy exports little other than primary mineral, agricultural, and forest products. It imports almost all its fuel, capital goods, and other inputs to production, together with the larger portion of its marketed food requirements. Only one-eighth of the economically active population in 1980 held formal wage employment. At the time of internal self-government in 1973, Australian grants met approximately half of the government's expenditure, and the World Bank did not recognize the country's sovereign credit-worthiness until 1976.

In the ten years since internal self-government Papua New Guinea has successfully contributed to designing relations between host countries and foreign investors in the minerals industries. Where there has been success in the development of sound mining and petroleum legislation, the foreign investment policies in forests and fisheries, the country's renewable resources, have been confused and poor.

The paper considers the emergence of the first five year development plan, its accompanying political changes, and the evolution of the national economic policy. Following an overview of the general economy and the achievements since independence, the paper examines the regulatory framework of the foreign investment policy, domestic impediments to investment, and the incentives that have been created to encourage investment. A comparative review of foreign investment policy in the renewable and nonrenewable natural resources is the basis for an evaluation of the pattern of foreign investment in Papua New Guinea and its future prospects.

Thomas, George C. III

THE PROHIBITION OF SUCCESSIVE PROSECUTIONS AND MULTIPLE PUNISH-MENTS FOR THE SAME OFFENSE: IN SEARCH OF STANDARDS

Washington University School of Law 1986 D

993 pages

Footnotes and bibliography

The double jeopardy clause of the fifth amendment of the United States Constitution forbids placing a person twice in jeopardy for the same offense. The United States Supreme Court has interpreted this protection to forbid more than one trial or more than one punishment for the same offense. An integral part of double jeopardy analysis is, therefore, the determination of whether the prosecutions or punishments are for the "same offense." The principal purpose of the dissertation is to formulate a definition of "same offense" for purposes of the fifth amendment double jeopardy clause.

The prohibition against double jeopardy has its origin in Greek and Roman law. The dissertation traces the history of the concept and identifies the policies served by a protection against double jeopardy. It then examines the evolution of the "same offense" component of double jeopardy analysis in the cases of the United States Supreme Court, beginning with the 1889 case of In re Nielsen.

Two primary conclusions are offered. First, the thrust of double jeopardy protection is against the power of government to force a defendant to endure more than one trial. Thus, although there are policy reasons to apply double jeopardy principles when multiple punishments for the same offense are imposed in a single proceeding, these reasons lose significance when the legislature has specifically authorized multiple punishments. Legislatures may, therefore, prescribe multiple convictions for the same offense in a single trial.

The second major conclusion is that the protection against multiple trials requires a broad and inflexible definition of "same offense" that encompasses the underlying criminal conduct. This protection is not subject to legislative power. Thus, the double jeopardy clause forbidgs, in all cases, a trial that requires proof of the same criminal conduct proved in an earlier prosecution.

The conventional analytical framework that applies a single definition of "same offense" regardless of the procedural context of the double jeopardy challenge is rejected. A different analytical framework is necessary in multiple trial cases than is appropriate in single trial/multiple conviction cases. These different frameworks are developed, defended, and compared to state law solutions to the problem of multiple trials and multiple convictions based on the same conduct.

Thwaite, Gregory J.

PARTY AUTONOMY IN INTERNATIONAL COMMERCIAL ARBITRATION: A STUDY OF THE LAW IN AUSTRALIA AND NEW ZEALAND

Harvard Law School 1986 M

70 pages

Footnotes

The focus of attention in international commercial arbitration is on the degree of party autonomy permitted in individual national jurisdictions. "Party autonomy" can be defined as the right of parties firstly to establish and conduct pursuant to contract an arbitration as their own dispute resolution procedure, without control by the courts of any nation, and secondly to subsequently enforce in any nation the award of that arbitration without any inquiry into its validity.

On a philosophical level, the concept of part autonomy calls for a re-assessment of national sovereignty: its justification, its genuine interests, its practical limits, and its relationship with the rights of other nations and with the rights of commercial entities that operate across national boundaries without allegiance to any particular nation. Traditional aspects of sovereignty have been tempered to the realities of international trade. At a minimum nations have acceded to international treaties such as the General Agreement on Tariffs and Trade, which restrict their rights to control customs restrictions and tariffs; blocs such as the European Economic Community impose a control over the general economic policies of their members.

The internationalization of trade at the expense of some areas of traditional state sovereignty must lead on to the internationalization of dispute resolution mechanism. The nation that lowers tariff and permits the free flow of goods across its boundaries cannot continue to insist on complete control over commercial disputes.

On a practical level, parties in international trade require an adequate dispute resolution procedure. For sound reasons arbitration is often preferred. Foreign parties seek to increase certainty and reduce risk by excluding or reducing the ability of a national court to intervene in the stipulated procedure. This has two economic consequences for a nation whose courts refrain from involvement in arbitration. Firstly, the prospects for international trade for that nation's commercial entities are improved. Secondly, there is a prospect that arbitrations will be held in that nation, and governed by its law.

Tsibris, Michael R.

ARBITRATION AGREEMENTS AND AWARDS IN BANKRUPTCY COURTS: AN INQUIRY INTO THE RELATIONS BETWEEN INTERNATIONAL COMMERCIAL ARBITRATION AND THE UNITED STATES BANKRUPTCY SYSTEM

Harvard Law School 1986 M

46 pages

Footnotes

In the forty years since the Second World War, there has been a spectacular increase in both the value and the volume of international trade. More and more firms are doing business, either as suppliers or as customers or both, with firms from other countries. The stability of the world economy can be said to have come to depend, to a certain degree, on this flow of goods between different national entities. Consequently, a strong desire to encourage this exchange and free it from impediments is reflected in several actions at the transnational level.

As in every transaction, disputes are certain to arise in international transactions. Resolving these disputes in a quick, inexpensive, and just way is crucial for encouraging international contracts and economic cooperation at the level of individuals. It is doubtful whether national courts can be relied upon to produce this result, since almost universally judicial systems are overburdened by cases, causing huge delays and subsequently increasing costs and - not infrequently - tending to favor their own nationals.

International commercial arbitration is an alternative method of settling disputes, one that claims to be less delaying, more efficient, less costly, and - as evidence suggests - more and more frequently chosen by parties. International commercial arbitration is the process in which two parties in dispute concerning an international transaction agree to submit their differences to one or more impartial persons for a decision which both parties agree to accept as binding upon them. This agreement is usually included in the contract itself as an arbitration clause.

The focus is not on the process of arbitration itself, but instead on its relation with proceedings in bankruptcy. Three conditions involving international commercial arbitration and bankruptcy are discussed in detail: bankruptcy occurring before the making of an award, enforcing an award in bankruptcy, and arbitration of claims on behalf of the bankrupt.

Relations between international commercial arbitration and national judicial systems are examined. Following an overview of the policy of cooperation, the problem of arbitration agreements and awards in bankruptcy are revisited.

Tsichrintzis, A. K.

CENTRAL BANKING IN A REGULATED ECONOMY: THE CASE OF THE BANK OF GREECE

Harvard Law School 1986 D

132 pages

Footnotes, appendices, and bibliography

The science of central banking is a fairly explored academic field. On the theoretical level, many have tried to define the precise meaning of central banking, i.e. the function of a financial intermediary that distinguishes it from the mass of the other credit institutions and qualifies it as the Central Bank of the country. In case studies, the position and function of central banks have been considered in economic terms. This paper explores the legal approach to the functions of the Central Bank of Greece. The focus is specifically on the extent and the significance of Government intervention in the activities of the Bank of Greece.

There are dissenting opinions about the characteristic function of a central bank in a State. However, the task of a central bank to regulate the internal and external value of the domestic currency seems to be the most encompassing, because it implies all the other control and supervisory powers of this institution. This is also supported by the fact that in countries where the independence of the central bank from the executive branch of the government is recognized legally, provisions are included in the relevant legislation that assign to the central bank the above regulatory role of the value of their currencies.

As far as the autonomous status of central banks is concerned, we are faced with conflicting opinions. The debate over the appropriate extent of discretion that should be entrusted normatively to central banks revealed disagreement among outstanding experts. The position this paper takes is that central banks should be allowed extensive discretionary power to draft the monetary and credit policy of the country.

Greece presents an example of total State control over the activities of its Central Bank. The Bank of Greece (BoG) functions as an apparatus for the implementation of the Government's policies in the banking sector. Its status as an independent State agency is not legally recognized; instead, it is administratively subject to the Ministry of National Economy. The BoG stands in the middle of a de facto nationalized banking sector performing completely regulated activities. Greek banks could be considered as agents collecting, on behalf of the State, and redistributing the national resources among the various sectors of the economy.

The modifications suggested in this paper can be realistically expected only if the current attitude of the State favoring absolute control over the banking sector is abolished and a more liberal policy of gradual elimination of the existing regulations followed. As long as the BoG is an apparatus of the State, any reformative action of the Bank furthering the autonomy and deregulation of the sector is a priori condemned to failure.

Tufvesson, Maria E.

INTERNATIONAL COMMERCIAL ARBITRATION: THE FINALITY PROBLEM UNDER THE NEW YORK CONVENTION

Harvard Law School 1987 M

49 pages

Footnotes and bibliography

The New York Convention of 1958 will celebrate its thirtieth anniversary next year. The Convention can be said to have had a very successful history both as regards the number of states which have ratified the Convention and its implementation in those states. The overall tendency amongst ratifying nations is to give effect to the Convention to the greatest extent possible. This favorable view of international commercial arbitration was recently expressed by the United States Supreme Court when the justices considered whether antitrust claims were arbitrable in the international context.

Any legal instrument when interpreted may have different judicial glosses placed upon its initial provisions; and indeed, this is especially true of an international instrument which is to be applied by many diverse legal orders. Thus, despite the fact that the national courts have demonstrated a willingness to give effect to the Convention, its practical application has resulted in much diversity of judicial decision-making.

The quintessence of the Convention is to make arbitral awards enforceable to the greatest extent possible, yet without prejudicing the defending party's right to due process. Thus it was recognized that in certain instances it may be appropriate to allow a right of objection. The drafters of the Convention sought to solve this problem in the allocation of judicial control over the enforcement process. As a result, the Convention enumerated a number of grounds for judicial control in the enforcing country.

The author looked first at the requirement of the "double exequatur" and secondly at the developments of the interpretation of the word "binding" once the "double exequatur" requirement was abolished. Finally, he provides a summation of the present position which shows that despite the fact that certain nations still adhere to the interpretation under the "applicable law," there is a definite movement towards the "autonomous" interpretation.

Urie, Matthew Clyde

NATURAL RESOURCE DEVELOPMENT: STATE RESPONSES TO THE UNDESIRABLE EFFECTS OF RESOURCE EXPLOITATION

George Washington Law School 1986 M

102 pages

Footnotes

Since 1973-74 Arab oil embargo, Americans have perceived a need to become energy self-sufficient. This desire for self-sufficiency has included not just energy producing resources, but also other strategic minerals of which the United States has few or no proven reserves. As a result of this desire for self-sufficiency, increased efforts in natural resource exploration have yielded discoveries of new and large oil and natural gas, and coal fields. These discoveries have been made in many of the western and southwestern states which generally lack the population and wealth of the eastern states.

The resource-rich states have attempted to capitalize on their newly found wealth by levying taxes or fees on the severance or use of the resources, or by otherwise regulating the transportation of these resources beyond the states' borders. Often these taxes, fees or regulations have been held to be invalid under the Commerce Clause as interfering with Congress' exclusive power to regulate interstate and foreign commerce. After all, the wealth of one state must be considered the wealth of all the states and the nation. However, a carefully drafted state severance or use tax may pass Commerce Clause muster, and secure for the resource-rich state additional financial benefits not shared by other states.

But the emphasis on the quality of life and preserving the environment dictates that resource development cannot occur at any cost. Society will no longer tolerate the social and environmental degradation that resulted from the early natural resource exploitation that dirtied the air and water in many parts of the eastern U.S. and west coast. Today, the resource-rich states require that resource development be planned so as to minimize the adverse impacts on the affected communities and environment. This planning and impact mitigation requires the expenditure of vast sums of money which would otherwise by a "clear profit" from the development of the natural resources.

These expenditures cannot assure the existence of a pristine environment during and after the resource development process; some environmental change will occur irrespective of the preventative measures taken. However, the resource-rich states must be allowed to profit from their resources and use those profits to develop economically; such is the nature of the free market. It must be hoped that these states will be educated from the mistakes of the past, and employ those mechanisms in cooperation with the federal government which preserve the environment in the face of natural resource development.

Vandevort, Dennis Eugene

LEGAL CONTROL OF HOSTILE ENVIRONMENTAL MODIFICATION

George Washington Law School 1986 M

83 pages

Footnotes

Weather and other environmental factors have historically played a large part in the outcome of military engagements. Although the role of these factors has been adapted and utilized to gain strategic or tactical advantage, recently it has become technologically feasible for man to intentionally alter the environment to his advantage not only as a means of enhancing military effectiveness but as a weapon in its own right.

Particularly in guerrilla warfare, features of the environment provide protection to the guerrilla force and the temptation on the part of the opposing force to either destroy those protective features or manipulate them for its own advantage is strong. For this reason it is considered that environmental modification will play an increasing role in the context of limited war or insurgencies. In other contexts, environmental modification offers unique possibilities with respect to atmospheric or oceanic effects on communications and remote sensing.

In addition to the effects of intentional hostile environmental modification recent world concern has also focused on the foreseeable collateral effects of methods and means of warfare on the environment. Most notable of these are the effects of nuclear warfare as exemplified by the findings of the International Council of Scientific Unions in its Scientific Committee of Problems of the Environment.

The juridical control of hostile environmental modification, both intentional and collateral is in a developmental stage, as is the technology. This study examines the current controls applicable to hostile environmental modification within the framework of the customary and conventional law of armed conflict to determine to what extent environmental protection has evolved as an aspect of the law of armed conflict.

Velazquez Valdes, Maria Jacqueline

DOMESTIC AND INTERNATIONAL ARBITRATION IN THE DOMINICAN REPUBLIC

Harvard Law School 1986 M

82 pages

Footnotes

The role of arbitration as a dispute resolution process has considerable importance in many countries as well as in the international community. Unfortunately, the Dominican Republic (DR) cannot be included among those nations where arbitration has become a popular method for the solution of controversies. Arbitration as a private form of justice is recognized in the DR, and is regulated by the Civil Procedure Code (CPC). Nonetheless, there has been an inexplicable reticence toward arbitration from Dominican legislative and judicial officials. Parties to disputes may suspect that rules of law may be avoided and public policy principles infringed through the use of arbitration. Nationalistic beliefs favoring local jurisdiction have caused courts to deny authority to foreign decisions. Skepticism about the degree of protection that arbitration grants to matters of national interest undoubtedly accounts for some of its unpopularity. Thus, the existence of some arbitral institutions, procedures, and regulations are ignored while others prove to be inaccessible because of economic factors. In addition to these obstacles, a lack of data about and explanation of the arbitral provisions contained in the CPC has hindered their widespread application.

The paper gives a general view of arbitration in the DR. The internal aspects of arbitration are examined and criticized. Provisions of the Constitution, the Code of Civil Procedure, the Civil Code, the Commercial code, and the Labor Relations Code are discussed, and jurisprudential precedents are explained. Furthermore, the role of the DR in the international arena and its participation in the promotion of international arbitration are treated in detail.

Regardless of the many advantages which the

parties may realize by resorting to arbitration, it cannot be said that the Dominican society is unanimously conscious of the advantages of arbitration. Therefore, it is the role of some community sectors to provide a basic understanding of the meaning and use of arbitration to Dominican citizens. A more active role is recommended on the part of law schools, the official Chamber of Commerce, Agriculture and Industry, and the Dominican Bar Association. The role of the legislature includes enactment of arbitral rules that respond to present judicial needs. With regard to the international aspect of arbitration, the Department of foreign Affairs ought to play a more active role as well.

Waer, Paul

RECIPROCITY AS A REQUIREMENT FOR RECOGNITION AND ENFORCEMENT OF FOREIGN JUDGMENTS

Harvard Law School 1987 M

113 pages

Footnotes

The use of reciprocity in private international law has in traditional idealistic conceptual theories often criticized as being a relic of the utilitarian approaches which emerged in the early era of the history of private international law under the influence of the notion of sovereignty of States and in a climate of rising nationalism. However, these traditional idealistic conceptual theories themselves did not turn out to provide a more successful alternative for the earlier approaches. Their universal acceptance and uniform application was not realized and subsequently, the decisional harmony their creators had hoped for was not achieved. The failure of these traditional conceptual theories of private international law, which assumed the equality of material norms and provided for a mechanical application of laws, disregarding the actual interests and policies involved, caused a search for new approaches to the conflict-of-laws problem. Attempts were made to create new techniques which, no longer blindfolded by a naive idealistic dogma, tried to provide for more satisfactory solutions.

In the light of these tendencies, the author considered the problem of international civil procedure anew and re-examine the question whether reciprocity can play any constructive role in solving the problem of conflicting interests. In this paper an attempt was made to analyze the rational interests and policies in international civil procedure law taking into account the political reality which influences the decision-making process in private international law.

The author discusses reciprocity in the broader context of its role in relations to international cooperation in international civil procedure law.

The basic problem of international civil procedure law are analyzed and the question whether theoretically, reciprocity could play a constructive role is examined. The focus was then on the most problematical aspects of the use of reciprocity. Unilateral reciprocity requirements are examined both from an empiric comparative law perspective and in the light of theoretical criticisms as to their use and efficiency.

Finally, an attempt was made to draw some conclusions. The decision-making process in international civil procedure law is discussed and the basic criticisms of unilateral reciprocity requirements are re-examined and evaluated.

Wallace, Ronald Stephen

TRADEMARK COUNTERFEITING: THE MOST EGREGIOUS FORM OF TRADEMARK INFRINGEMENT

George Washington Law School 1986 M

154 pages

Footnotes

Imitation may be the sincerest form of flattery, but the counterfeiting of goods with internationally recognized brand names, which are sold to unsuspecting customers around the world, seems to reached epidemic proportions.

Commercial counterfeiting in the trademark context, is a particular form of trademark infringement; therefore, for the purposes of discussing the problem of the sale of counterfeit goods bearing unauthorized trademarks, the following terms are used. "Counterfeiting" is the unauthorized use of a registered trademark on a product that is identical or substantially similar to, the product for which the trademark is registered and used; "commercial counterfeiters" are persons who attempt to deceive customers into purchasing inferior merchandise by affixing to it counterfeit trademarks of quality-brand manufacturers; and, "counterfeit goods" are any goods bearing the unauthorized representation of a trademark that is legally registered with respect to such goods in the country of importation or sale, which counterfeit goods when compared with genuine products, often will not permit distinction between the original product and the counterfeit.

In short, commercial counterfeiting involves the unauthorized and intentional use of a protected trademark on identical or substantially similar goods. It is the theft for profit of a firm's reputation and product through use of deception. As such, it is most egregious form of trademark infringement.

The aim of this paper is to describe briefly the evolution of trademarks and the rise of the problem of the commercial counterfeiting of trademarked goods, to provide an overview of past attempts to deal with the problem, and to examine various existing remedies used to combat commercial counterfeiting, including one of the newest weapons, the Trademark Counterfeiting Act of 1984.

Wallin, Ann-Marie

RESIDENCE AS BASIS FOR JURISDICTION TO TAX: THE EXAMPLE OF THE UNITED STATES AND SWEDEN

Harvard Law School 1986 M

66 pages

Footnotes

The purpose of this paper is to describe and explain the concept of residence and its importance in international taxation. A further purpose is to discuss alternative ways of determining whether an individual or other legal person is to be considered a resident for tax purposes.

The issue of whether an individual or other legal entity is a resident (or domestic) legal person is essential in tax systems that use residence within the country as the basis or one of the bases for jurisdiction to tax. The method or tests that are being used to determine this issue can, in principle, be characterized as either subjective or objective, i.e., mechanical. This is the case irrespective of what kind of legal person is in question.

The two kinds of methods that are thus being used both give rise to advantages and disadvantages that are caused by the characteristics of the method in question. A subjective method is characterized by problems concerning foreseeability and uncertainty but does, on the other hand, take into account a broad range of elements important to the case that is to be decided. An objective method is characterized by foreseeability and predictability and it is relatively simple to administer. On the other hand, the fact that the method is mechanical opens up possibilities of undesirable results. It should be remembered that, whatever method is used, the purpose is to determine whether there is a sufficient nexus between the individual or legal entity and the state to constitute a basis for jurisdiction to tax.

As can be seen supra, both the United States and Sweden changed their rules for determining residential status of individuals very recently.

Before the change took place, both countries used a form of the "center of gravity of life" test, i.e., subjective test. The United States changed their rules to an objective test and Sweden further developed and broadened the application of the subjective test. It is interesting to note that both countries have expressed a desire to develop rules that apply to individuals who have a real and firm nexus to the country. It is further interesting to note that the United States besides residence uses citizenship as a basis for jurisdiction to tax. This means that the problem of deciding who after moving from the country still retains a nexus sufficient to be a basis for residence taxation does not exist in the case of an American citizen leaving the country.

Wang, Chen-guang

COMPARISON OF THE AMERICAN LEGAL PROFESSION AND THE CHINESE LEGAL PROFESSION

Harvard Law School 1986 M

60 pages

Footnotes

In modern society, law plays an important role. Industrialization and commercialization of society generated the idea of democracy aiming to protect the best interest of society as a whole and the idea of civil libertarianism aiming to protect the individual's right and interest. These ideas brought the principle of the rule of law which is becoming dominant in the political and legal thinking in almost every country. To some extent, every country has an established legal system. But a legal system is not self-operative and law is not a set of self-sufficient rules. To give them vitality, there is a need for trained experts - legal professionals. And within the legal profession, the lawyer or attorney is one of the most important components.

Though the legal profession is an indispensable component of the rule of law, its position and function vary considerably in different countries, due to different legal traditions and to different cultural, social, and economic conditions. Comparative studies of the legal profession, such as this one, identify the common and special traits of the legal profession, consider the need for improvement to the profession, and promote cooperation among lawyers in transnational legal affairs.

This comparison of the legal professions of China and America begins with a historical survey of the legal profession from its first appearance within the Roman Empire, and proceeds to examine the differences and similarities in the practice of law in the United States (US) and China.

There are some interesting contrasts. One is that Chinese lawyers as government officials have the duty to spread the legal knowledge and the idea of rule of law among the people. In the Mass Legal Education Campaign, lawyers organized by judicial bureaus made a great contribution. The forms they take are free legal consultations and lectures for ordinary citizens. American lawyers as private professionals have no such voluntary work organized by the state.

Another difference is that because of the shortage of lawyers in China, many litigants or citizens cannot get legal services. In the US, some citizens also cannot obtain legal services, but mainly because of their poor economic condition. There is no pro bono work in China as in the US. But according to law and practice, if the defendants in serious criminal cases do not have lawyers, the courts provide appointed lawyers.

Though there are many differences between the working process of the two legal professions, their basic functions in the society are very similar. They are advocates of individuals' interests, guardians of the public interest and the integrity of legality, reconciliators and settlers of social disputes, and participants in legislation and policy making.

Warden, Karl Duval

THIRD PARTY CONSENT TO MEDICAL TREATMENT

George Washington Law School 1986 M

78 pages

Footnotes and appendices

Probably the most common form of third party consent arises from the process of educating the patient and their family. An otherwise competent patient will refuse medical treatment the attending physician deems necessary. The doctor will try to persuade the patients that they must accept treatment for their own good. If this does not work the doctor, or nurse, will speak with the friends and family of the patient. The doctor will attempt to persuade the family that the patient is making a wrong decision and that they must change the patient's mind. Then the family persuades the patient to accept the doctor's point of view. The patient has, in effect, had someone else make his decision for him or her. The tactic usually works.

Sometimes the education of the patient and family does not work. If the patient is considered fully competent to refuse the physician can do nothing more. If the patient is not considered fully competent to make medical decisions a range of alternatives is open to the physician seeking to treat that patient. They may obtain the consent of a person authorized to give consent. They may even take the case to court to obtain the court's consent.

The process of obtaining this third party consent is the subject of this paper. The paper also studies how variations in the standards used to make third party choices can affect the outcome of that process. Third party consent is studied from the point of view of the physician, the health care administrator, the judge, the family, and most importantly the patient.

Courts and other third party consenters should be given guidelines for how to make their consent decisions. It must first be determined which available guideline is most suited to the case at hand. When the proper guideline is established, the consenter should have a checklist of factors to consider before making their decision. A consenter may make an appropriate choice only by keeping all relevant facts in mind.

Warriner, Wallace Fones

THE UNILATERAL USE OF COERCION UNDER INTERNATIONAL LAW: A LEGAL ANALYSIS OF THE UNITED STATES RAID ON LIBYA

George Washington Law School 1986 M

150 pages

Footnotes and appendices

International terrorism creates unique problems for governments trying to function within the framework of international law. It is undeniably true that the Charter of the United Nations preserves the inherent right of national self-defense; however, a rigid, restrictive interpretation of this right places unacceptable limitations on state action to protect legitimate national interests.

During the United Nations Security Council debates over the Israeli raid on the headquarters of the Palestinian Liberation Organization located near Tunis, Tunisia, the United States made its interpretation of the legitimate use of force to combat terrorism crystal clear.

On April 14, 1986. thirty-two American aircraft attacked selected targets located at Tripoli and Benghazi, Libya. Thirty-seven people were killed; an undetermined number were injured. The more than sixty tons of ordnance used during the attack also caused significant material damage.

The United States defended its action as legitimate self-defense against the state-sponsored terrorism of Libyan leader Moammar Gadhafi. During the last several months, administration and congressional statements have indiscriminately used the words "retaliation" and "reprisal".

Libya, however, requested an urgent meeting of the United Nations Security Council to consider the American action and described it as a "barbaric, savage" raid against civilian targets, such as schools, houses, foreign missions and airports; Libya also urged the adoption of a resolution condemning the United States for the practice of international terrorism.

The Security Council has the primary responsibility to maintain international peace and security. If it fails to function as designed, more and more states will resort to the unilateral use of force in an attempt to solve their legitimate problems, thereby jeopardizing the chances for successful world public order.

White, Peter C.

TRIADS THEN AND NOW - AN EVALUATION OF THE SUITABILITY OF US SOLUTIONS TO CURRENT HONG KONG PROBLEMS

Harvard Law School 1987 M

107 pages

Footnotes and appendices

In 1842, sovereignty over the island of Hong Kong passed from China to Britain. By the end of the first year of British administration, the Chinese population had increased to fifteen thousand, and by the end of the century it totalled five hundred thousand. Hong Kong's population is now approximately six million, and it is significant that during different periods of its history the administration has barely been able to cope with waves of immigration from the Chinese mainland.

Although Hong Kong now prides itself on having one of Asia's finest police forces, this was not always the case. Sometimes inefficient and corrupt, very often undermanned, and nearly always troubled by cultural and linguistic differences, Hong Kong's police force and the community it serves have often inadvertently provided an ideal haven for the nurturing and development of criminal activity. During the entirety of the Colony's history most of this activity has been controlled by criminal gangs which are commonly known as "triads."

The paper outlines the history and development of triads from their inception as political opponents of the ruling Ching Dynasty in seventeenth century China. Different triad society groups invariably broke up into smaller sub-groups as the motive for involvement and membership changed from political and social to one which, over the last forty years, has been exclusively criminal. It is argued that the remaining fifty groups and sub-groups have continually demonstrated an ability to engage in extreme violence. This capability and their "gang" orientation are attributes which have made them indispensable to ongoing organized crime.

This triad involvement has contributed to the success enjoyed by organized crime in Hong Kong.

The government has responded to the problem by establishing the Fight Crime Committee (FCC) to investigate and recommend counter measures. The FCC commenced its work in late 1983 and in April of 1986 published a discussion paper which included suggestions derived from the US experience in dealing with the detection and prosecution of organized crime. The FCC paper (and especially the "American Solution") was sharply criticized by the powerful Hong Kong Bar Association. As a result, an extensive and healthy debate has occurred which has centered upon the FCC American options and the Hong Kong Bar's response. The most controversial issues of this debate are set forth through a comparative analysis of certain components of the US model: the racketeer influenced and corrupt organization statute, electronic surveillance, accomplice witnesses, and grand juries.

Hong Kong law-makers will face complicated questions when they come to address US solutions to organized crime. While the preponderance of feeling is likely to emphasize the seriousness of the threat posed by triads and ongoing crime to the well being of the people of Hong Kong, legislators will be concerned to ensure that any legislative initiatives taken are likely to be effective, are well tailored to Hong Kong's present needs, and yet do not threaten the possibility of civil rights abuse. It is argued that these goals are not inconsistent in view of recent US experience which teaches that a fresh approach to electronic surveillance and accomplice witness evidence might now be justified.

Wichitwechkarn, Netipong

THE LAW OF CONSPIRACY: THE THAI AND AMERICAN LAWS COMPARED

Harvard Law School 1987 M

88 pages

Footnotes

In Thailand, when people or lawyers speak of conspiracy, they do not have the slightest idea that they are speaking of a criminal conduct. This is because conspiracy is not a crime in Thailand, nor has it ever been recognized by the Thai Penal Code. The only meaning it conveys is just a dictionary meaning, that is, "the making of secret plans (with others, especially to do something wrong)". Thus, if two persons agree to commit any crime, be it murder, burglary, or rape, their conducts have not yet fallen within the reach of the Thai Penal Code.

But in the United States, the concept is different. Conspiracy is a criminal conduct. Moreover, the crime of conspiracy is distinct from the crime contemplated. Thus, if the same conduct is committed in the United States, the criminal process must be initiated against those who got involved in such an activity.

The fact that conspiracy is a crime in the United States but not in Thailand can be attributed to many factors, e.g. the difference between common law and civil law systems, the historical backgrounds, the spirit of the nation. It also depends on the policy of each country whether or not to make certain conducts criminal, which reflects the legal sovereignty of each state. As a natural consequence, certain conduct or activity becomes a crime in Thailand but not at all in the United States and vice versa. The crime of conspiracy affords a good example of this phenomenon. The doctrine of conspiracy may effectively serve the United States as a crime prevention measure but the doctrine does not commend itself to jurists of civil law countries. However, the Thai criminal law seems to put less emphasis on the prevention of crimes and law enforcement officers sometimes completely overlook this equally essential function; hence, the relevant provisions have scarcely come into play. On the other hand, the applicability of the crime conspiracy in the United States sometimes seems to be so rampant that Thailand could hardly adopt it into her own law without great problems. The author feels that it is time that the Penal Code of Thailand be altered to include the new crime prevention offense that, on the one hand, must be flexible enough to punish those who demonstrate ascertainable propensity to commit crimes of serious nature but must not be so rampant that it punishes just an agreement between two or more persons to commit unlawful conduct on the other.

Williams, Jeffry Alan

THE INTERNATIONAL MILITARY TRIBUNAL AT NUREMBERG: THE CREATION AND EVOLUTION OF THE NUREMBERG PRECEDENT AND ITS APPLICATION TO THE 1982 ARMED CONFLICT IN LEBANON

George Washington Law School 1986 M

145 pages

Foortnotes

The International Military Tribunal at Nuremberg sentenced twelve of twenty-two Nazi defendants to death by hanging and seven to imprisonment for terms ranging from ten years to life. Three of the defendants were acquitted. Of six accused Nazi organizations, three were found to be criminal in nature. In his report to the President on October 15, 1946, the Chief Prosecutor for the United States, Supreme Court Justice Robert H. Jackson, spoke highly of the Tribunal's decision. He indicated that the law applied by the International Military Tribunal had been "incorporated into a precedent" and further indicated that "such a judgment shifts the power of the precedent to the support of existing rules of law." In his concluding remarks, Justice Jackson stated, "No one can hereafter deny or fail to know that the principles on which the Nazi defendants were adjudged constitute law - law with a sanction."

In his evaluation of the Judgement of the Tribunal, Justice Jackson was only partially correct: the decision certainly did constitute an international precedent; nonetheless, a number of authorities questioned the universality of the principle on which the decision was based. This paper, too, begins with a critical evaluation of the juridical bases for the Tribunal's decision. In this regard, the analysis focuses initially on the customary and conventional law in existence in 1945 in an attempt to determine whether the Tribunal applied international law, or as the author contends, created international law with its decision.

The paper then considers the Nuremberg Subsequent Proceedings. Principle attention is given to analysis of the laws of war and the concept of individual responsibility for war crimes. The principles of law discussed and analyzed are then applied to the facts of the international armed conflict in Lebanon in 1982.

The author then discusses the formulation and codification of the Nuremberg Principles. Because the formulation of the United Nations International Law Commission reproduced in almost identical terms the provisions of the Nuremberg Charter, this portion of the paper concentrates on an analysis of the Draft Code of Offenses Against the Peace and Security of Mankind and the Commission's attempt to impute criminal responsibility to individuals for acts which previously involved only State resonsibility.

Application of the Nuremberg Precedent and related concepts of international law to the 1982 armed conflict in Lebanon are finally discussed. In this analysis, it is established that the State of Israel has waged an aggressive war in Lebanon and that waging such a war gives rise to international criminal responsibility. Israeli responsibility for war crimes against humanity are also established utilizing the law of the Nuremberg Tribunal as a basis for the legal analysis which follows.

Winitzer, Marcia J.

RETHINKING THE TAXATION OF THE FAMILY

Harvard Law School 1987 M

77 pages

Footnotes

With reference to the cynical colloquialism that the only things about which individuals can be certain are death and taxes, this paper examines the latter. More specifically, the subject is the way in which the law regulates the family through rules governing personal income taxation. The thesis is that the tax code is used as a mechanism for implementing social policy even though it is viewed primarily as performing the function of raising revenue. It is argued that underlying many of the basic rules and regulations for the calculation of tax liability are certain assumptions about the family which often remain unarticulated. In so far as these assumptions are operative in the formulation of the tax rules, their existence should be exposed and scrutinized in light of the consequences, both intended and unintended.

A further claim in this paper, and perhaps the more crucial one, is that the rules themselves reflect specific preferences about social arrangements. The complex structure of the Code and its unwieldy procedures tend to obscure the vision of the world that is articulated, at least implicitly, and promoted, more or less explicitly. Nevertheless it is clear from an analysis of some of the Code provisions that are most directly related to and governed by one's status as a member of the social group defined as a family, that there is a view of society which prevails. Rather than emerging from objective criteria, the standards to which this view adheres are informed by norms and values which are not neutral. Thus these norms and values should be rendered explicit in order to adequately evaluate the choices that have been made on the basis of them.

The author points to the direction in which her analysis can be pushed with respect to possible revisions of the manner in which the Code treats the family and the resulting consequences. As a result of the contention that the tax code is not neutral or objective, the preferences implicit in the regulations ought to be made explicit in order to evaluate the underlying policy goals. More fundamentally, it is claimed that any taxing regulations should be considered by focusing on not only aspects of revenue raising and allegedly objective criteria, but underlying normative considerations as well. If the observation that assumptions about the family, women and social roles form a part of an ideology that informs the tax rules is valid, then rethinking the way in which the income tax rules treat the family would be a significant part of tax policy.

Wolf, Richard V.

INTERNATIONAL ADJUDICATORY JURISDICTION: A COMPARATIVE STUDY OF THE U.S.A., THE E.E.C., AUSTRIA, AND SWITZERLAND

Harvard Law School 1986 M

103 pages

Footnotes

The paper compares international adjudicatory jurisdiction in civil and commercial matters as it is regulated and exercised in the United States, Austria, and Switzerland, and the Brussels EEC Convention on Jurisdiction and the Enforcement of Judgements in Civil and Commercial Matters. The comparison is limited by the scope of the Brussels Convention, that is, to civil and commercial matters. By looking at the major issues of contracts, property, counterclaims, and litispendence, an examination is made of the four individual jurisdictions' approaches to assuming "competence directe," in terms of the courts' interpretations.

The various bases of jurisdiction are discussed in regard to their conformity with ideas of fairness concerning the assumption of jurisdiction over the parties, the objects, and the litigation involved. A general evaluation of the results arrived at by the four jurisdictions is made.

Viewed in terms of fairness-power paradigms, the US jurisdiction practice is closest to a fairness approach. The fairness analysis was for a long time a limited one, and exorbitant results have occurred. Slowly the US Supreme Court is directing a process of change. New jurisdictional factors are gaining ground: litigational abilities and burdens, fairness, the forum's interest, convenience, foreseeability, and so forth.

European jurists more closely adhere to statutory provisions. Jurisdictional bases are distinguished by their legal attributes and not by independent jurisdictional considerations that have to be made from case to case. Their application is mechanical and does not provide a degree of predictability. The legislator preempts the independent development of solutions, and the judge's attention is only aroused in "hard" cases. Jurisdictional bases resting on power arguments survive and find their promoters. The legal system diverts attention away from a general analysis of jurisdictional principles.

From a plaintiff-defendant orientation, it can be observed that nearly all recent major American decisions grant the defendant's situation more importance than formerly. The pendulum that started its first swing with International Shoe is swinging back. From a pro-defendant oriented power period, the development went too far in serving plaintiffs, and now the reverse trend can be seen. In Europe, consumer protection, for example, benefits classes of defendants, but does not really change the general practice.

The two most distinct theoretical approaches, the American and the German-Austrian, are both based on statutory interpretation. However, jurisdictional thinking in Europe and America seems to be following different patterns, owing possibly to differences in legal and social backgrounds. Another factor may be the style of the scholars' discourse. American jurists tend to discuss policy questions, while the others concentrate on dogma and theory. Against this background, the paper consolidates the different approaches.

Wolfisberg, Eva

LIMITED GUARDIANSHIP: A COMPARISON OF THE SWISS CIVIL CODE WITH THE ABA'S MODEL STATUTE, WITH PARTICULAR RESPECT TO PERSONS WITH MENTAL RETARDATION

Harvard Law School M

62 pages

Footnotes

In Switzerland, the debate about the objective of modern legislation on guardianship has generally been rather scarce. Despite such a dearth of academic analysis the Swiss government has proposed, in the course of the general revision of the Swiss Civil Code, that the guardianship law should be adapted to current societal and legal developments.

The Swiss Civil Code was enacted in 1912 and its provisions on guardianship are still currently in force. The guardianship law reflects the then prevailing attitudes towards social welfare which were extremely paternalistic. Thus, the range of persons subject to guardianship is very broad encompassing mental illness, mental retardation, prodigality, mismanagement of financial affairs, immorality, alcohol abuse and imprisonment due to criminal conviction. Despite such differences, the guardianship provisions apply to all these categories uniformly.

In the United States, guardianship law has been the object of legal discourse in the last two decades over two different issues. Some perceived a lack of guardianship protection for many disabled persons and supported the establishment of public guardianship systems. Others were concerned with the severe impact of traditional plenary guardianship on civil and political rights and advocated the concept of limited guardianship.

In Switzerland, there is no lack of guardianship protection, since in line with the civil law tradition, special guardianship provisions within the family law were formed centuries ago. At issue is rather a modernization of the traditional plenary guardianship scheme in order to better fashion it to the specific needs of persons with a mental or another disability.

The U.S. concept of limited guardianship which purports to promote the abilities and rights of the individual who is disabled has characteristic features. The concept has implications on the definition of legal incompetence and correlated guardianship standards. Traditionally, a guardian has been appointed when an individual is incapacitated by reason of mental retardation. In contrast, limited guardianship does not focus on a medical condition like mental retardation but requires a substantial impairment of the cognitive functions leading to a failure to perform basic life functions. Since not every mentally retarded person meets these requirements, the new concept limits the scope of guardianship and the number of persons subject to guardianship.

This paper examines whether the U.S. concept of limited guardianship could provide a source of ideas for the upcoming revision of the Swiss Civil Code, especially with respect to persons suffering from mental retardation. It also explores whether there is in fact a basis for limited guardianship in Swiss law implicit in the constitutional principle of proportionality or, as it is stated in U.S. terminology, "the principle of least restrictive alternative".

Young, Alan

JUDICIAL REWRITING OF CONSTITUTIONALLY DEFICIENT STATUTES

Harvard Law School M

95 pages

Footnotes

In most areas of the criminal law the court has a demonstrated expertise to engage in a lawmaking enterprise. There may be institutional constraints that can retard the courts legislative enterprise, as was demonstrated in the search and seizure cases, however, absent these constraints the court should not be diffident in asserting a power to rewrite unconstitutional legislation.

Although the discussion in this paper centered around issues of criminal justice the rewriting proposals extends beyond this discrete topic. What is presented here is a methodology or strategy that can be employed to determine whether judicial intervention in a legislative manner is an appropriate and legitimate response to constitutionally deficient statutes of any kind. It may be that upon weighing the relevant considerations one may conclude that there is little room for judicial lawmaking in our polity, but the significance of this proposal does not lay in the amount of lawmaking that the judiciary can legitimately engage in. What is significant is that we begin to abandon our perception of the court as an apolitical institution that merely administers pre-existing law. There are few, if any, people that still accept the Montesquieuian notion of the court as the mouth of the law; however, there are also few who see all the political ramifications of judicial behavior. It is essential that we dismantle the traditional paradigm of adjudication but it is unclear what new model will emerge.

During the Bill of Rights era the courts were criticized as being too restrained and now the tide has turned and the courts are being criticized as being too creative with their mandate under the Charter. There are many who believe that judicial creativity will lead to hegemony of nine old men but this is not a realistic fear because there are sufficient institutional constraints to preserve the supremacy of Parliament. A lawmaking partnership between the courts and the legislature will not lead to tyranny by a judicial junta but will hopefully result in a judiciary that is responsive to the legal and political concerns of the community.

Zaal, Frederick Noel

LAW AND INHIBITION OF INTERRACIAL SEXUAL RELATIONS UNDER THE DUTCH EAST INDIA COMPANY: THE HISTORICAL ORIGINS OF SEXUAL APARTHEID IN SOUTH AFRICA

Columbia Law School 1985 M

134 pages

Footnotes and bibliography

The purpose of this study is to explore the early historical genealogy of the anti-miscegenation strand in that network, during the formative Dutch colonial period which lasted from 1652 until 1806, and the period of British colonial governance which followed. White-ruled South Africa has been completely or partially subject to overseas colonial government agencies for most of its three hundred and thirty-three years of existence. Despite this palpable historical fact, the deep-rooted external European influences which underpin the current race laws in South Africa have not yet been fully explored by legal scholars.

It has been suggested that the Nationalist Government's discriminatory distinctions between supposedly discrete segments of the South African population are contrary to the egalitarian and liberal value systems of the Roman-Dutch and English legal systems. Since it was from a process of historical 'miscegenation' between these two systems that modern South African law emerged, this is a criticism which attempts to spotlight as deviant, the course taken by the Nationalist lawmakers after 1948.

Perhaps unfortunately, it is also a criticism which fails to take proper account of the ancient insidiousness of legislatively manifested European racism. In the course of the analysis which follows the author shows that, at least in the area of miscegenation, colonial statutes from the Roman-Dutch era have had a significant juridical impact in South Africa, and one which has encouraged rather than countered racial discrimination.

The author provides in this investigation of the available materials, ·a comprehensive evaluation of the earliest juridical inspirations for the Prohibition of Mixed Marriages and Immorality Acts. On a point of terminology the term "black" was used to refer generally to all persons of mixed or Negro or Asian ancestry. This was done purely to provide a substitute for the description "non-white." The latter is a label which many persons find highly derogatory.

Zakson, Laurence Scott

RAILWAY LABOR LEGISLATION 1888 TO 1930: A LEGAL HISTORY OF CONGRESSIONAL RAILWAY LABOR RELATIONS POLICY

Columbia Law School M

85 pages

Footnotes

In recent years, economic dislocation and "borrowing" by U.S. companies of quality of work life programs from their Western European and Japanese counterparts have brought the issue of employee participation in major workplace decisions into the foreground of labor relations discourse. However, employee participation or industrial democracy, as it is sometimes called, is not wholly compatible with federal labor relations policy. Federal labor relations policy relies on the adversary model, employer-employee relations being self-governing process operating through the mechanisms of collective bargaining and employee unionization. To a large degree, these policies are a function of the experiences of American industrial life.

The purpose of this paper is to examine the history of one part - indeed, one of the oldest parts - of federal labor policy, railway labor legislation, for the purpose of shedding some light on why certain choices were made. This, in turn, should serve as a tool for modern policy makers as they try to determine the future direction of labor policy and the continued validity and vitality of current rules and practices.

During the 19th and first three decades of the twentieth century, the federal courts, on the one hand, and the federal executive and legislative branches, on the other, were often at odds in their development of labor relations policies.

The earliest area of extensive federal labor relations legislation is in the railroad industry. Given the extensive judicial involvement in this arena and the profound economic effects of disruptions of the railway systems, this is not surprising. However, despite the hostile reception labor organizations, concerted action and other forms of mutual aid and protection received in the courts, the relatively consistent Congressional policy was to seek to foster industrial peace by encouraging negotiated settlements and the voluntary arbitration of employer-employee disputes by railroad management and railway employees' labor organizations.

What followed is an exploration of railway labor relations legislation prior to 1930, with as especial emphasis on the Railway Labor Act of 1926. It seeks to identify Congressional policies and the political environment in which they were formulated. It examines these issues primarily from the perspective of the employees' labor organizations rather than seeking a perspective which presents equally the views of railway operators and employees. The primary purposes of this examination are twofold. First, it seeks to demonstrate that Congress decided to safeguard industrial peace in the railway industry by fostering collective bargaining between the railroad operators and their employees' labor organizations and the use of related voluntary dispute resolution mechanisms. Second, it seeks to discover how and why Congress sought to do this by strengthening employees' organizational rights and their independent trade unions.

Zenger, Christoph Andreas

REFLEXIVE LAW: CRITIQUE OF A STRATEGY

Harvard Law School 1987 M

87 pages

Footnotes

At the outset there is a scenario of crisis. The modern welfare state is in a financing, taxation and guidance crisis, and its law is in a regulatory crisis. These crises are the real basis of a renaissance of the idea of social self-organization, of self-regulation and self-help, of autonomy and subsidiarity.

The concept of reflexive law is to respond to this crisis. It represents a particular strategy to do so, the strategy of "controlled self-regulation". There are concurring strategies aimed at coping with the crisis of "materialized law" which, however, are related to differing concepts of law. Attempts at delegalizing, reprivatizing and reformalizing the law are based on the concept of formal law. Efforts to improve the implementation of substantive norms, in their turn, refer to the concept of substantive law.

The strategy of "controlled self-regulation" complies best with the ideals of social self-organization as revived under the impression of the welfare state's crisis. But it cannot rely on one of the two traditional concepts of formal and of substantive law.

The strategic model of reflective law dispenses outright with substantive, prescriptive norms which so far have served the welfare state to change individual behavior and to produce desired outcomes of regulation. Reflexive law rather means a new type of proceduralizing the law which seems to be quite similar to other current proposals; in particular the "reconstitutive law"

In his analysis the author takes a close look at the concept of reflexive law, at its concrete details, and its possible political impact.

# Subject Index

# Title Index

ABOUT THE AUTHOR

KENNETH BROWN was involved in academic and legal publishing for many years. Most recently as the Publisher and Director of Huddleston-Brown, Publishers, Inc., he issued The New Law Books Reviewer.

www.ingramcontent.com/pod-product-compliance
Ingram Content Group UK Ltd.
Pitfield, Milton Keynes, MK11 3LW, UK
UKHW020231290926
15470UKWH00002B/477

9 780313 264863